SAILING ESSENTIALS

SAILING ESSENTIALS

STEVE SLEIGHT

LONDON • NEW YORK • MUNICH •
MELBOURNE • DELHI

Editors: Gareth Jones, Satu Fox
Senior Art Editor: Jill Andrews
Production Editor: Lucy Sims
Production Controller: Mandy Inness
Cover Designer: Mark Cavanagh
Managing Editor: Stephanie Farrow
Managing Art Editor: Lee Griffiths

DK India
Project Editor: Vibha Malhotra
Editors: Pallavi Singh, Gaurav Joshi
Managing Editor: Pakshalika Jayaprakash
Project Art Editor: Ranjita Bhattacharji
Art Editors: Jaypal Singh Chauhan, Swati Katyal, Tarun Sharma
Deputy Managing Art Editor: Priyabrata Roy Chowdhury
Managing Art Editor: Arunesh Talapatra
DTP Designers: Rajesh Singh Adhikari, Arvind Kumar, Bimlesh Tiwary
DTP Manager: Balwant Singh
Production Manager: Pankaj Sharma

Produced for Dorling Kindersley by Schermuly Design Co
Project Editor: Cathy Meeus
Project Art Editor: Hugh Schermuly

First published in Great Britain in 2013 by Dorling Kindersley Limited, 80 Strand, London WC2R 0RL

Penguin Group (UK)

10 9 8 7 6 5 4 3 2 1

001–186989–May/2013

A CIP catalogue record for this book is available from the British Library.

ISBN 978-1-4093-2445-4

Printed and bound in China by Leo Paper Products.

Discover more at www.dk.com

Contents

Please note As with many sports, there are inherent risks with sailing. Don't take risks – wear a buoyancy aid or lifejacket and ensure that you have adequate supervision as a beginner.

tacktick®

Introduction

Sailing is, in essence, a means of harnessing the wind to take you across water, whether sea, lake, or river, to wherever you want to go. To do this safely, there are many skills to learn and remember. This book explains the essential elements of cruiser sailing for those who have never sailed before, as well as providing a handy "crib sheet" for more experienced sailors.

In this book, those who are new to sailing will find out how to stay safe and comfortable on board, how to work as part of a crew, and will learn key sailing and seamanship skills. Sailors at all levels can benefit from the step-by-step guidance on techniques such as how to approach a marina berth and what ropes to use to secure your boat.

There is also vital reference information, for example, on what lights to use at night and how to access and understand weather forecasts, as well as a guide to buoyage, an introduction to the basics of navigation, knots and ropework, practical maintenance skills, advice on what to do in an emergency, and much more.

The aim of this book is to help novice sailors to become useful and effective members of the crew, solve problems, identify mistakes, and learn new skills.

Experienced sailors can also use this book to hone their sailing skills, by reminding themselves of the basic procedures and techniques before a sailing trip, or at the end of a day's sailing to review what went well and what could be improved with some additional practice.

I hope *Sailing Essentials* becomes your valued companion as you explore the pleasures of sailing and expand your horizons by cruising safely under sail.

Steve Sleight

KEY
The following symbols appear throughout the book.

 **Wind direction**  **Tide direction**  **Boa**

Comfort and safety

Whatever boat you sail, you will have more fun if you understand how to stay comfortable afloat by protecting yourself from wind, rain, sun, and spray. It is also essential that you familiarize yourself with the personal safety equipment on board.

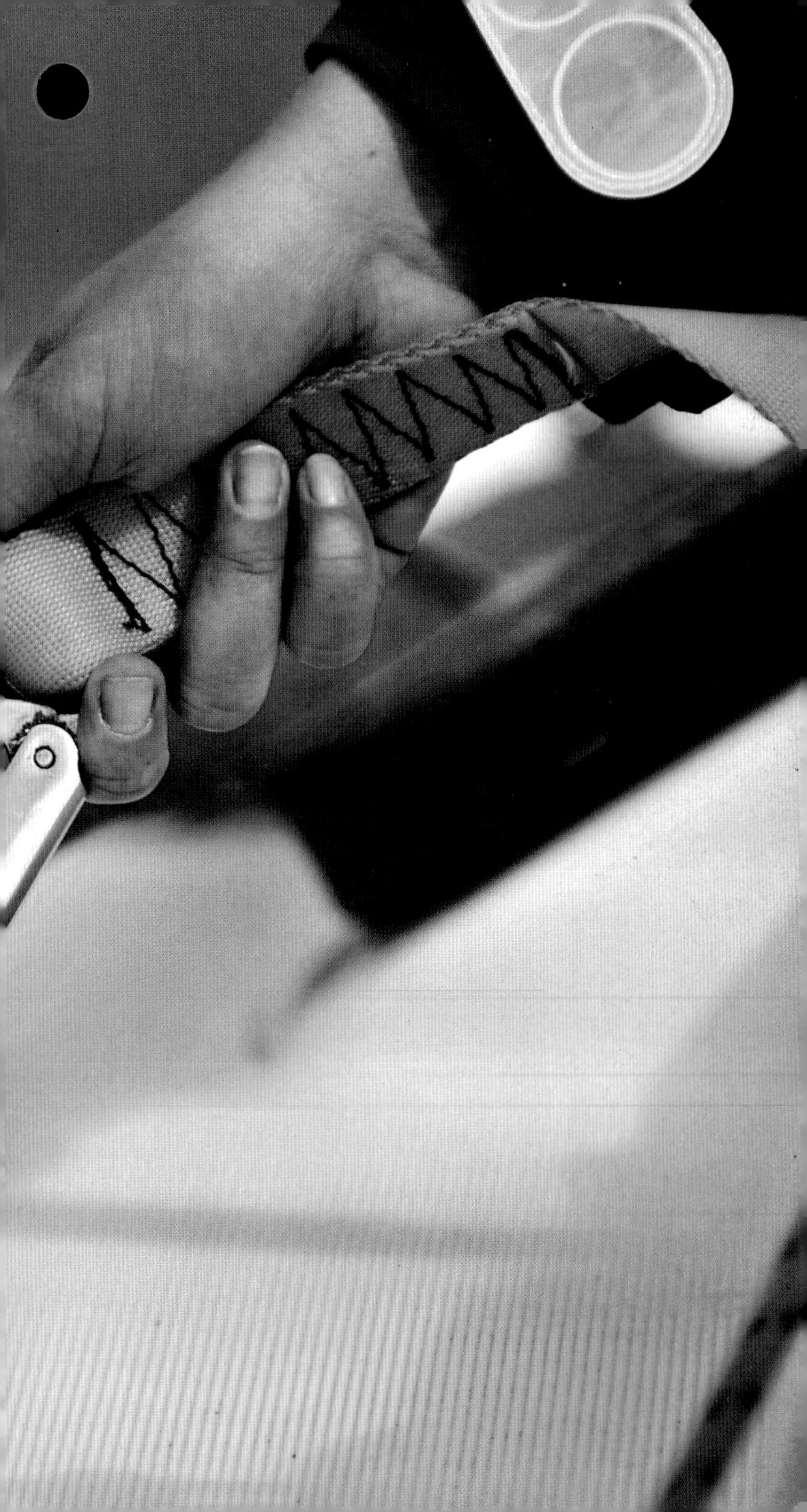

Clothing

If you sail in a hot climate, all you may need for cruising is a T-shirt, shorts, sailing shoes, and sunglasses, plus a fleece for cooler evenings. But much sailing takes place in colder climates where more clothing will be required to keep you warm and dry in a range of conditions. Modern breathable fabrics help reduce sweating inside waterproof garments.

WHAT TO WEAR FOR SAILING IN COLD WEATHER

- **Keep warm** In cold or wind, you must stay dry inside wind- and waterproof clothing that retains your body heat. Wet skin gets cold 30 times more quickly than dry skin, so your clothing must be able to transport moisture away from skin while retaining dry, warm air close to body.

- **Adjustable wrist and ankle seals** These provide a comfortable and water resistant fit when worn with shoes, boots, or gloves. If conditions are extremely wet, neoprene seals provide a good grip at the wrists without constricting blood flow.

- **Thermal underwear** Modern lightweight thermal clothing wicks perspiration away from the skin and is perfect to wear under a waterproof outer layer.

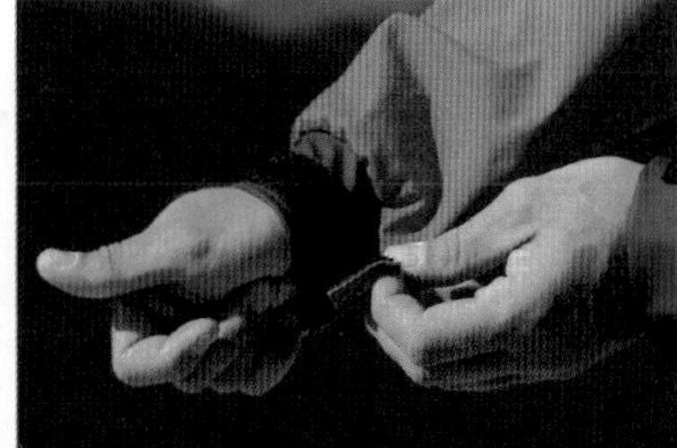

CHOOSING TROUSERS

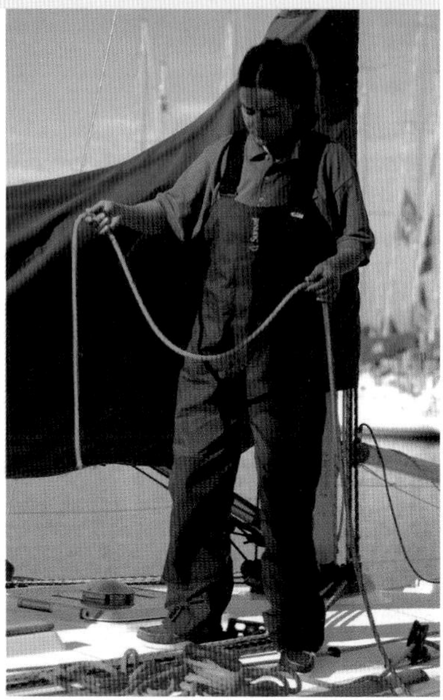

- **High-cut trousers** Choose a design with heavily reinforced knees and seat to add durability.
- **Bib-and-braces design** Many sailors favour this style. Like all sailing trousers, they should be a loose fit to allow you to wear warm layers underneath.
- **Desirable features** Look for a heavy-duty two-way zip with flaps, hand-warmer fleece-lined pockets, and adjustable ankle closures and braces.
- **Add layers** In cold conditions, you should wear warm layers underneath the trousers and a water- and windproof jacket over the top.

WHAT TO WEAR IN WARM WEATHER

- **Keeping cool** Shorts and T-shirts are the best clothes for sailing in hot weather.
- **Don't forget** Whether or not the sun is shining, always use protection against sunburn on exposed skin (see p.13).

Head, hands, and feet

It is important to protect your head, eyes, and skin from the elements. Much heat can be lost through the head. Eyes can be damaged by strong sunlight reflected off the water, as can the skin. Wear sunglasses and use protective sunscreen. Footwear needs to provide a secure grip on deck as well as protection against cold and wet.

HATS AND HOODS – HOW DO THESE HELP?

- **Hood** Most waterproof jackets have a hood to keep your head dry and protect it from wind in rough conditions. Make sure the hood fits well and does not impede your peripheral vision.

- **High collar** Protect the lower part of your face from wind, rain, and spray with a high collar secured by velcro seals. Try a jacket on with the collar raised before you buy, to make sure it is a comfortable fit and does not chafe your skin.

- **Baseball cap** This is a popular choice for protecting the head from the sun when sailing in good weather. Choose one that is adjustable and which has a retaining clip to prevent it being lost if it blows off.

- **Thermal hat** A warm hat is very useful when sailing in cold weather as it will keep your head warm and can be used under the hood of a waterproof jacket in wet or rough weather.

CHOOSING EYEWARE

- **Eye protection** It is vital when sailing to protect your eyes from UV reflection off the water.
- **Good-quality sunglasses** Consider choosing polaroid lenses as they allow you to see under the surface of the water more easily.
- **Wrap-around design** Look for glasses that have a wrap-around, close-fitting frame, and are large enough to cover your eyes to minimize light leakage around the sides, top, or bottom.
- **Retaining cord** Use a secure cord to prevent your sunglasses from being knocked off and lost.

USING SUNSCREEN

- **Sun protection factor (SPF)** Protect your skin with a product with a high SPF. Sensitive areas such as lips and nose should be protected by total sunblock.
- **Water resistance** Choose a sunscreen that is water resistant and use on all exposed skin.
- **Regular application** Apply sunscreen liberally and keep reapplying regularly.
- **Grey days** Cloudy conditions are no protection from UV light, and reflection off the sea increases UV exposure.
- **After sailing** Use moisturizing cream after sailing to combat the drying effects of wind and salt.

CHOOSING FOOTWEAR

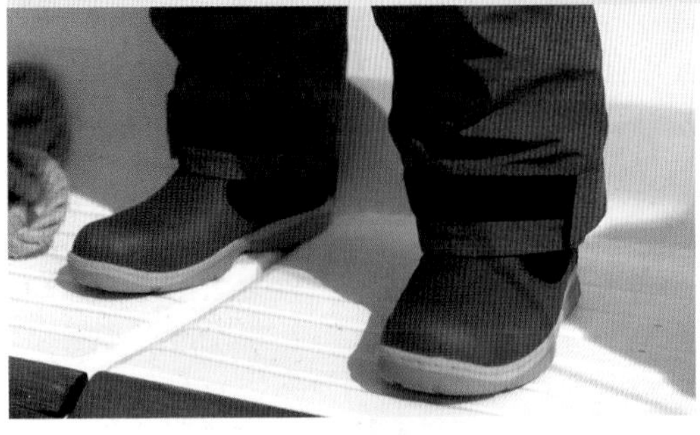

Made for purpose Always wear footwear designed for sailing. Good-quality sailing shoes and boots have non-slip soles, made from materials that do not mark the deck.

Best choice for cold weather Uppers made from leather or synthetic materials and a waterproof, breathable lining allow the boot to breathe. These provide maximum foot comfort in wet and cold weather.

Budget choice Rubber boots are the most inexpensive choice. Make sure they have a good non-slip sole, and pick a size that offers sufficient room for a thick pair of socks and that allows for easy removal.

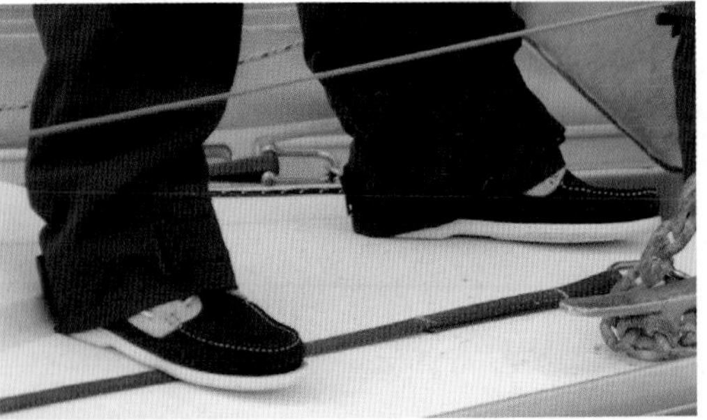

Deck shoes For cruiser sailing in moderate conditions, good-quality deck shoes will provide a good grip on deck and protect your feet.

- **Lightweight shoes** These are suitable footwear when you are yacht sailing in warm conditions. Synthetic materials dry more quickly than leather.

- **Soft soles** Sailing shoes and boots have soles made of softer material than regular shoes. They will wear out more quickly if you use them ashore.

WEARING SAILING GLOVES

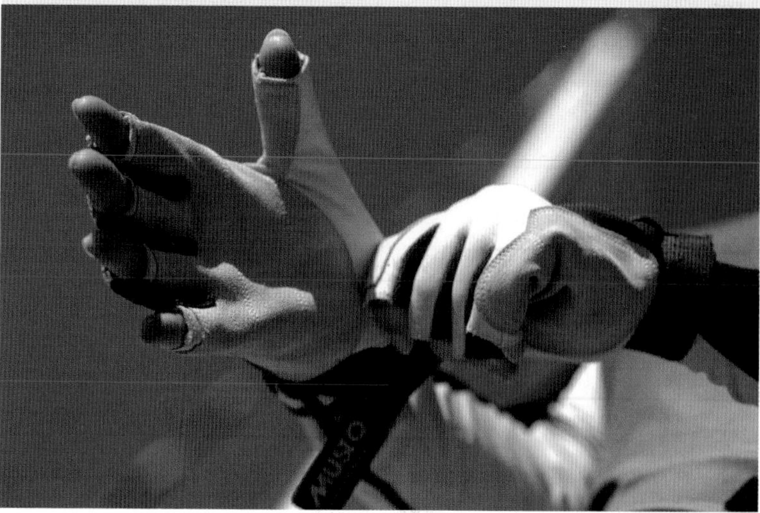

- **Good grip** Sailing gloves have reinforced palms to help you to handle thin, loaded lines. You can choose gloves with full-fingers or half-fingers.

- **Warm hands** When sailing at night or in cold weather, a pair of fleece-lined gloves will help keep you comfortable.

Lifejacket and harness

The best way to keep safe is to stay on the boat. This makes a safety harness and tether (a line that attaches you to the boat) the most vital items of your safety gear. If you fall overboard, a lifejacket will keep you afloat. The skipper should instruct the crew when to wear a harness and lifejacket; but you must always wear them in poor conditions and at night (see p.190).

WEARING A LIFEJACKET AND HARNESS

- **Separate or integrated** You can buy a separate lifejacket and harness, although an integrated harness and lifejacket may be a more convenient option.

- **Comfort and security** Always pick a harness with wide, comfortable straps and crotch straps.

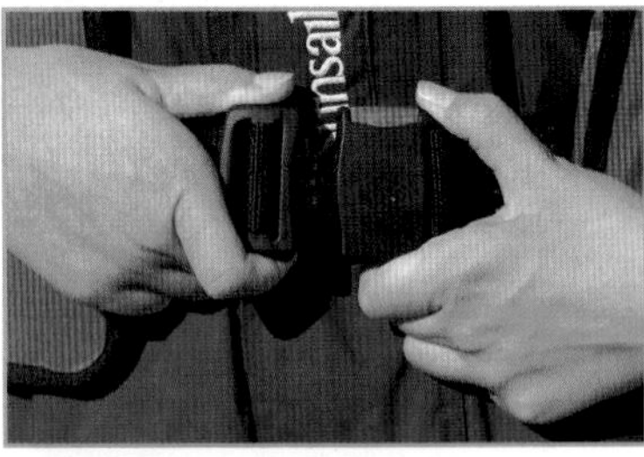

- **Adjustment** Tighten the straps so that the lifejacket is a snug but comfortable fit. Make sure that the waist buckle is properly engaged and secure. Make these adjustments before you set off so that the lifejacket is ready for use when you need it.

- **Crotch straps** These provide maximum safety as they will prevent the lifejacket riding up when it is inflated.

KNOW THE FEATURES OF YOUR LIFEJACKET

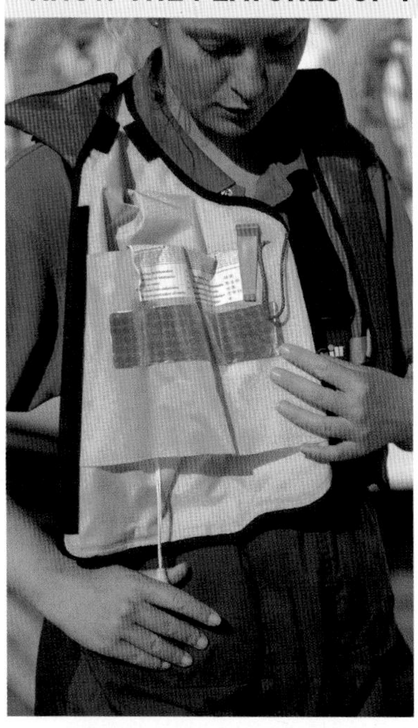

- **Automatically inflated lifejacket** This is the most practical lifejacket for cruising. The CO_2 cylinder that inflates the lifejacket may be activated automatically on entering water or by pulling a toggle. The lifejacket also has an oral inflator.

- **Additional features** For added safety, there should be a whistle, an automatic water-activated light (to help you to be seen if you go overboard at night), and retro-reflective strips.

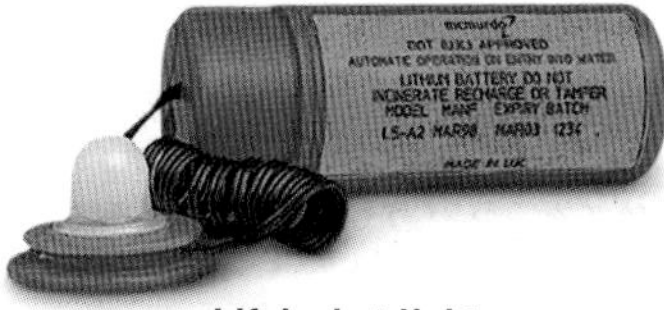

Lifejacket light

TETHER DESIGN – WHAT TO LOOK FOR

- **Tether design** The best tether to use is one with a one-handed double-action safety hook at each end.

- **Elasticated tethers** These reduce the length of the tether when not under tension.

- **Double tethers** Incorporating both a long and a short tether (see p.19), is very useful when moving about the boat.

- **Overload indicator** Tethers with an overload indicator let you know when they need to be replaced.

Safety on deck

The most important safety rule is to avoid falling over the side. Remember the old sailors' maxim – "One hand for yourself and one for the boat". Always hold on with at least one hand and tell the helmsman when you are moving forward. Keep well clear of the boom at all times. When under way, clip on whenever you need to leave the cockpit.

SITTING IN SAFETY

- **The cockpit** This is the safest and most comfortable place for the crew while sailing.

- **Brace yourself** If the boat is heeling, try to sit on the windward side of the cockpit with your feet braced.

- **Going forward** When the boat is under way, go on the side decks or foredeck only when the skipper asks you to perform a necessary task.

WORKING SAFELY

- **On deck** Be sure to clip on (see p.21) when working on the coachroof or foredeck. With practice, the tether will not get in the way at all. Think of it as wearing a seat belt in a car.

- **Short tether** Keep the tether as short as is practical.

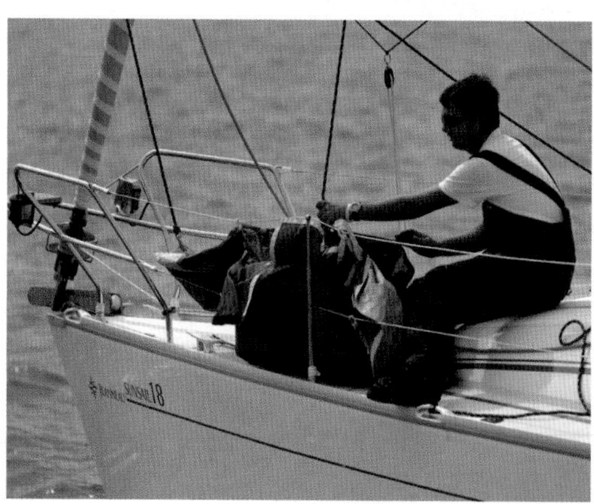

- **On the foredeck** When working on the foredeck, where the motion is greatest, sitting down with a foot braced against the gunwale adds to security. It is prudent to wear and use a harness in all but the most benign of conditions.

- **Safety in the cockpit** Halyards and control lines are usually led back to the cockpit in order to reduce the need for the crew to go on deck. However, even when working in the cockpit, you should be well secured.

HOW TO MOVE ABOUT THE BOAT

- **Clip on** When moving forward along the side decks, clip your tether onto the jackstays (safety lines that run along the deck) and hold on to the grab rail. Keep low as you move about the deck.

- **Handholds** Use handrails, shrouds, and the mast as handholds, but avoid holding on to the guardrails if possible.

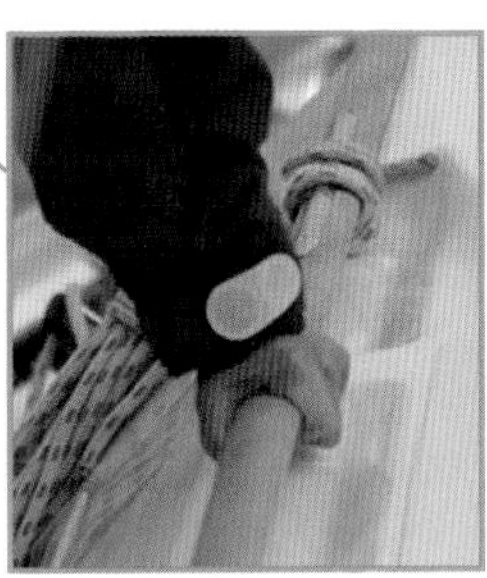

AVOID THE LEEWARD SIDE

- **Take care** If you need to move about on deck when under sail and well heeled, stay on the windward side, whenever possible. Take special care if, as here, it is necessary to work on the leeward side.

CLIPPING ON

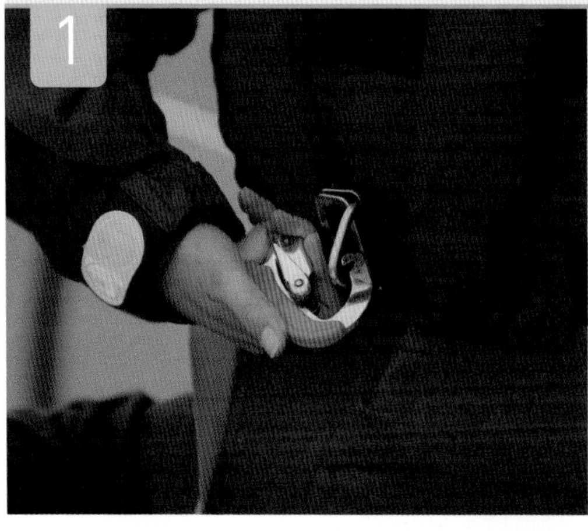

- **Before you go on deck**, clip one end of the tether to the attachment point on your harness.

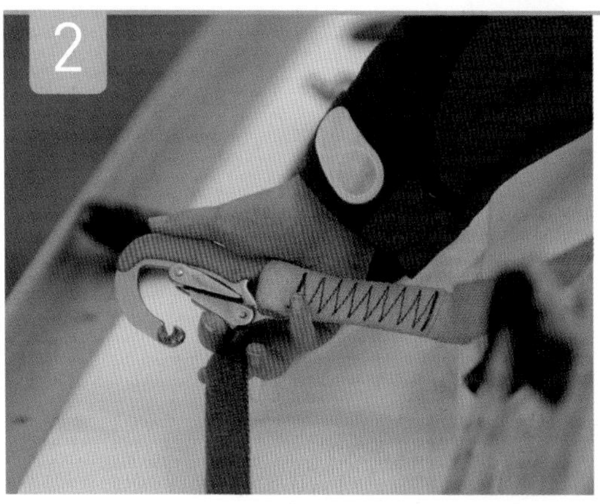

- **Hook the other end** of the tether to a strong attachment point – if possible, on the windward side of the boat. A jackstay is an ideal attachment point to use.

- **Allow the hook** to run along the jackstay as you move.

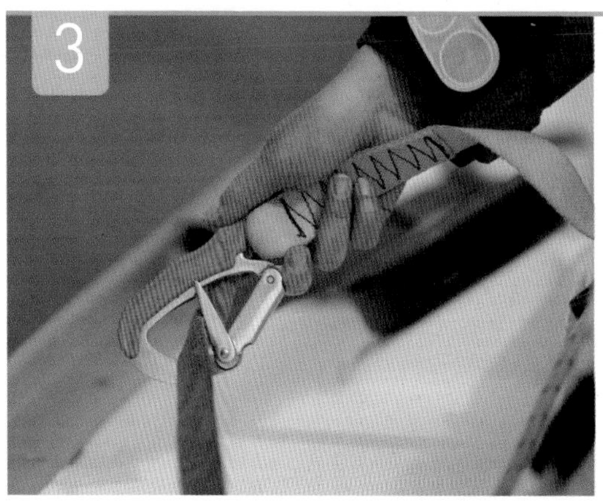

- **To change your anchorage point** at any time, release the safety clip on the hook with your index finger; this will allow the hook to open.

Boat safety equipment

All cruisers should carry sufficient safety equipment to cope with an emergency involving either the boat or the crew. It is important that the skipper and crew regularly practise emergency procedures and learn to use the equipment. There is more information on how to deal with specific emergencies on pp.262–91.

HOW TO USE LIFEBUOYS

- **Ready for use** All cruisers must have a couple of lifebuoys stowed for immediate use in case a person falls overboard. Lifebuoys are only effective when thrown at once as they soon drift out of reach. A lifebuoy should have a flashing light for visibility at night and a nylon drogue to reduce its drift.

- **Stowage** Stow the lifebuoys in quick-release brackets on the pushpit. Keep them below when the boat is not in use to protect them from UV light.

- **Danbuoy** This is a brightly coloured marker pole with code flag O – the man-overboard signal – and should be attached to the lifebuoy. It is more visible than a person or a lifebuoy in the water.

- **Monitoring** Check the lifebuoys frequently to ensure they are in good condition and practise using them regularly.

WHAT IS A MAN-OVERBOARD ALARM SYSTEM?

- **Self-activating alarm** A system of this type can be a life-saver.

- **Crew units** A transponder is issued by the skipper to each crew member and should be carried at all times.

- **Base unit** The control panel detects the drop in signal level if a person falls overboard (see pp.274–75), which sounds an alarm and identifies the person.

KEEP A KNIFE HANDY

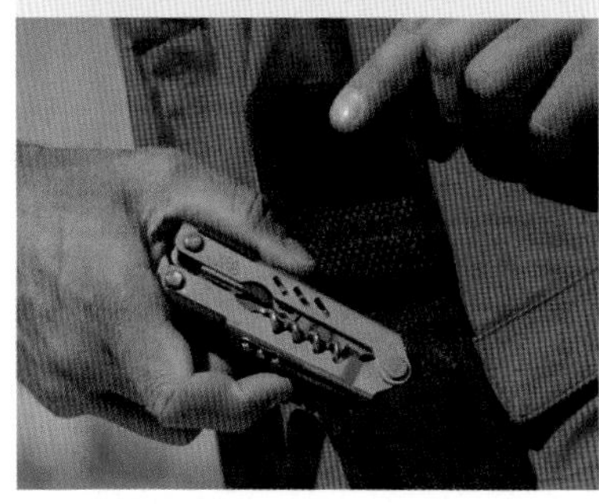

- **In the cockpit** Stow a sharp knife or multi-tool somewhere near the steering position. You may need to cut a rope quickly in an emergency.

- **In your pocket** Some types of waterproof jacket or trousers have a small pocket designed for a personal multi-tool.

FIRST-AID KIT – WHAT GOES IN

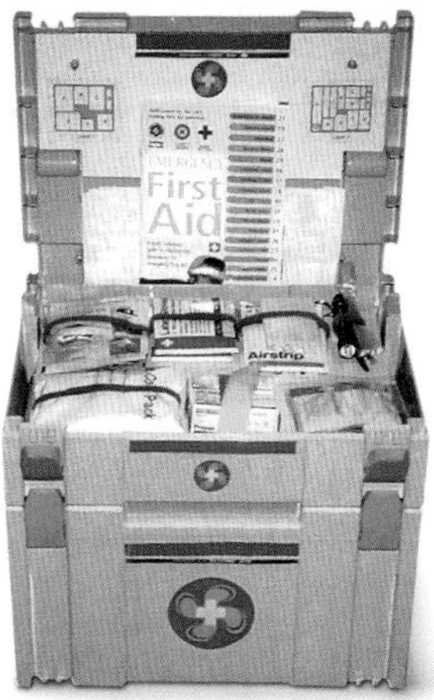

- **Carry the essentials** Make sure that you have a well-stocked first-aid kit on board in case a crew member is injured. Learn more about first aid on pp.264–71.

- **Short trips** For day sailing and short cruises, you may only need adhesive dressings and bandages.

- **For longer passages** It is advisable to take a comprehensive kit (left) on long cruises so that you can deal with any injuries on board until you reach assistance.

STORING AND USING FIRE EXTINGUISHERS

- **Large dry powder extinguishers** Place these in each cabin and near the engine compartment.
- **Smaller foam extinguisher** Keep one in the galley for easy access.
- **Storing fire extinguishers** Make sure that the crew knows where the fire extinguishers are. Check that they are in-date.
- **Using extinguishers** Follow the instructions on the extinguishers clearly. Familiarize yourself with them in advance. See also p.278.

USING LIFERAFTS

- **Liferaft storage** A liferaft is packed inside a solid canister or a soft valise. A canister is often stowed on deck, with quick-release fastenings. A valise may be stowed in a cockpit locker.
- **Know what to do** Read the instructions on using the liferaft in advance and practise releasing and launching it quickly and efficiently (see pp.288–89).

WHAT IS A GRAB BAG?

- **Canister or bag** A grab bag must be waterproof and able to float. You can use a solid canister or a flexible dry bag. Leave space for air inside so it has positive buoyancy or tie it to a fender to keep it afloat.

- **Filling the grab bag** A liferaft usually has basic survival equipment on board, but this is the minimum required. Check what yours contains and prepare your grab bag accordingly. In an emergency, supplement it if possible with equipment, food, and water taken from the yacht before you abandon the ship.

WHAT FLARES DO I NEED?

- **Be seen** Flares are important for signalling for help when in sight of land or other vessels (see also pp.286–87). Select the right type for the sailing you do. For offshore sailing, store a full set of flares in a watertight container.

- **Preparing yourself** Read the instructions for all of the different flares you carry, so you can use them in a hurry, and in the dark.

WHAT IS AN EPIRB?

- **Emergency position indicating radio beacon (EPIRB)** This device transmits a distress signal to satellites that are part of the GMDSS (see p.284). The distress signals locate the EPIRB's position and relay it to a rescue coordination centre.

- **Operation** An EPIRB can be manual or automatic – with a float-free bracket that releases the beacon if the boat sinks. Check the instructions on your device before sailing so you know how it will work in an emergency.

Crew roles

The skipper is responsible for the safety of the yacht and the welfare of the crew, but sailing a yacht successfully requires team work from the skipper and the crew. This will ensure that all manoeuvres – such as leaving a mooring, hoisting sails, changing tacks, reefing, or entering a marina – can be completed with maximum enjoyment and minimum stress.

WHAT MAKES A GOOD SKIPPER?

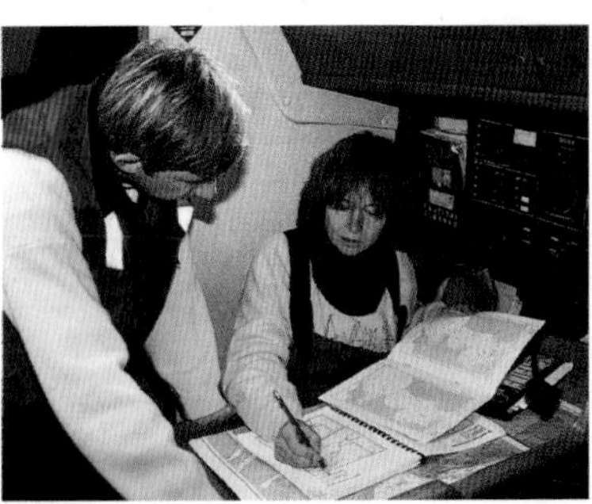

- **Responsibility** The skipper is responsible for all aspects of the running of the yacht, its safety, and the crew's wellbeing.
- **Skills** He or she should be comfortable with sailing and navigation skills, inspire confidence in his or her crew, and be a good communicator.
- **Delegation** A good skipper should keep on top of all his or her duties and give the crew tasks that are appropriate to their experience.
- **Patience** He or she should be patient with inexperienced crew members and be able to run the yacht with a light touch while retaining respect and authority.
- **Briefing** It is the skipper's role to plan the passage in detail before setting sail.
- **Involvement** A good skipper will also encourage the crew to get involved in passage planning and navigation, and will always listen to their opinions.

WHAT MAKES A GOOD CREW MEMBER?

● **Key qualities** All crew members require a positive attitude, sense of humour, and the ability to get on with others in the confined space aboard a cruiser.

● **Willingness to learn** Good crew are willing to learn and to take an active role in all aspects of running the yacht.

● **Attentive** Diligent crew listen to the instructions carefully and ask questions if they do not understand anything.

WORKING AS A TEAM

● **Team spirit** All members of the crew must remember that they are part of a team. A happy gathering in the cockpit at the end of the passage is an indicator that each member of the crew has done their job.

Sailing basics

In this section, you will learn the basics of boat equipment and the principles of sailing, which will enable you to become a useful member of the crew. Once you have mastered the basics, there is a fascinating wealth of skills and knowledge available to you.

Parts of the boat

Modern cruisers have a lot of fittings above deck, including the components of the spars and sails together with the ropes and hardware that control them. Other equipment is needed for anchoring, mooring, and helping ensure the safety of the crew. Make sure you understand the purpose of the equipment on your boat.

Winch
Winches provide additional power for the control of heavy loads on the ropes (sheets and halyards) that are used to control the sails.

Topping lift
The topping lift runs from the boom end up to the masthead, then down to deck level where it is adjusted. It supports the boom when the mainsail is lowered but is left slack when the sail is hoisted.

Boom
Attached to the mast by the gooseneck fitting, the boom supports the mainsail's foot.

Mainsheet
This controls the angle of the mainsail.

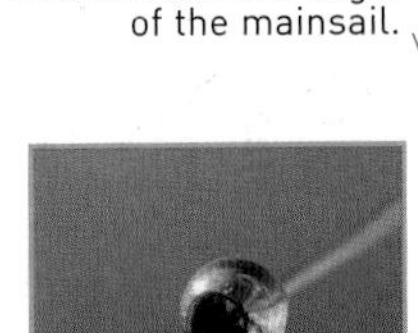

Lifelines
Two lifelines run either side of the boat from the pulpit to the pushpit; they pass through stanchions secured to the deck.

Compass
The binnacle compass is often mounted where it can be easily seen by the helmsman.

Toerail
An aluminium rail is often fitted to the edge of the deck to strengthen the hull-to-deck joint and to provide a restraining bar to prevent feet slipping off the deck.

Mooring cleat
Warps (mooring ropes) are led through fairleads before being secured on the deck cleats.

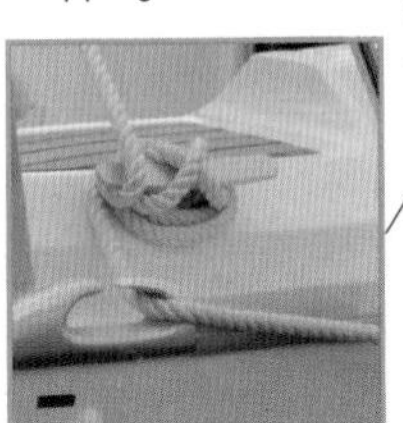

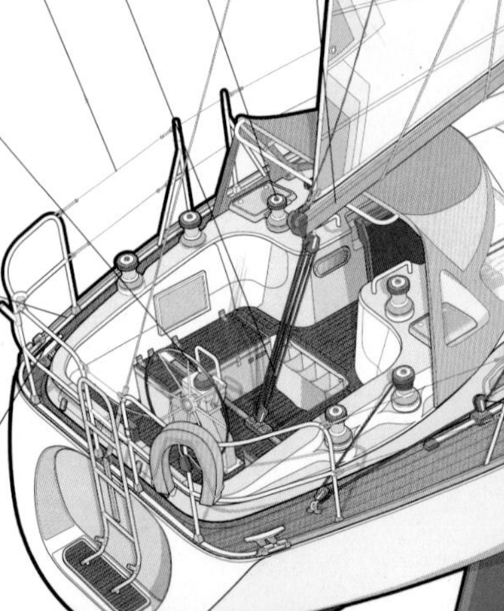

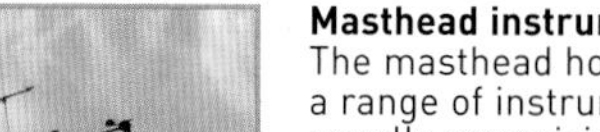

Masthead instruments
The masthead houses a range of instruments, usually comprising wind-speed and direction sensors, a VHF radio aerial, and a tricolour navigation light.

Shrouds
The main sideways support for the mast.

Spreaders
These widen the angle of the shroud to the mast and help to support the mast.

Forestay
The forestay runs from the bow to the masthead, and together with the backstay (which runs from the masthead to the stern), supports the mast fore and aft.

Pulpit
The pulpit is a strong metal frame at the bow designed to make the foredeck more secure; forward navigation lights are attached to it.

Anchor well
A self-draining well just aft of the pulpit holds the anchor cable and often the anchor.

Halyards
Used to raise and lower sails, halyards are usually led inside the mast and emerge at deck level, where they are led aft to winches for adjustment.

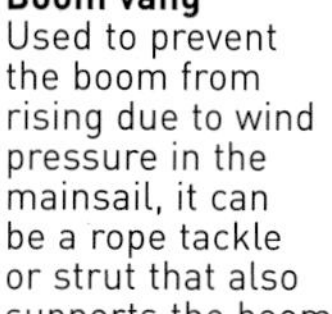

Boom vang
Used to prevent the boom from rising due to wind pressure in the mainsail, it can be a rope tackle or strut that also supports the boom.

Jib turning block
The adjustable fairleads for the headsail sheet run along a track on both sidedecks or the cabin roof.

Basic forces

A number of forces created by wind, tide, and waves have an effect on a sailing yacht and it is important that you understand how these forces act on your boat and how to use them or counteract them as necessary. Different designs of yacht may react quite differently to the forces so you need to know how your yacht will behave.

HOW WIND DRIVES A BOAT

Direction of movement
Low-pressure area
Total force
Airflow
Individual forces
High-pressure area
Leeward side
Windward side

- **Drive** Wind flows around both sides of a sail. The difference in pressure between the windward side (high pressure) and the leeward side (low pressure) sucks the sail to leeward and exerts a force on the sail, roughly at right angles to the boom, which drives the boat.

- **Sideways force** Some of the force created by the sails pushes the boat sideways, and this is resisted by the keel (see p.34).

- **Drag** Some of the force of the wind on the sails and on the boat pushes the boat backwards, slowing its forward movement.

UNDERSTANDING TRUE AND APPARENT WIND

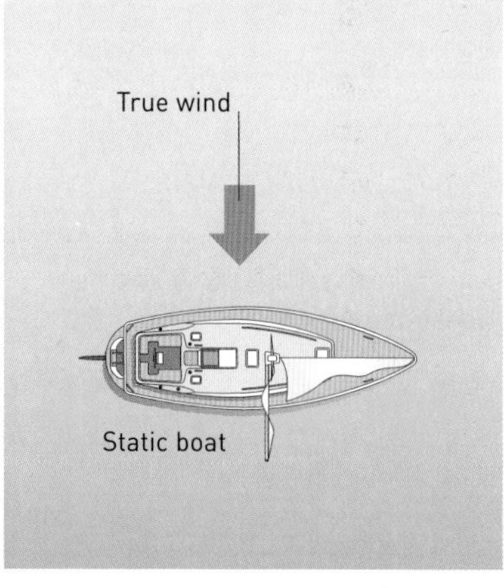

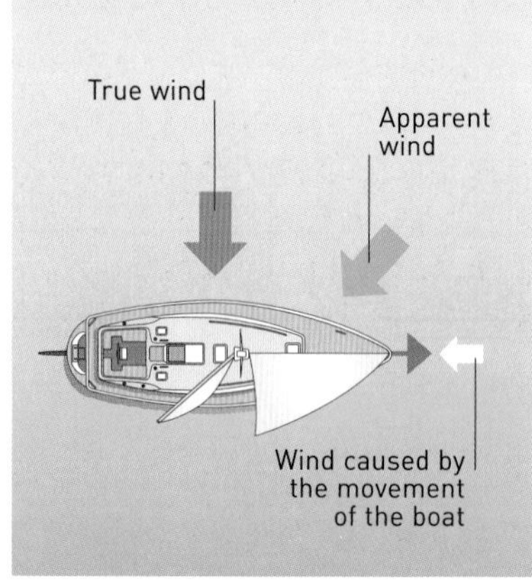

• **True wind** The wind direction and speed you feel when the boat is stopped is the effect of true wind. If the boat is moving, the wind speed and direction will appear to change.

• **Apparent wind** The wind you sail with is the result of the wind caused by the boat's motion altering the apparent direction and speed of the true wind.

WHAT IS LEEWAY?

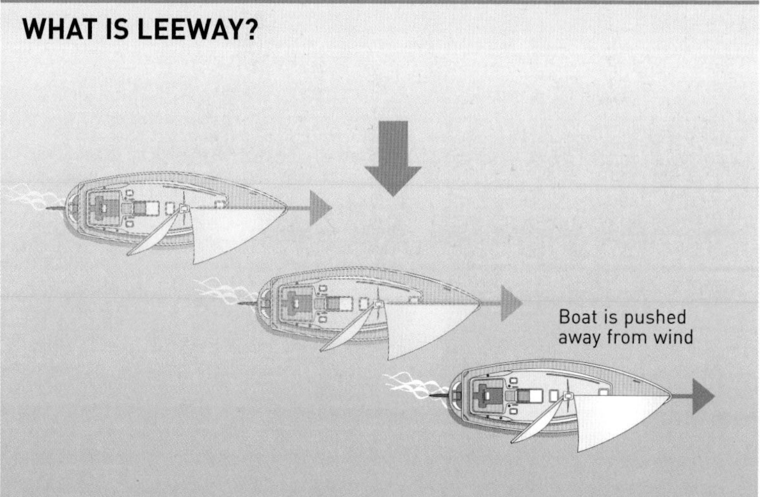

• **Excess sideways force** The keel resists the sideways force from the sail, but there is always a small excess force that causes the boat to slide to leeward on upwind courses.

• **Understanding leeway** Taking into account the effects of leeway is a key aspect of navigation (see pp.182–83).

UNDERSTANDING SIDE AND HEELING FORCES

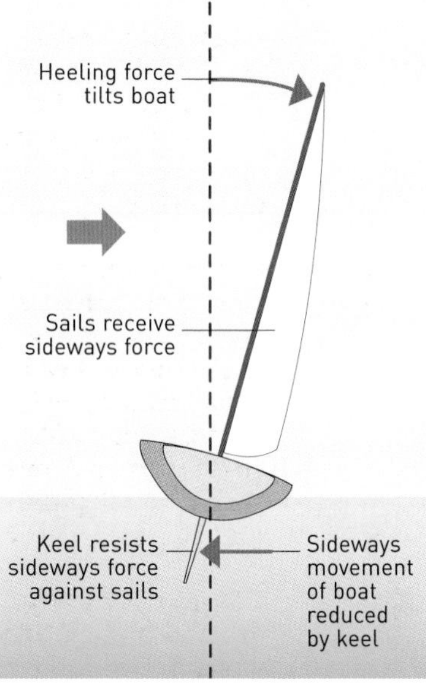

- **Heeling force** The sideways force on the sails and the keel's resistance combine to produce a heeling (tilting) force.

- **Keel resistance** The keel acts to prevent the boat being blown sideways and helps to transform some of the sideways force into forward drive.

- **Effects of keel and hull design** A weighted keel provides most of a yacht's stability – the remainder is provided by the beam and shape of the hull. The lower the centre of gravity of the keel, the greater the stability it provides.

WHAT IS BALANCED HELM?

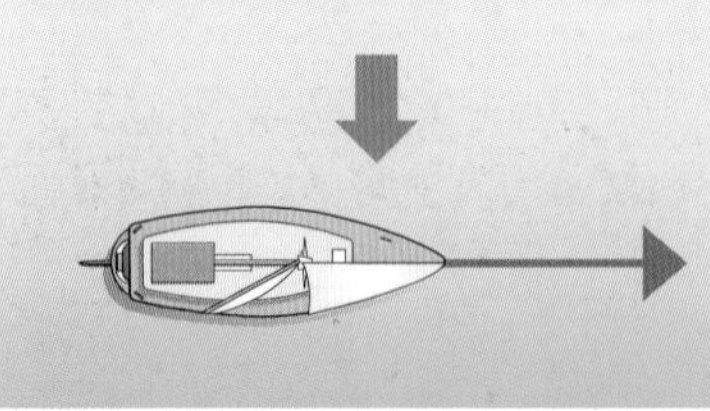

- **Balanced helm** This is when the forces generated by the sails and the forces on the keel and rudder are in balance and the boat sails a straight course without the need for the rudder to hold it on course.

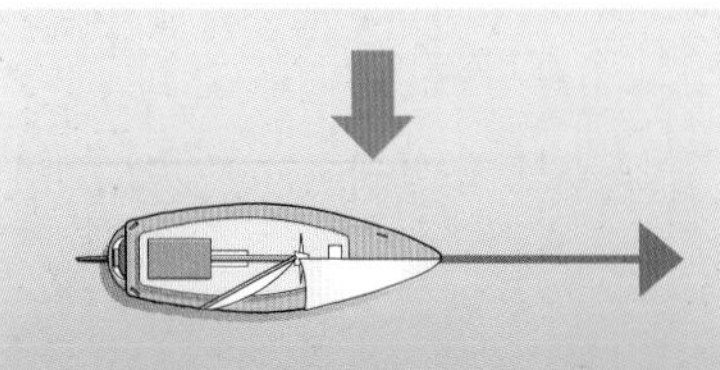

- **Weather helm** When the forces trying to turn the boat towards the wind are greater than those trying to turn it away from the wind, a boat is said to have weather helm. A small amount of weather helm is an advantage.

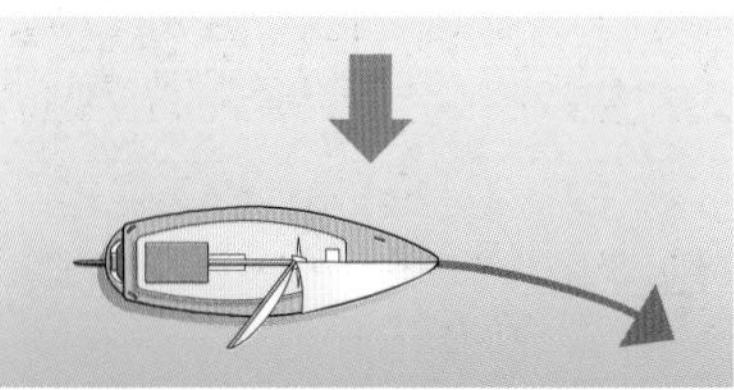

- **Lee helm** When the boat tends to turn away from the wind it is said to have lee helm. This makes the boat difficult to steer and is potentially dangerous. Reduce the size of the headsail to counter the effects of lee helm.

WHAT ARE THE EFFECTS OF CURRENTS AND TIDES?

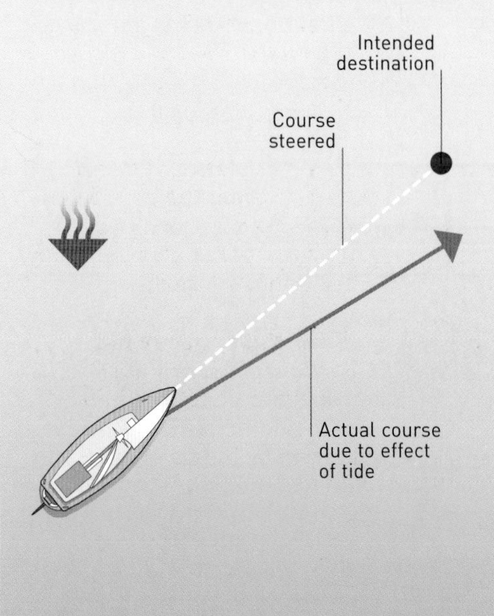

- **Currents** A tidal stream or a current will affect a boat's course and/or speed relative to land and the sea bed.
- **Effects** When a tidal stream or current is in opposition to the boat's course it will slow the boat down; from behind it will speed it up; and from the side it will push it off course.
- **Course planning** You need to take tidal streams and currents into account when navigating (see p.182).

HOW CAN I SPOT TIDAL FLOW?

- **Useful indicators** Navigation marks and other structures fixed to the seabed or river bed are useful indicators of the strength and direction of a tidal stream. A wake streams out downtide of the object.

Using the engine

Most sailing boats have an inboard marine diesel engine, often situated under the companionway steps or the cockpit. This drives the boat when under power and charges the batteries (see p.150) through an alternator when the engine is running.

WHEN TO USE THE ENGINE

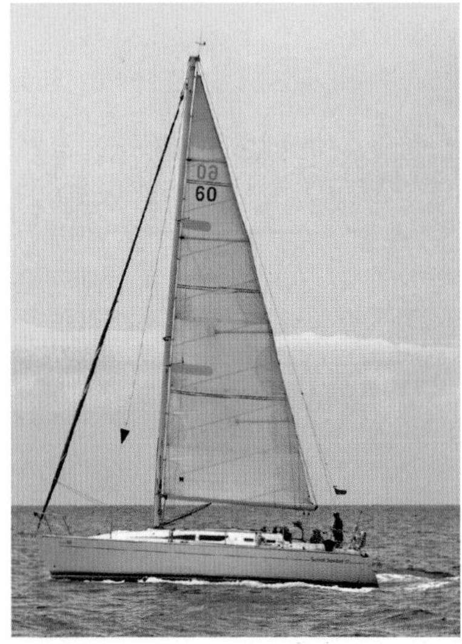

- **Harbours** In crowded harbours in popular sailing areas, it is sensible to enter and leave under power. In fact, many harbour by-laws require a boat with an engine to use it in the harbour.
- **Tight manoeuvring** Mooring in the tight confines of a marina is virtually impossible under sail, so use your engine.
- **Anchoring** When anchoring, it may be easier to anchor under power than sail.
- **Little wind** In calm conditions when it is impossible to sail, the engine will allow you to keep to your passage plan. If the wind dies down and the tide is against you, engine power will keep you moving.
- **Man overboard** If a crew member falls overboard, you may decide that it is safer to pick up the person under power rather than under sail.
- **Using your sails** A sailing boat is designed to sail, so do not rely too much on the engine – it may not work when you need it.

WHERE ARE THE ENGINE CONTROLS?

- **In the cockpit** The engine throttle and gear shift are situated in the cockpit, within reach of the helmsman.
- **Wheel binnacle** If the boat is steered by a wheel, the throttle and gear shift are usually situated on the wheel binnacle.
- **Start and stop controls** These are often located in the side of the cockpit within reach of the helmsman. They may be located down below for more protection.

HOW DO I REFUEL?

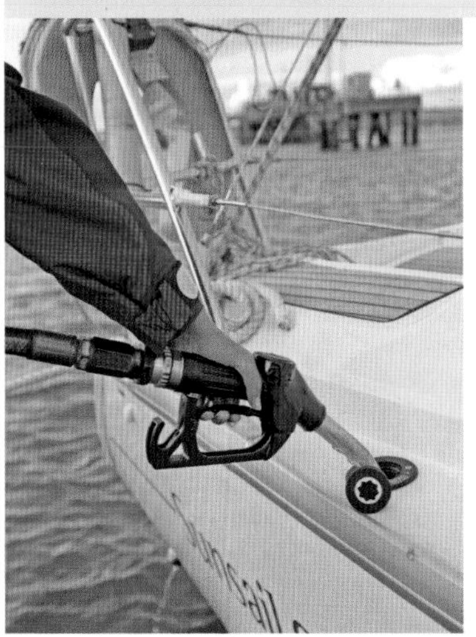

- **Keeping water out** Dry the deck around the filler before removing the cap to prevent water and dirt from getting in the tank.
- **Maintaining fuel reserves** Monitor your reserves and fill up before you get too low (see p.218). Try to maintain a reserve of 20 per cent and keep a spare can and funnel in a cockpit locker.
- **Avoiding spillage** Be careful when filling the tank. Have lots of paper towel to hand. Fill the tank slowly so that it does not overflow.

Manoeuvring under power

A yacht does not steer in the same way as a car. When you push the tiller or turn the wheel, the yacht pivots around a point near its centre, the precise position of which is determined by the position and size of the keel. Windage and prop walk also influence a boat's handling.

HOW A BOAT TURNS

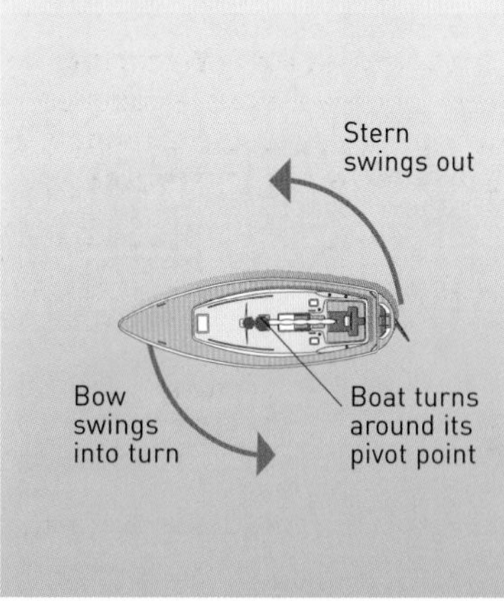

- **Rudder** The angle of the rudder controls the rate of turn – the greater the angle, the faster the turn.
- **Keel** A boat pivots around its keel as it turns. The greater the separation between keel and rudder, the greater the rudder's effectiveness.
- **Stern** The rudder acts at the stern and causes it to swing in the opposite direction to the bow.

WHAT FACTORS INFLUENCE MANOEUVRING?

- **Steerage way** A boat cannot be steered unless it is moving through the water, either ahead or astern.
- **Keel design** A cruiser with a long keel will have a larger turning circle than a fin-keeled yacht. Long-keeled yachts, with the rudder attached to the keel, are much harder to steer in reverse than fin-keeled yachts.
- **Windage** The drag or "windage" caused by parts of the boat and crew exposed to the wind will influence the way a boat can be turned.
- **Propeller** The size and type of propeller affects its efficiency and the amount of prop walk (see opposite) it creates.
- **Size** Larger, heavier boats are less manoeuvrable than smaller boats.

WHAT IS PROP WALK?

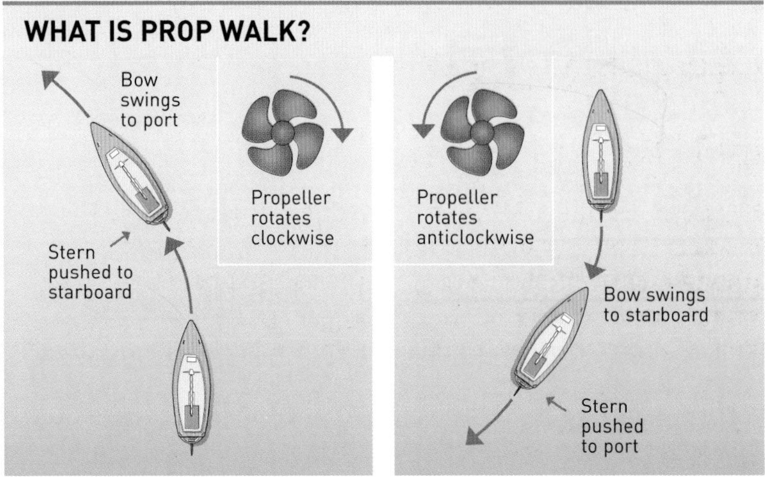

● **Prop walk ahead** A standard propeller rotates clockwise when running ahead, causing the stern to move slightly to starboard.

● **Prop walk astern** When running astern, a conventional propeller rotates anticlockwise, causing the stern to move slightly to port.

HOW TO TURN USING PROP WALK

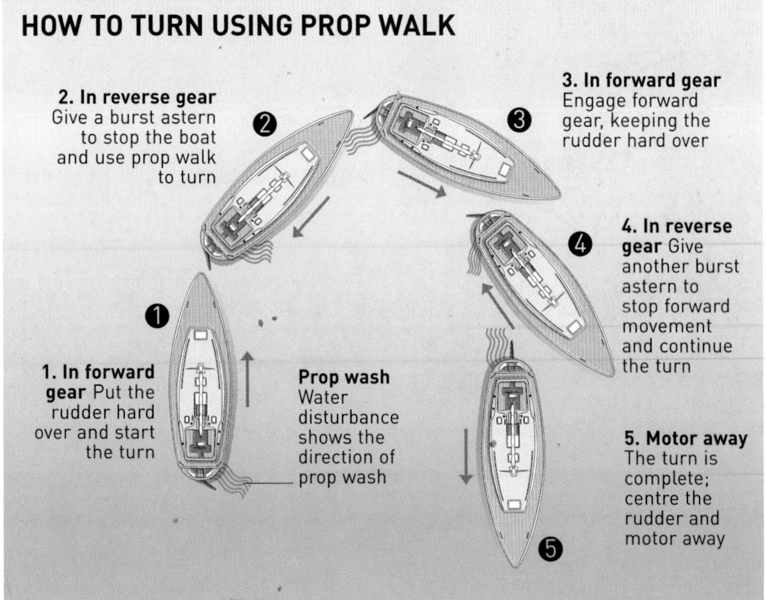

● **Using prop walk to turn** While turning the wheel, use short bursts of power in forward gear. Return to neutral when the boat starts to move. Then, in reverse gear, use short bursts of power to stop the forward movement and kick the stern to port.

Steering under power

Many modern fin-keeled cruisers, especially those with a spade rudder, steer astern well, even at slow speeds. If you are steering this sort of boat using a tiller, however, beware when motoring quickly astern. The forces on the rudder can be strong and will be transmitted to the tiller. Unless you hold it firmly and avoid large movements, the tiller may be wrenched from your grasp and swing violently to one side.

STEERING AHEAD

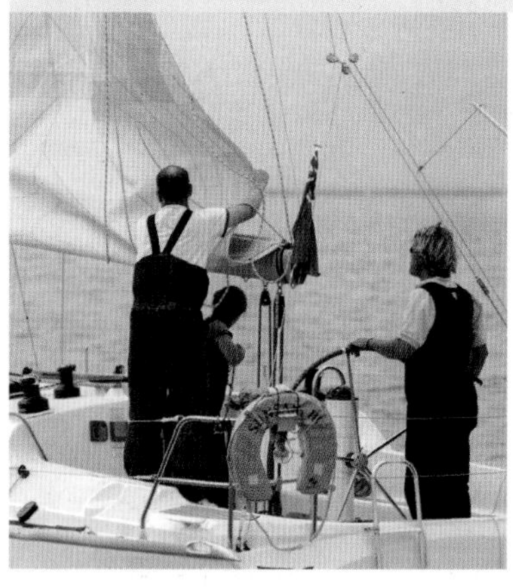

- **Lower the sails** In most cases it is best to lower sails when under power to ensure that the helmsman has an unobstructed view ahead and to save the sails from damage when flogging.

- **Keep clear** The crew should avoid standing in front of the helmsman and should be aware that a sudden course alteration could make them lose their balance. Sit down when possible.

STEERING ASTERN

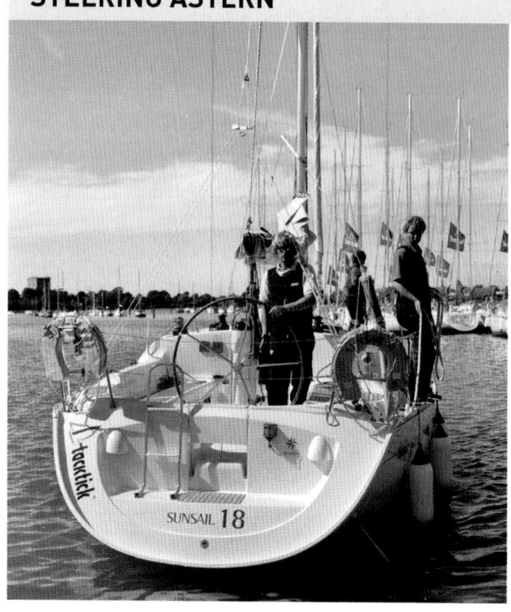

- **Good visibility** Motoring astern into a berth gives the helmsman good visibility.
- **Manoeuvrability astern** It is often easier to manoeuvre a modern cruiser into a berth stern first.
- **Beware shallow water** Be careful not to reverse stern first into shallow water where the rudder and the propeller risk damage.

CONTROLLING YOUR SPEED AND STOPPING

- **Go slowly** Proceed at a low speed in crowded waters or narrow channels.
- **Slow manoeuvres** In a marina or when hoisting or lowering sails, proceed at minimum engine revs to go slowly while keeping steerage way.
- **Allow for momentum** Remember that when you put the engine in neutral, the boat will continue moving for some distance.
- **No brakes** The only way to stop is to turn into the tide or wind or to put the engine in reverse for a quicker stop.

MOTOR-SAILING – WHAT DO I NEED TO KNOW?

- **Stability and speed** Motoring with the mainsail hoisted and sheeted close to the centreline helps stop the boat rolling and may add a bit of speed, depending on the conditions. Remember to hoist the motor-sailing day shape of an inverted cone ahead of the mast to let other vessels know that you are under power.

Points of sailing

The direction in which a boat is being sailed is often described in relation to its angle to the wind. Collectively, these angles are known as the "points of sailing". When you change from one point of sailing to another, the sails need to be adjusted to suit the new angle of the boat in relation to the wind.

WHAT ARE THE VARIOUS SAILING COURSES?

- **Close-hauled** This course is the closest a boat can sail to the wind, without entering the no-sail zone. For most boats, this is about 40°–45° away from the wind. When sailing close-hauled, both sails are pulled in tight to the centreline.

- **Close reach** This windward course is achieved when a boat on a close-hauled course is turned away from the wind by a further 10° and the sails are eased out a little.

- **Beam reach** When a boat sails with the wind coming directly across its side and the sails eased halfway, it is said to be on a beam reach.

- **Broad reach** This downwind course is when the boat sails about 120° away from the wind with the sails eased almost fully.

- **A run** A boat is said to be on a run when the wind is directly behind the boat and the sails are eased out fully.

WHAT IS THE NO-SAIL ZONE?

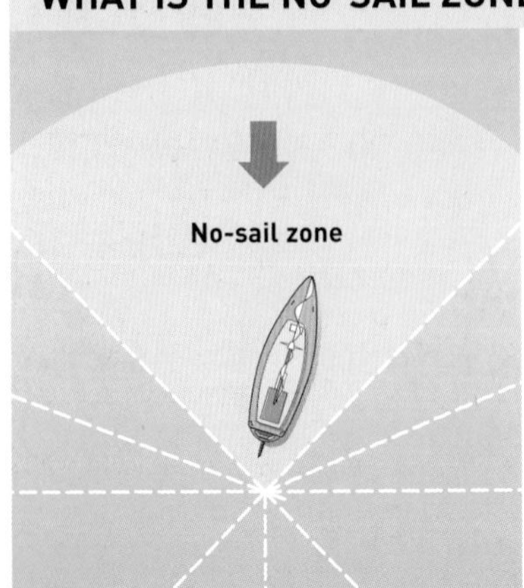

- **Too close to the wind** If a boat sails closer to the wind than an angle of about 40°–45°, it enters what is termed the no-sail zone.

- **In irons** In the no-sail zone, the sails cannot fill and the boat will stop. This situation is known as being "in irons".

Sailing close-hauled This boat has its sails pulled in tight as it sails as close as possible to the wind.

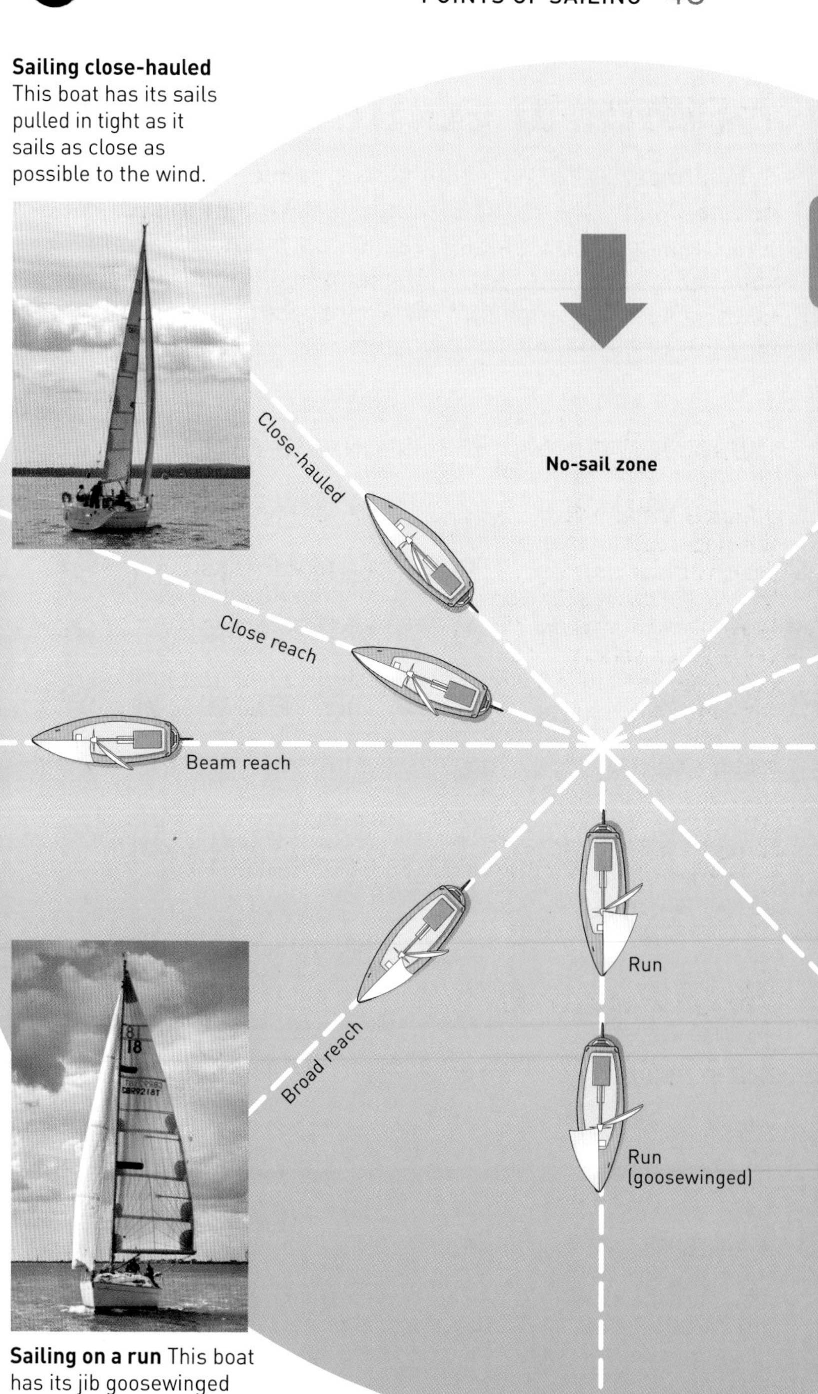

Sailing on a run This boat has its jib goosewinged on the opposite side to the mainsail.

Steering controls

When under sail, the rudder is the main means of steering the boat, but is not the only turning control at your disposal. Indeed, if sail trim and angle of heel are not considered, it can be impossible to turn the boat using the rudder in some circumstances. The type of keel – long or fin – also affects how quickly a boat will turn.

HOW KEEL AND RUDDER DESIGNS AFFECT STEERING

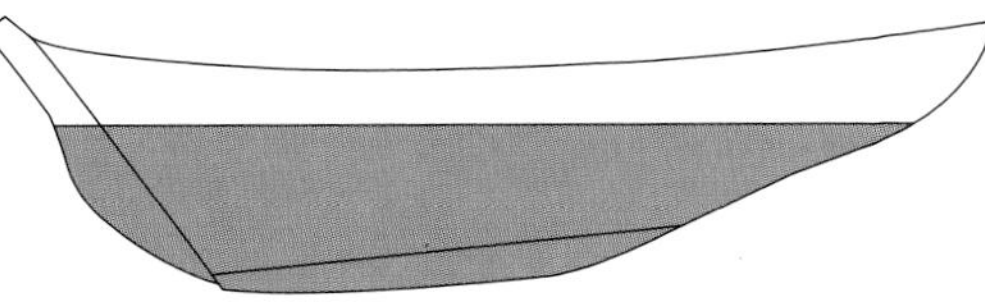

- **Long keel** A long-keeled yacht will hold its course better but will be slower to turn than a fin-keeled boat.

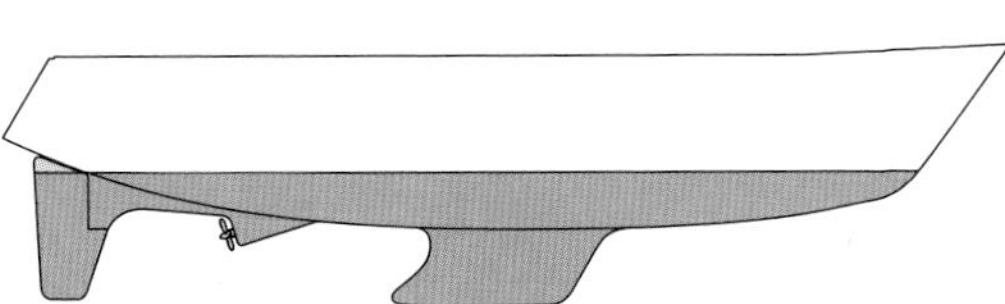

- **Fin keel** A fin-keeled yacht with a rudder that is not attached to the keel is more manoeuvrable.

HOW THE RUDDER AFFECTS BOAT DIRECTION

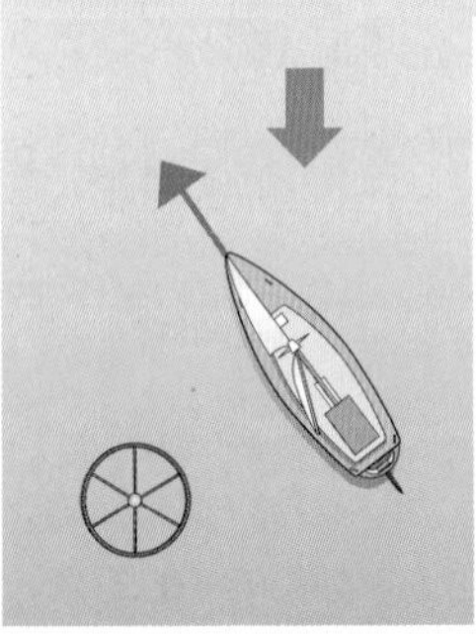

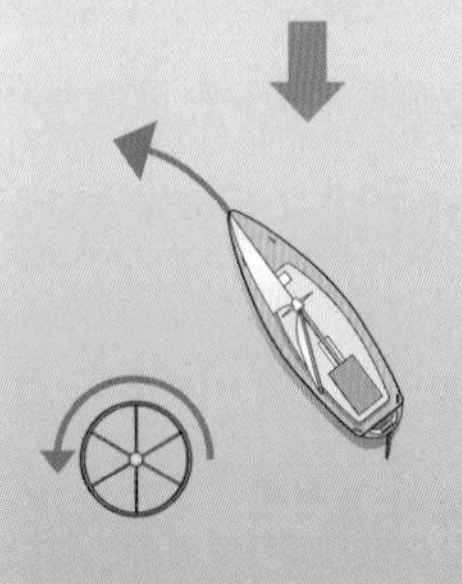

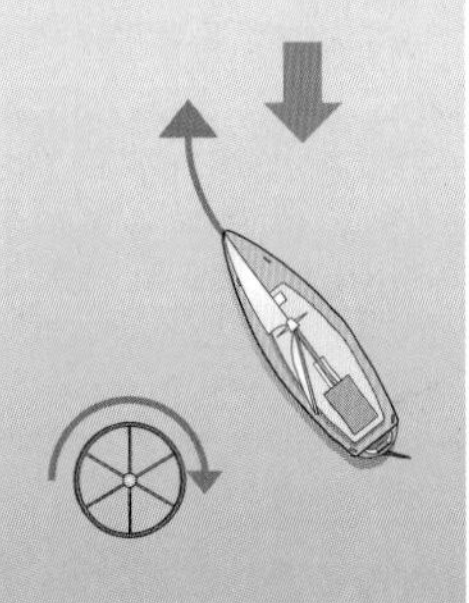

- **Straight ahead** If a boat has a neutral helm (see p.34), keep the wheel centred. If the boat heels, it will tend to turn into the wind and you will need to steer slightly away.
- **Towards port** Turning the wheel to the left turns the boat to port, which here is away from the wind.
- **Towards starboard** Turning the wheel to the right turns the boat to starboard, which here is towards the wind.

UNDERSTANDING STEERING AND STEERAGE WAY

- **Wheel** Most yachts over 10m (33ft) in length use a wheel mounted on a binnacle to steer the boat.

- **Response of the rudder** This depends on the speed of the water flow over the rudder.

- **Steerage way** If a yacht is not moving through the water, the rudder will have no steering effect at all. The amount of speed through the water that is needed for the boat to be steerable is known as "steerage way".

HOW TO STEER USING SAILS

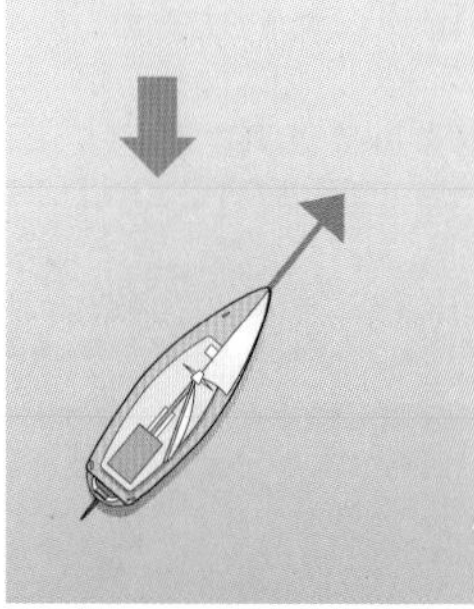

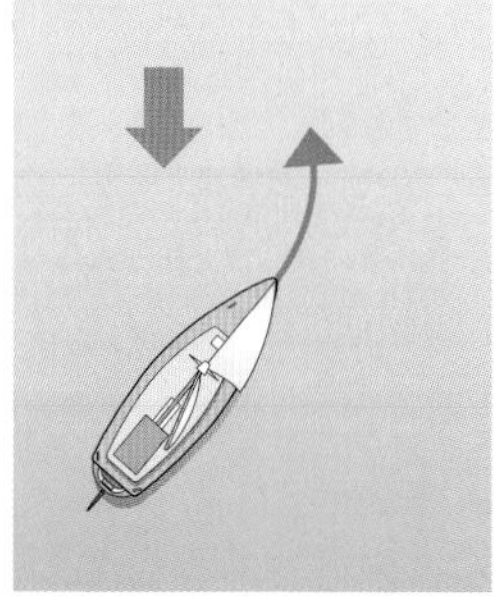

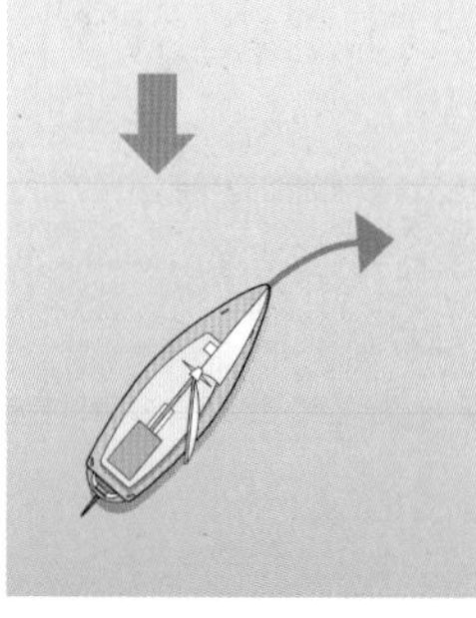

- **Straight course** When the sails are balanced, it is possible to get the yacht to sail a straight course in flat water just by adjusting the sails to keep the boat on course, without using the rudder.

- **Towards the wind** Pulling in the mainsail and letting out the headsail will cause the boat to turn towards the wind.

- **Away from the wind** Letting out the mainsail and pulling in the headsail will cause the boat to turn away from the wind.

Sail controls

Most modern sailing yachts use a bermudan sloop rig, with just one mast, a headsail (usually called a jib), and a mainsail, but older yachts may have quite different configurations with one or two masts and different types of sail arrangements. Apart from the halyards, which are used to hoist the sails, the main sail controls are the sheets.

CONTROLLING THE ANGLE OF THE JIB

- **Sheets** These are ropes that control the angle of a sail to the boat's centreline. They pull the sails in and let them out.

- **Attachment** A jib has two sheets, one on each side. They are tied to the sail at the clew by a bowline.

- **Working and lazy sheets** Only one jib sheet is used at a time, which is the working sheet. The other is the lazy sheet.

- **Turning block** Each sheet runs from the clew down to a deck- or track-mounted turning block, and back to the cockpit.

- **Winch** Each sheet is led to a winch on the cabin roof or the side of the cockpit so the crew can work them effectively.

SETTING THE ANGLE OF THE MAINSAIL

- **Mainsheet** This controls the angle of the mainsail to the boat's centreline. There is only one mainsheet, which is attached to the boom and is rigged as a multi-part tackle to provide power to adjust it. On larger boats a winch is used to adjust the mainsheet.

USING THE SHEETS

- **Trim** Adjust the sail trim every time the boat alters course by pulling in the sheet until the sail stops shaking at its luff (front edge). At this point it is correctly trimmed for the wind angle on the course you are sailing. Ease out the sheet when you bear away.

- **Twist** The twist of a sail is the difference in its angle to the wind between its top and bottom. A small amount of twist is usually required for the best trim.

- **Ease** Use the mainsheet and the boom vang to adjust the twist of the mainsail. Ease both slightly to introduce more twist and pull them in to reduce twist.

Winches and clutches

Winches are used to control sails which produce loads larger than the crew can manage by hand. Most modern yachts have self-tailing winches that allow one-person operation. Winches without self-tailing jaws require two people to winch the rope – one person to wind the winch and the other to pull on the end, which is known as "tailing".

WHAT ARE WINCHES?

- **Large loads** A winch allows you to control large loads. There are two types of winch – manual and power-assisted.

- **Self-tailing** In a manual self-tailing winch, turning the drum with a handle placed into a slot on top of the drum increases the power applied to the rope.

WHAT ARE CLUTCHES?

- **Securing lines** Clutches are used to secure halyards and control lines and to allow one winch to control several lines. Clutches are placed between the winch and the turning blocks so that when they are closed, the line can be taken off the winch.

WHAT ARE TURNING BLOCKS?

- **Deck organization** Turning blocks are fittings that are bolted to the deck. They are used to change the direction of halyard and control lines and lead them aft to clutches and winches that allow the lines to be operated from the cockpit.

LOADING A SELF-TAILING WINCH

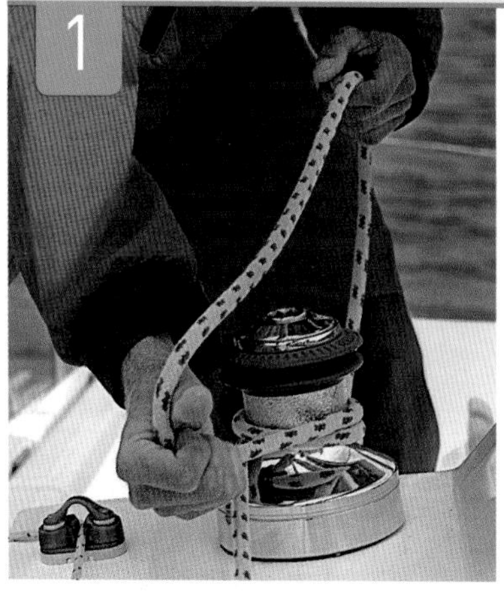

- **Wind the rope** clockwise around the drum. Keep your fingers clear by pointing the thumb away, as shown here.
- **Make enough turns** to provide sufficient friction to hold the rope. Three or four turns are usually enough.
- **Make sure that the turns** are placed neatly one above the other and do not allow one turn to cross another.

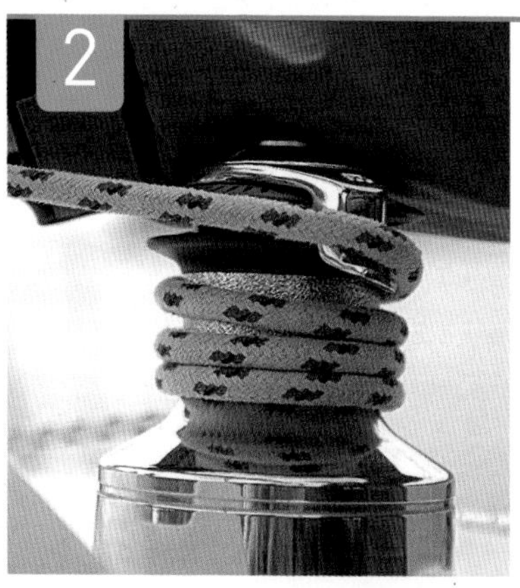

- **Pull in the slack** by hand with two turns on the drum before adding extra turns.
- **Secure the rope** by taking a turn over the feeder and pulling it into the self-tailing jaws.

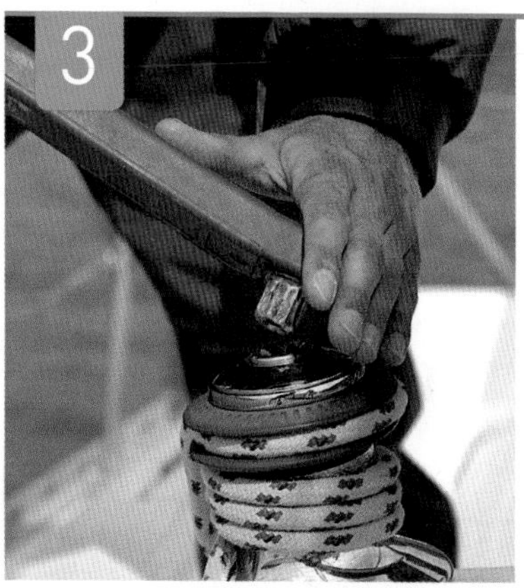

- **Put the handle** into the top of the winch with both hands, ensuring it is fully locked before you start to wind. Longer handles give greater power, but there may not be space to turn them through 360°.
- **Position your shoulders** over the winch for maximum power, and wind with both hands.

Basic manoeuvres

The most basic manoeuvres in sailing are luffing up and bearing away and both describe a turn in relation to the wind direction. Luffing up is turning the boat towards the wind, and bearing away is turning the boat away from the wind, on either a port or starboard tack. Start sailing on a beam reach (see pp.42–43) and practise these manoeuvres.

HOW TO LUFF UP

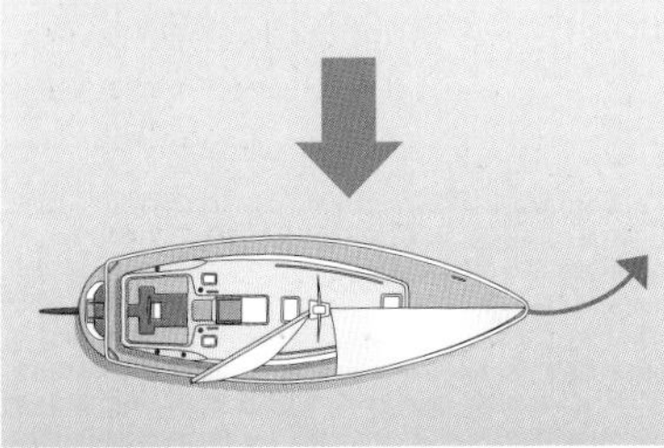

- **Turning under sail** To do this, use a combination of turning the rudder and adjusting the sails. Do not rely solely on the rudder.
- **Luffing up** To luff up, turn the wheel towards the wind, and sheet in the mainsail and the jib.

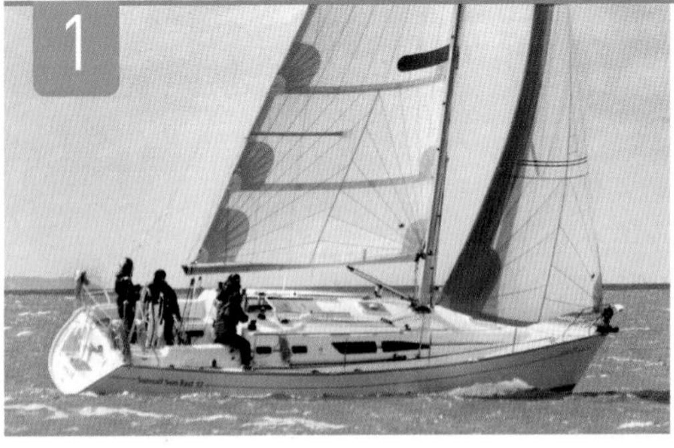

1

- **Make a smooth turn** and do not turn faster than you can trim the sails.
- **Sheet in** the mainsail faster than the jib so that it helps the boat to luff up.

2

- **Practise** luffing up from a reach to a close reach, then to close-hauled.
- **Be prepared** for the loads on the mainsheet and jib sheets to increase as the boat sails closer to the wind.

HOW TO BEAR AWAY

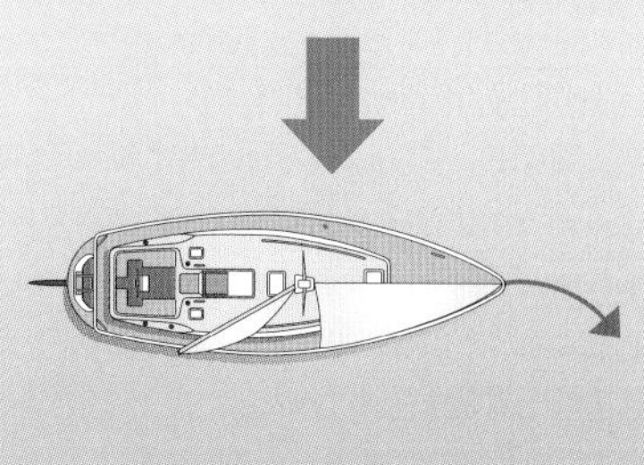

- **Bearing away** To do this, turn the wheel away from the wind and let out the mainsheet and jib sheets.
- **Best practice** Make it your practice to let out the mainsheet before turning the wheel. This will make it much easier to bear away, especially in strong winds.

- **Use the jib** Always ease the mainsheet before the jib sheet. The jib will help the boat bear away.
- **Loads on the sheets** These will decrease as the boat bears away and sails further downwind, reducing the wind pressure on the sails.

UNDERSTANDING HEAD-TO-WIND

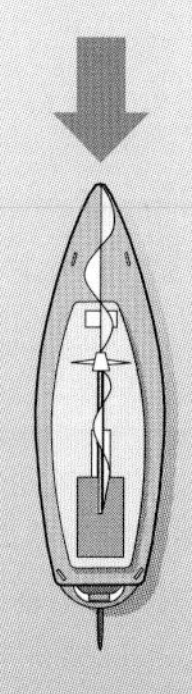

- **Turning head-to-wind** This is the best way to stop when under sail. The sails flap in the middle of the boat.
- **Managing the mainsail** Turn head-to-wind to hoist or lower the mainsail.
- **Safety** Avoid being struck by the boom swinging in the middle of the boat, or by the jib or its sheets as the jib flaps.

Changing tack

There are two ways to turn the boat from one tack to the other – tacking and gybing. Tacking is used when the yacht is sailing upwind, while gybing is used when sailing downwind. Tacking involves turning the bow of the boat through the wind until the sails fill on the new tack, while gybing involves turning the stern through the wind.

UNDERSTANDING TACKING

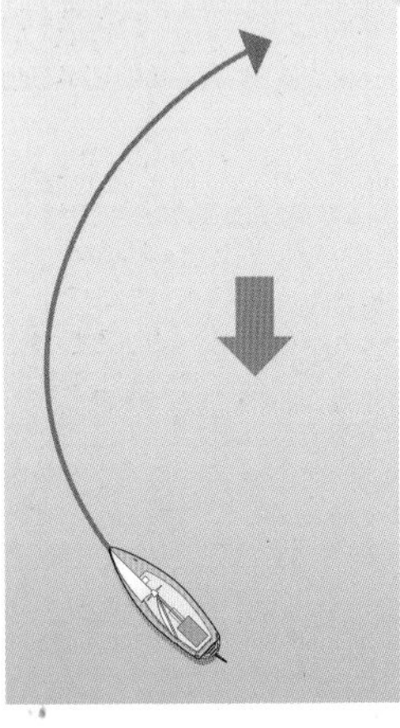

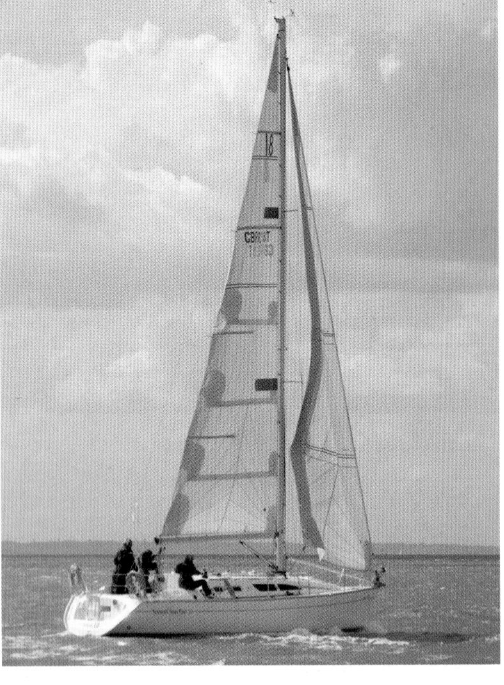

● **The manoeuvre** The tack starts as the boat luffs up (see p.50). It continues as the boat turns through the wind and bears away onto the new tack. Here the boat is tacking from starboard tack to port tack (see opposite). It is important that the helmsman does not allow the boat to stop head-to-wind (see p.51), a situation known as being "in irons".

● **Sails** As the boat turns head-to-wind, the sails will flap in the middle of the boat, as shown above. They will fill again on the new side as the boat bears away from the wind onto the new tack.

● **Jib control** Release the old jib sheet and pull in the new one as the jib blows across to the new side.

UNDERSTANDING GYBING

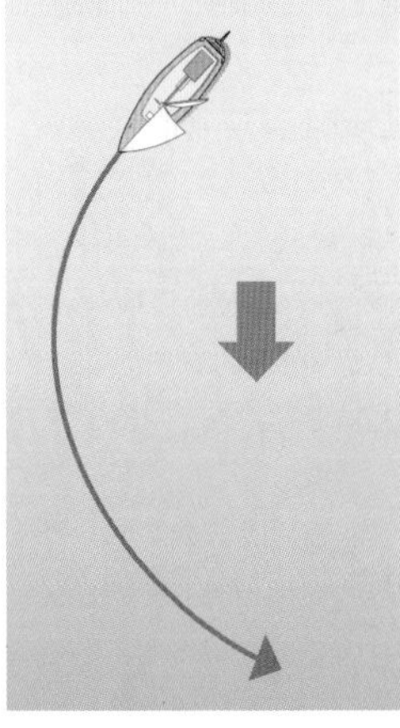

- **The manoeuvre** The gybe starts when the boat bears away (see p.51). It continues as the stern turns through the wind.
- **Sails** The sails, especially the mainsail, swing across the boat faster and more violently than when tacking.
- **Mainsail control** Pull in the mainsail before the gybe to limit how far it can swing, then let it out again after the gybe.

PORT OR STARBOARD – WHICH TACK AM I ON?

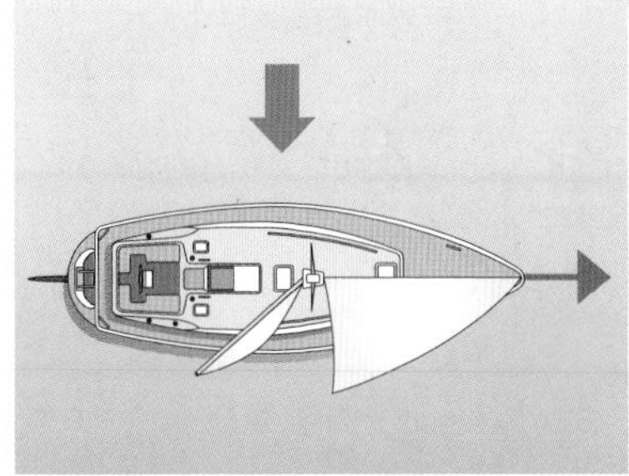

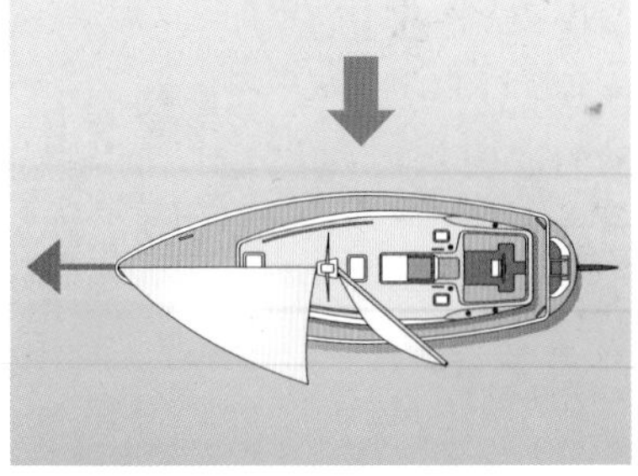

- **Port tack** The boat is said to be on port tack when the wind is coming from the port side of the boat and the sails are set on the starboard side.
- **Starboard tack** The boat is said to be on starboard tack when the wind is coming from the starboard side and the sails are on the port side.
- **Wind over the stern** If the wind is not clearly on either side, as on a run, a boat is said to be on port tack if the boom is on the starboard side and vice versa.

Hoisting the mainsail

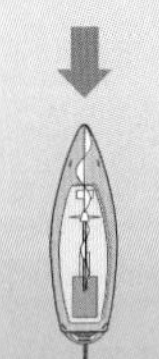

The skipper briefs the crew on where and when to hoist, and decides if any reefs are required. When you are ready to hoist the mainsail make sure you have plenty of space around the boat and turn it head-to-wind to allow the sail to be hoisted without filling with wind.

- **Foredeck crew** Attach the main halyard to the head of the sail.
- Pull the halyard taut to prevent it catching on the spreaders.
- Remove the sail ties.

- **Cockpit crew** Close the clutch and take three turns of the halyard around the winch.
- Pull the slack out of the halyard and prepare to hoist.

- **Cockpit crew** Ease the mainsheet and boom vang (the tackle that prevents the boom from lifting) to allow the boom to lift and swing freely.
- **Crew** Keep clear of the boom during the hoist.

● **Foredeck crew** Pull the halyard at the mast to raise the mainsail.

● **Cockpit crew** Pull in the slack on the winch in time with the foredeck crew hoisting the sail.

● **Cockpit crew** When the foredeck crew can no longer manually pull on the halyard, feed it over the self-tailer and tighten it using the winch until the luff (front edge) of the mainsail is taut.

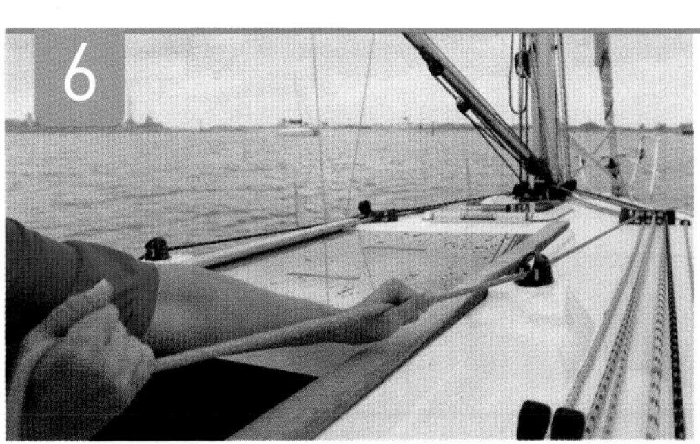

● **Cockpit crew** When the mainsail is fully hoisted, tighten the boom vang and tidy up the halyard.

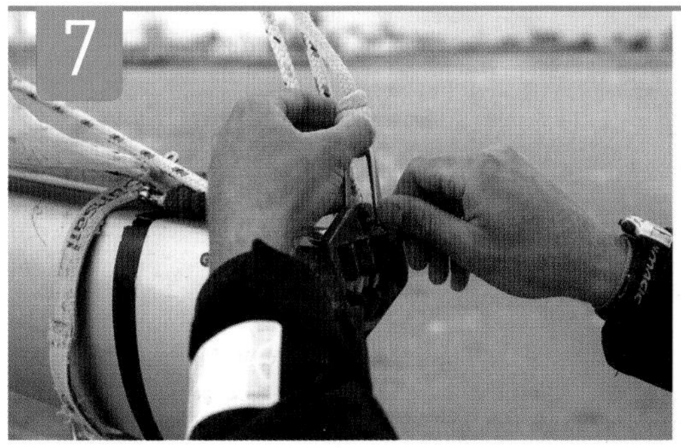

● **Cockpit crew** Slacken the topping lift. On some boats you remove it from the boom end and secure it to the base of the mast while sailing. Do not forget to re-attach it before lowering the sail.

Dropping the mainsail

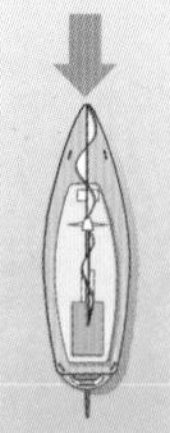

Lowering the mainsail is the reverse procedure of hoisting it. Allow enough room so that the drop can be done without haste. If you are returning to harbour, for example, start the engine and ensure you have room to turn head-to-wind during the drop. Aim to motor as slowly as possible into the wind, maintaining enough speed to give steerage way.

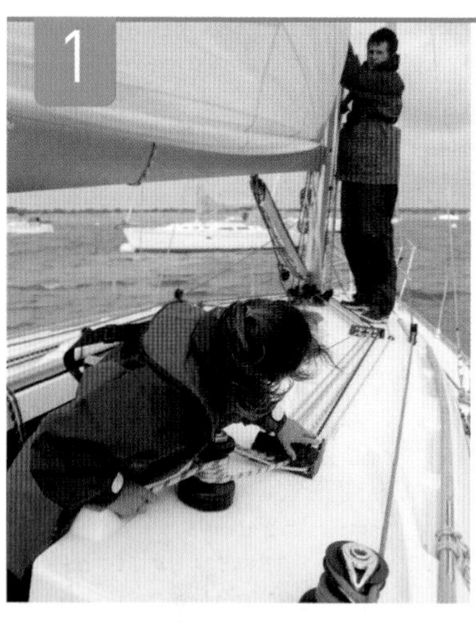

1

- **Cockpit crew** If the topping lift (see p.55) was removed after hoisting, replace it.
- Carefully ease the mainsheet and tighten the topping lift to take the weight of the boom off the sail.
- Put the mainsail halyard on to the winch and release the clutch lever.
- **Foredeck crew** Prepare to pull down on the luff (forward edge).

2

- **Cockpit crew** Ease the turns round the winch drum with one hand while holding the end of the mainsail halyard in the other.

3

- **Foredeck crew** Pull the sail down by the luff.

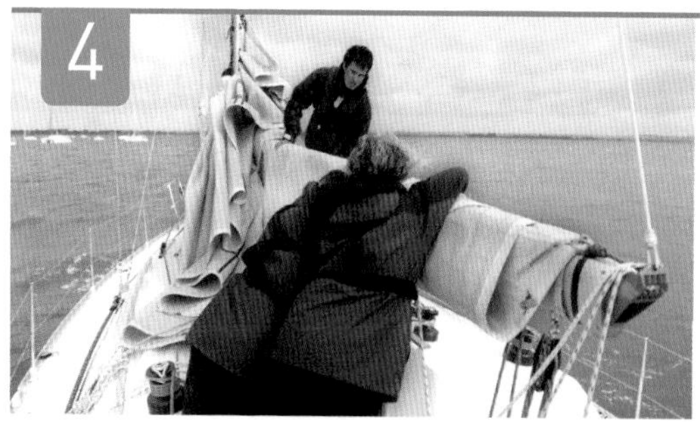

- **Crew** Tighten the mainsheet to prevent the boom moving.
- Flake the mainsail by arranging it in folds on top of the boom. (See also Stowing alternatives, below.)

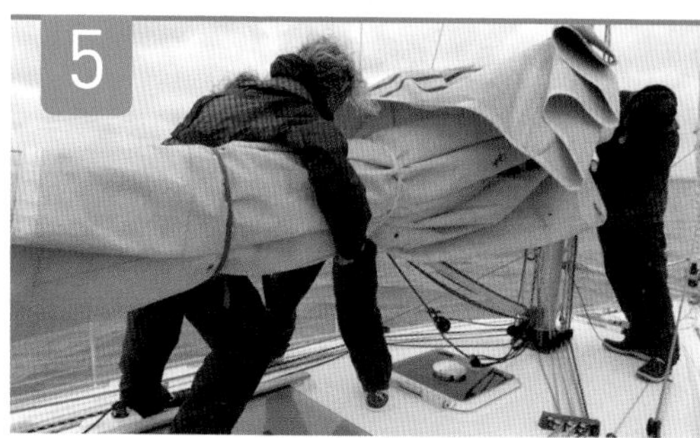

- **Crew** With the sail stowed neatly on the boom, hold it in place with a number of sail ties tied around the sail and boom.

STOWING ALTERNATIVES

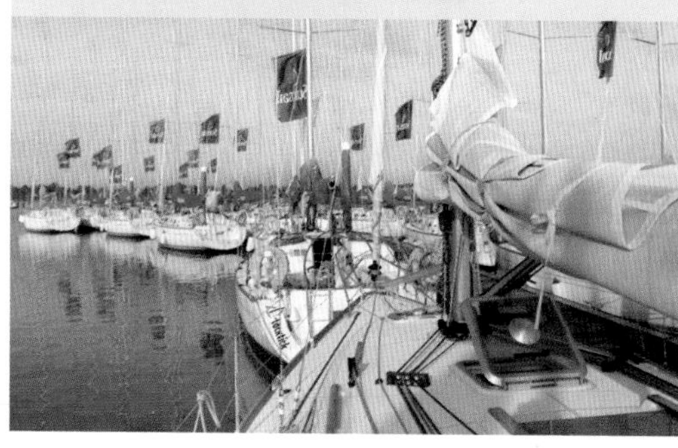

- **Stuffing or flaking** How you stow the mainsail depends on the type of sail material, and whether it is fully battened or not.

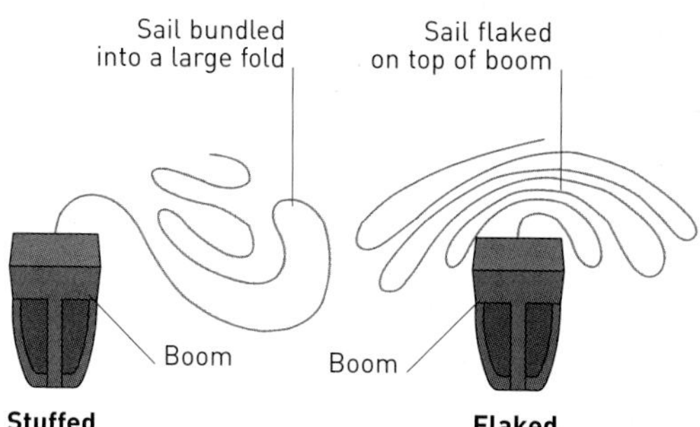

- **Stuffed** Cloth sails can be stuffed into a fold of sail pulled out from the foot of the sail.
- **Flaked** With laminate or fully battened sail, flake it over the boom.

Unfurling the headsail

Most modern cruisers use only one headsail – known as a jib – at a time. The most common arrangement is to have the jib fitted to a roller-reefing system, operated by a furling line, which allows it to be rolled away. An older, more flexible arrangement is to have a number of jibs to suit different wind strengths. These are attached to the forestay by metal hanks.

UNFURLING A ROLLER-REEFING HEADSAIL

1

- **Cockpit crew** Put a couple of turns of the leeward sheet onto the winch.
- Check that the furling line is free to run.

2

- **Cockpit crew** Open the clutch that is controlling the furling line and pull on the leeward jib sheet to unroll the headsail.

- **Cockpit crew** As you unroll the headsail, the wind will catch it and help it unroll. Pull in the jib sheet to prevent the sail from flogging.
- Adjust the jib sheet to trim it for the course being sailed.
- Take the slack out of the furling line and close its clutch.
- If you require only part of the jib to be unfurled, ease the furling line on a winch until a sufficient amount of the jib is unfurled, then close the clutch.

HOW TO UNFURL A HANKED HEADSAIL

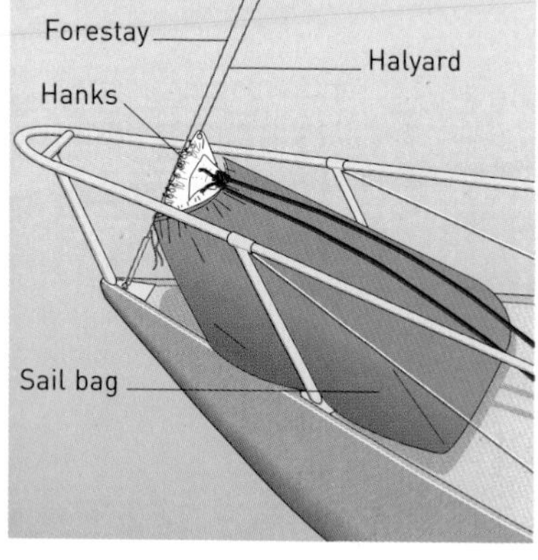

- **Hanked at the luff** The luff of the sail is attached to the forestay with metal hanks. The halyard and sheets are attached to the head and clew. Remove the sail from its bag before hoisting.
- **Hoisting** Pull the halyard to hoist the sail up the forestay.
- **Lowering** Release the halyard so that the hanks slide down the forestay. Gather and stow the sail.

Furling and stowing the headsail

A furling headsail is easy to roll away when it is not needed or to partially roll when you need to reef. The system has disadvantages, but it is convenient and popular for coastal cruising, and most modern yachts are fitted with a headsail of this type. Older yachts may have headsails attached to the forestay by hanks.

FURLING A HEADSAIL

- **First cockpit crew** Use the winch to wind in the furling line from the furling drum.

- **Second cockpit crew** Ease off the jib sheet, while keeping some tension on it so that the sail furls tightly and evenly.

- **If working alone** Leave one or two turns of the jib sheet around the winch to keep the roll tight while you pull on the furling line.

2

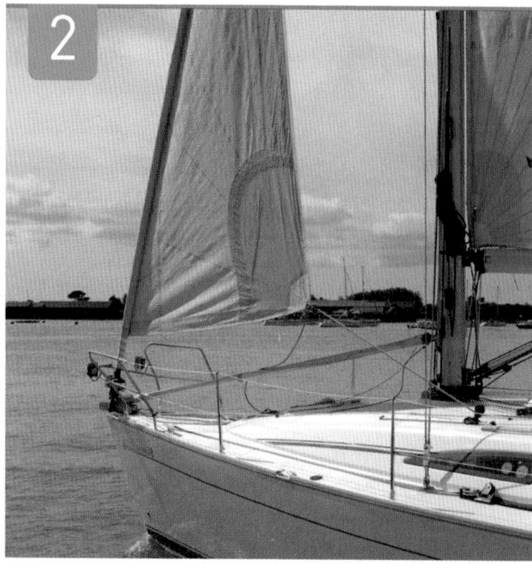

- **First cockpit crew** Continue to wind in the furling line.
- **Second cockpit crew** As the headsail begins to roll up, keep some tension on one or both sheets.

3

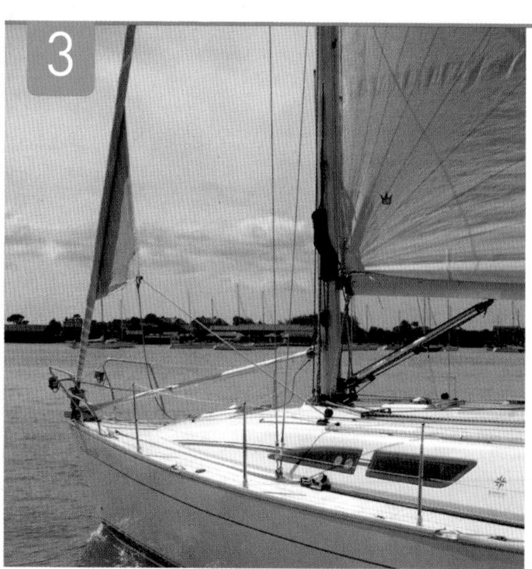

- **Second cockpit crew** When the sheets start to roll around the sail, pull in the sheets until tight, and cleat.
- **First cockpit crew** Close the clutch to secure the furling line under tension. This will help to prevent the line falling off the roller-furling drum and jamming.

LOWERING AND STOWING A HANKED HEADSAIL

- **Hanked headsail** Lower this type of headsail by releasing the halyard. A crew member should be on the foredeck to prevent it falling into the water.
- **Stowing** You can temporarily stow the headsail while it is attached to the forestay by tying the sail to the guardrail with sail ties, or by bundling all but the luff into a sailbag.

Sail trimming

Sail handling and trimming is not only about hoisting the sails and pulling them in. Sails should be adjusted using a number of controls to alter the shape of the sail to suit different wind strengths and the points of sailing. Understanding sail trim allows you to sail fast in all conditions and more comfortably in rough weather.

HOW SHOULD I SET THE SAILS?

- **Slot** One of the key factors that determine sailing performance is the slot between the mainsail luff (front edge) and the headsail leech (back edge). Aim to keep the slot even all the way up.

- **Too tight** The slot will be too tight if the headsail is over-sheeted or the mainsail is under-sheeted. The airflow will be choked, and the boat will sail slowly and heel more. The mainsail may shake at the luff.

- **Too open** The slot will be too open if the headsail is under-sheeted or the mainsail is over-sheeted. If the jib sheet leads are too far aft, the top of the headsail will twist, as shown here, and power will be lost (see also p.34).

HOW CAN I JUDGE WIND DIRECTION?

● **Masthead wind indicators** The modern solution is the permanent Windex, which sometimes incorporates a VHF aerial. Traditionally, a burgee (triangular flag on a short flagstaff) at the masthead is used to indicate the wind direction.

● **Anemometer** An electronic speed and direction sensor is often mounted at the masthead with a readout in the cockpit.

ADJUSTING THE LUFF

● **Mainsail halyard** Tighten the halyard sufficiently to remove any horizontal creases running from the luff. Apply more halyard tension as the wind increases. This prevents the fullness in the sail moving back towards the leech, which causes the boat to slow down and heel more.

● **Jib halyard** Adjust the halyard tension to remove any horizontal creases running from the luff. The halyard should be tighter in strong winds and eased slightly in light winds to maintain the correct shape in the sail.

FLATTENING THE MAINSAIL

● **Cunningham** This control is fitted on some boats. It pulls a cringle (eyelet) in the luff of the sail down towards the boom and helps flatten the sail in stronger winds and twist the leech off at the top, which reduces heeling.

TENSIONING THE FOOT OF THE MAINSAIL

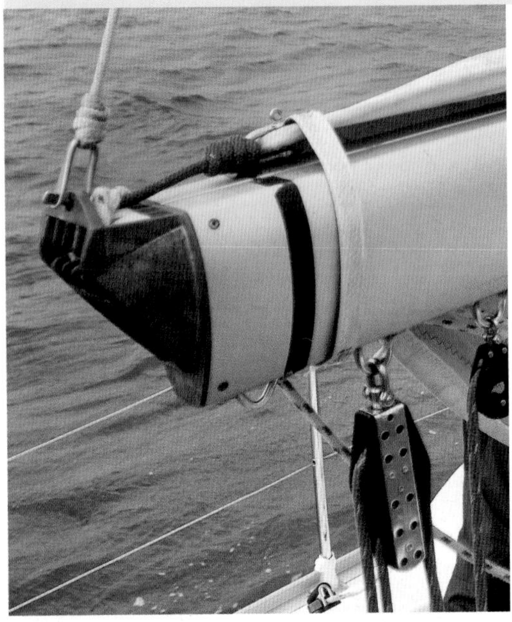

- **Use the clew outhaul** This controls the tension of the mainsail's foot. It usually runs inside the boom from the clew and exits at the mast end (the red line pictured left at the end of the boom) .

- **Adjustment** The clew outhaul may be adjusted at the mast, or more commonly, is led back to a clutch near a cockpit winch. Ease it in light winds and when sailing offwind, and tighten it in strong winds.

CONTROLLING MAINSAIL TWIST

- **Twist** The boom vang in conjunction with the mainsheet controls the amount that the mainsail leech can twist off between head and clew.

- **Adjust** Ease the boom vang in light winds and tighten it in stronger winds.

- **Leech tell-tale** Adjust the boom vang to keep the top tell-tale streaming aft most of the time.

READING TELL-TALES

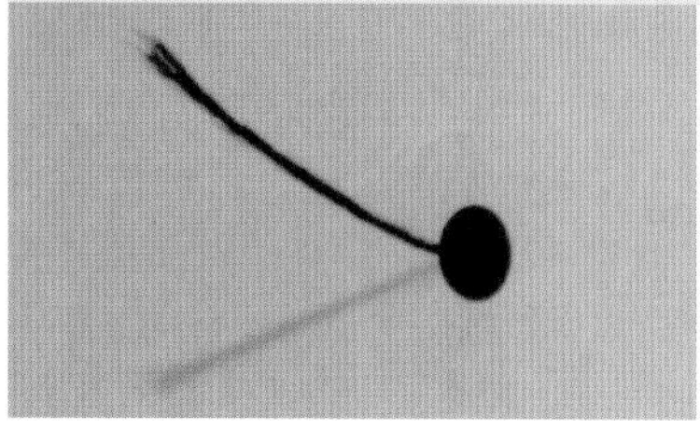

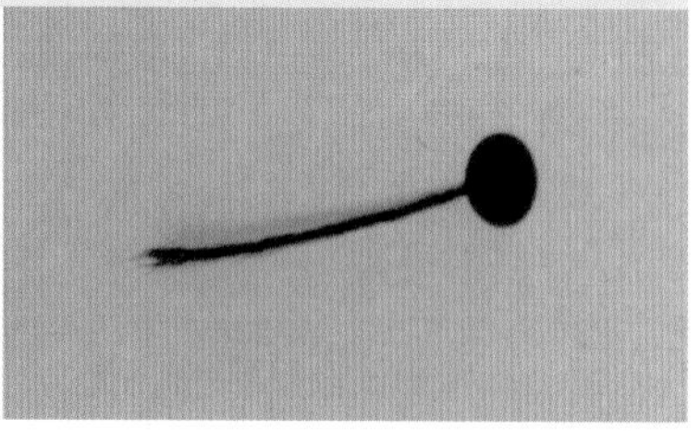

● **Lifting** The windward tell-tale will lift when the sail is slightly under-sheeted, or when sailing too close to the wind.

● **Streaming** When both tell-tales are streaming aft, the sail is perfectly trimmed.

ADJUSTING THE SLOT USING THE JIB TURNING BLOCK

● **Position** The jib sheet turning block is mounted on a track that allows it to move fore and aft.

● **Fore-and-aft position** Move the block fore and aft to adjust the slot between headsail and mainsail when sailing upwind. When sailing offwind, move the lead forward to control the jib leech.

Steering a course

Keep a yacht and its sails in balance to steer a course well. You must have the correct amount of sail area for the prevailing conditions, and the crew must trim the sails in accordance with the course being followed by the helmsman. When this is achieved, the yacht will be easy to steer and "light on the helm".

STEERING A STRAIGHT COURSE

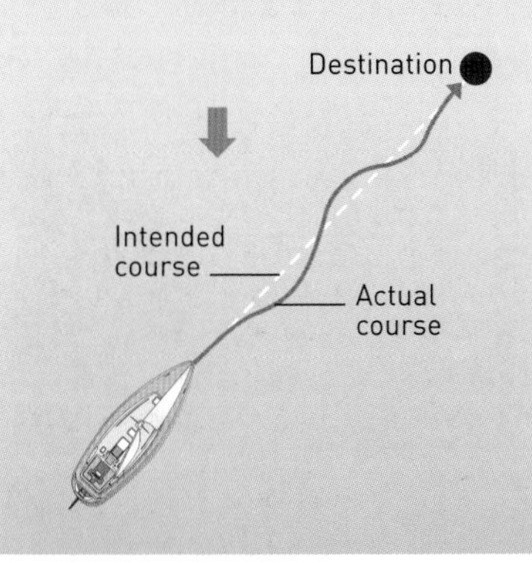

- **Course correction** The effects of wind and waves mean it is hard to sail a straight course unless the yacht is motoring over a flat sea. Constant correction is usually needed.
- **Heeling** In all but the lightest winds, a yacht will heel, which affects steering and increases weather helm, the tendency to turn towards the wind.

FEELING THE LOADS ON THE WHEEL

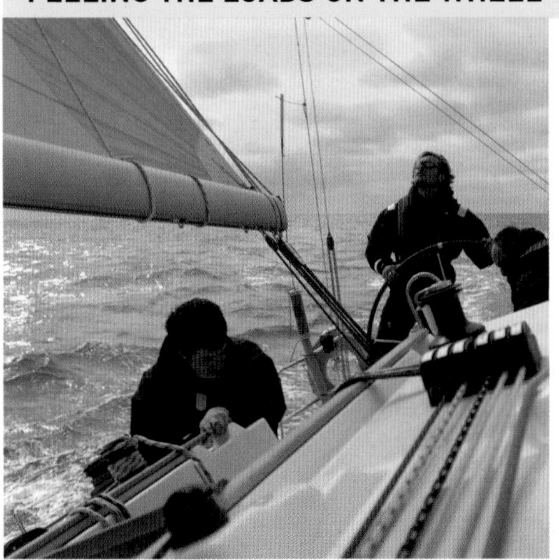

- **Balance** As the helmsman, you should learn to feel the loads on the wheel and luff up or bear away to help the crew achieve the correct sail trim (see p.62).
- **Gusts** Anticipate the yacht heeling when a gust hits, and weather helm increases, by countering with the wheel any tendency to luff up.

USING A COMPASS

- **Course** As the helmsman, you will usually steer by a compass course, unless you are familiar with the sailing area.

- **Visibility** When steering, make sure you can see the compass comfortably.

USING TRANSITS

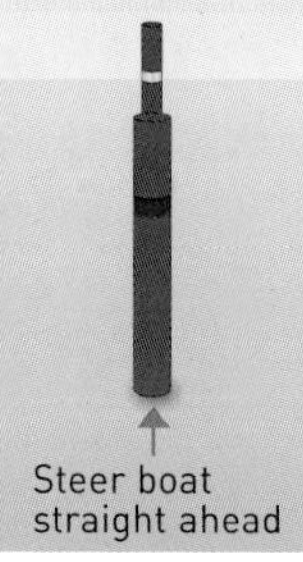

- **Safe course** Two objects are in transit when they are in line. Transit marks are used in harbours and channels to indicate the safe course to follow (see also pp.162–65).

USING LANDMARKS

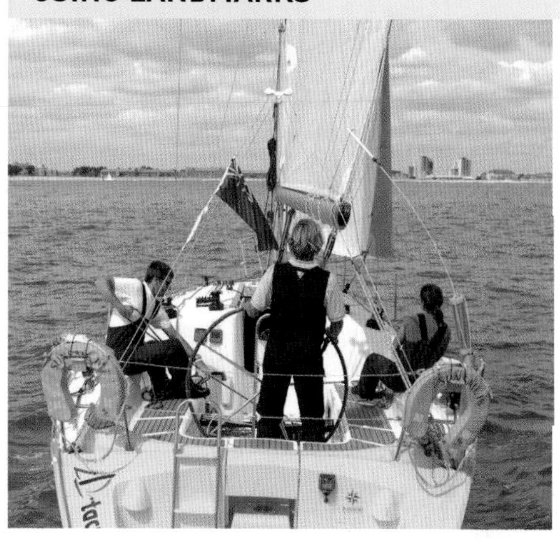

- **Pilotage** Landmarks and sea marks such as lighthouses, buoys, and transits, as shown above, provide a visual guide for steering in sight of the shore.

- **Lookout** Keep a good lookout ahead, and to leeward, where the headsail obscures the view. Check the chart for underwater hazards.

Sailing on a reach

Reaching courses are usually the fastest and most comfortable angle to the wind at which to sail. They range from a close reach to a broad reach, with the beam reach being the fastest point of sail for most yachts in moderate wind strengths.

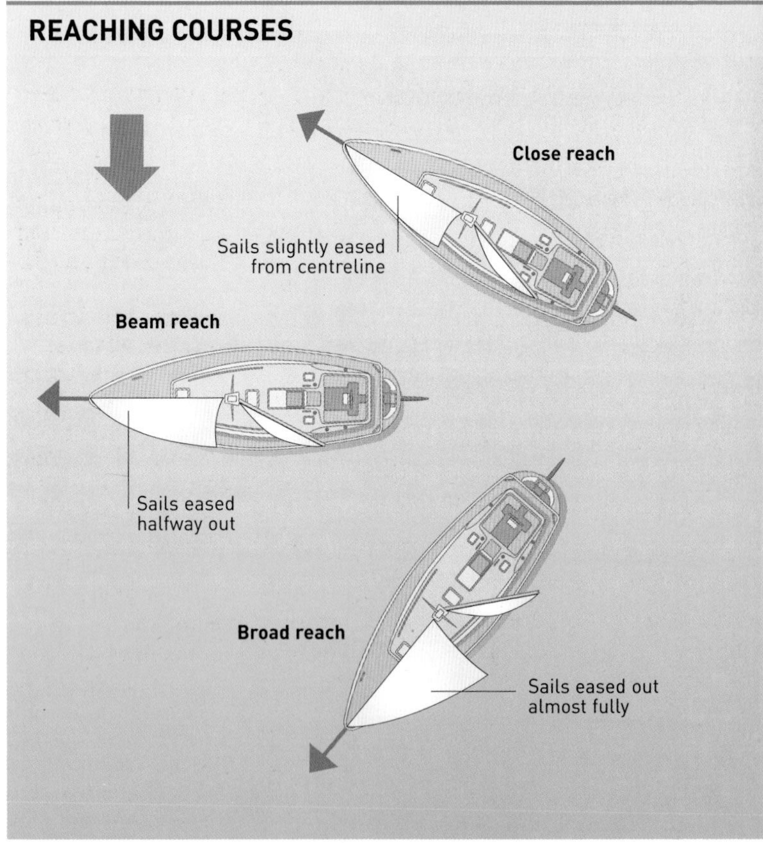

- **Close reach** Sailing at 60° off the wind is called a close reach.

- **Beam reach** You are sailing on a beam reach when the wind comes over the side of the boat at 90°.

- **Broad reach** This course is between a beam reach and a run, at 120° off the wind.

HOW TO GET THE BEST FROM YOUR BOAT

- **Steering** Sail a compass course or use sea marks or landmarks to set the course.
- **Jib** Ease out the sheet until the luff starts to shake. Then pull it in until the shaking stops.
- **Mainsail** Ease the mainsheet as much as possible until the sail starts to flutter at its luff, then pull it in until the fluttering just stops (see p.47).
- **Boom vang** Adjust the boom vang (see p.64) until the top tell-tale on the mainsail leech streams aft most of the time. If it won't stream aft, ease the vang.
- **Outhaul** Ease the mainsail's clew outhaul (see p.64) in light winds to create a more powerful sail.
- **Slot** Adjust the jib sheet and the jib sheet lead to maintain a slot between jib leech and mainsail luff that is even all the way up. The jib sheet lead (see p.65) usually needs to be moved forward on its track.

Sailing to windward

Sailing towards a point upwind of the yacht is known as sailing to windward. If your destination is further upwind than the yacht can sail when close-hauled on either port or starboard tack, you will have to tack to reach it (see pp.74–77). This is known as beating to windward, sailing upwind in a series of tacks, like walking up a cliff on a zig-zag path.

SAILING CLOSE-HAULED

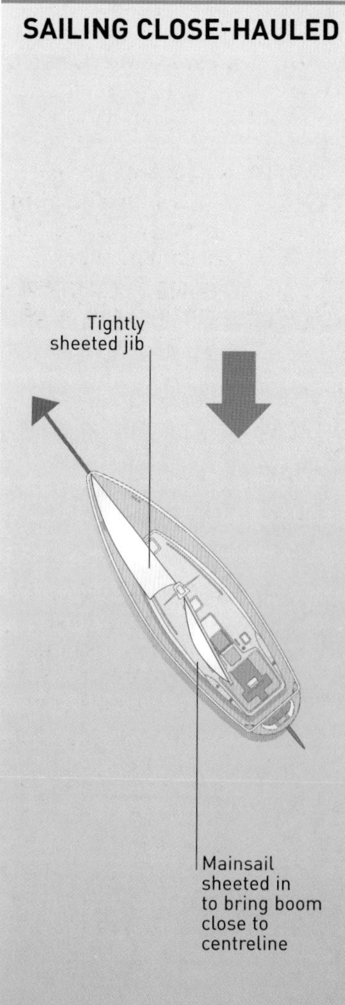

- **Close to the wind** The close-hauled course is governed entirely by how close your boat can sail to the wind direction. This is known as pointing ability.

- **Pointing ability** Race boats point higher than cruising yachts and different rigs and sail shapes have varying pointing capabilities. Get to know how well your boat can point and how to trim the sails for best results.

- **Sail trim** This is most important when sailing close-hauled as it has a large effect on speed and pointing angle.

- **Course** The helmsman steers as close to the wind as possible by watching the jib luff (front edge) tell-tales, and keeps an eye on the compass in order to tell the navigator the course achieved.

HOW TO GET THE BEST FROM YOUR BOAT

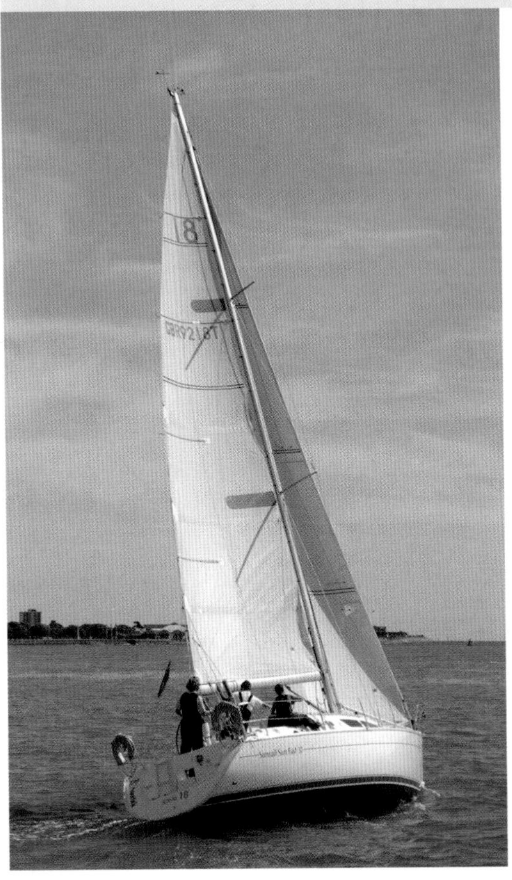

- **Mainsail** Sheet in the mainsail to bring the boom onto or close to the centreline for the best speed and pointing ability.
- **Jib** Sheet in the jib and adjust the sheet leads so that the leech (back edge) matches the curve on the leeward side of the mainsail.
- **Tell-tales** Aim to keep both windward and leeward tell-tales streaming aft or having the windward one lifting some of the time.

- **Sheet tension** Adjust the sheet tension according to wind strength – less in light winds and more in strong winds.
- **Boom vang** Adjust the boom vang and mainsheet tension to control the amount of twist in the mainsail leech, and to keep the top leech tell-tale streaming aft for most of the time.

Sailing downwind

When the yacht bears away from a beam reach so that the wind comes from aft of the beam, it is on a downwind course. A broad reach covers the angle from a beam reach to a run and is often the fastest point of sailing for cruising yachts in a moderate or strong wind.

DOWNWIND COURSES

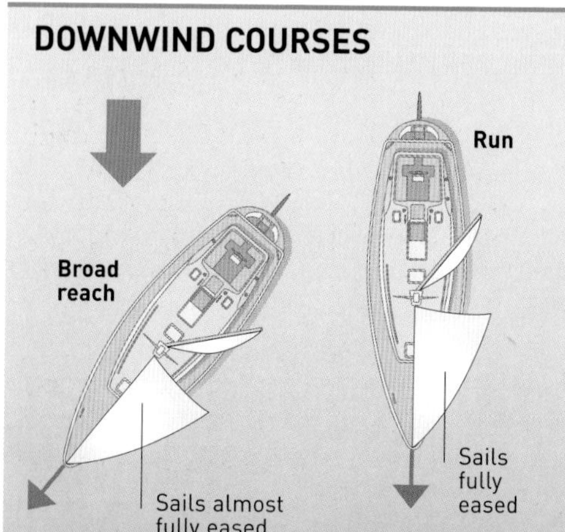

- **Broad reach** The helmsman steers a compass course or uses sea or land marks to choose his course while the crew trim the sails. The sails are almost fully eased.
- **Run** In strong winds and waves, on a run the boat will tend to roll and be hard to steer. Both sails are fully eased.

PREVENTING ACCIDENTAL GYBES

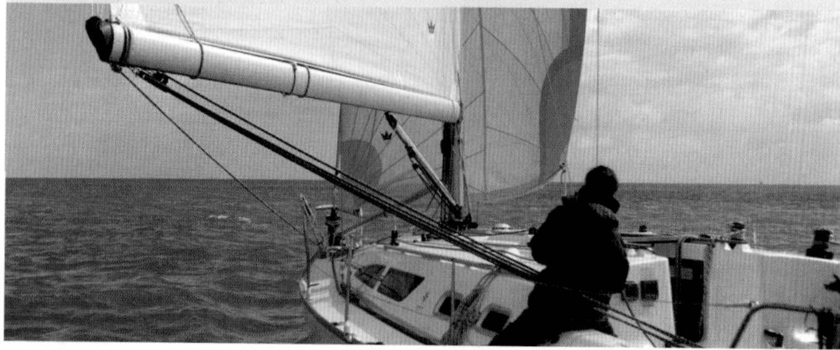

- **Gybe preventer** Rig a rope from the end of the boom to the bow to prevent an accidental gybe (see p.78).
- **Adjustable preventer** Make a preventer adjustable by leading it through a block on the foredeck and back to the cockpit.

HOW TO GET THE BEST FROM YOUR BOAT

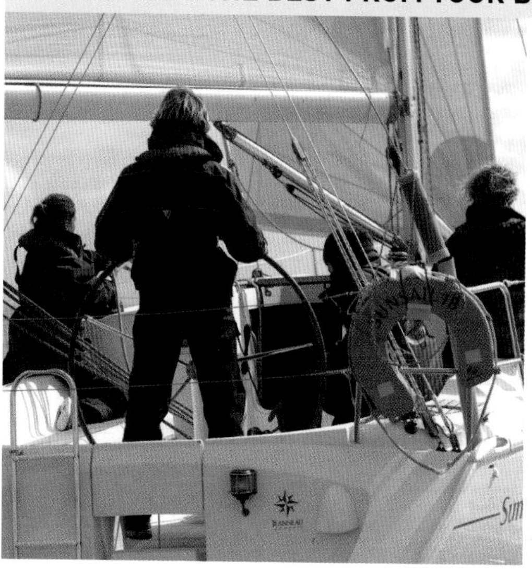

- **Sails** Ease the sails as much as possible for maximum speed.
- **Waves** In rough seas concentrate on steering to prevent the boat being pushed off course.
- **Boom vang** Keep the boom vang (see p.64) tight on a broad reach or a run to stop the top of the mainsail twisting forwards, which causes rolling.

MAXIMIZING SAIL POWER

- **Goosewinging** On a run the jib can be set on the opposite side to the mainsail to give more drive.
- **Using a spinnaker pole** You can use a spinnaker pole (see p.84) to keep the jib stable on the windward side.

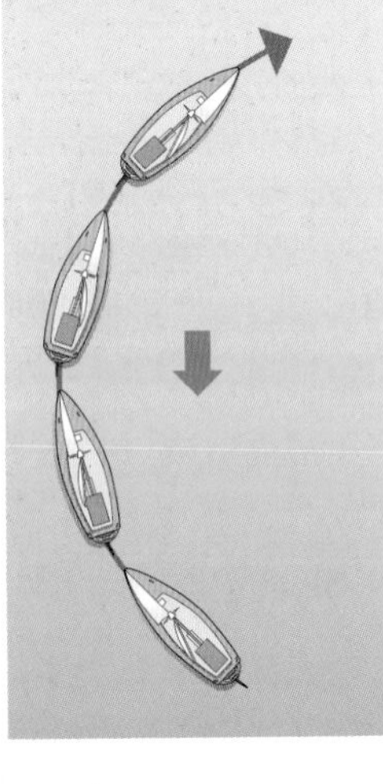

Tacking

When tacking, your aim is to turn the bow through the wind and steer the boat onto the new course with a minimum loss of speed. In most cases, you will tack from a close-hauled course on one tack to a close-hauled course on the other tack. However, on occasions you may tack from a reach to a reach.

1

- **Helmsman** Get ready to tack by sailing on a close-hauled course. If you have to tack from a reach, make sure that the boat is moving quickly. Look to windward and astern to check that the new course is clear.

- **Crew** Prepare the new winch before the tack. If there are enough crew members, each should man one jib sheet winch.

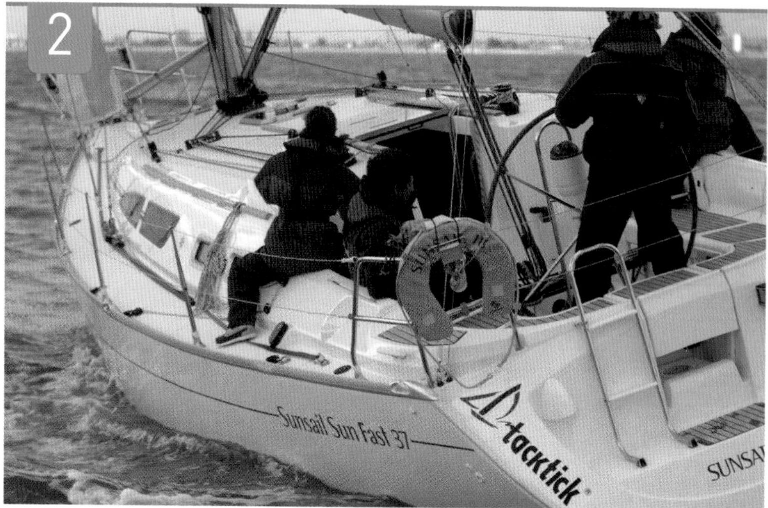

● **Helmsman** Call "Ready about" to warn the crew and give them time to prepare for the manoeuvre.

● **Crew** Check that both sheets are ready and clear for the tack. Inform the helmsman that this has been done by saying "Ready".

● **Helmsman** Check the area to windward is clear, call "Lee-oh", and turn the wheel to start the boat turning into the wind.

● **Crew** Take up the slack in what will become the new working sheet.

- **Helmsman** Monitor the rate of turn to ensure that the bow passes through the wind.

- **Crew** Release the old working sheet as the jib blows across the bow, making sure it is running freely.

- **Crew** Rapidly pull in the new working sheet around the winch.

● **Crew** Winch the sheet in until the sail is correctly trimmed for the course.

● **Helmsman** Assist the crew by slowing down the turn so, that the crew has time to sheet in the jib before it becomes fully loaded.

● **Helmsman** Settle the boat on the new course, either close-hauled or bearing away to the chosen course.

● **Crew** If the new course is not close-hauled, ease the sails to suit the new wind angle and tidy up the sheets.

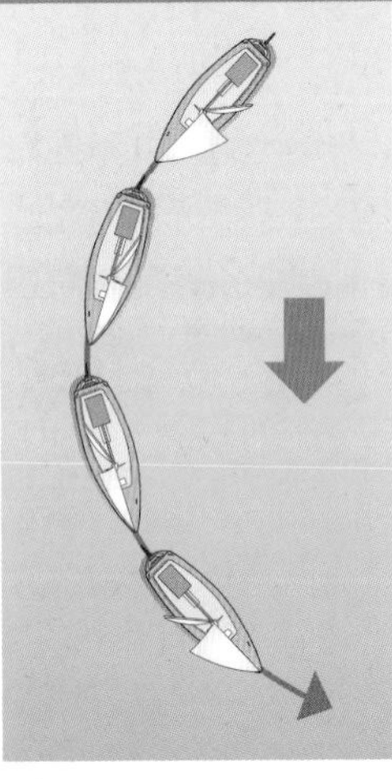

Gybing

When gybing, your aim is to turn the stern through the wind while controlling the swing of the mainsail and boom across the boat. The boom will swing across much faster than when tacking. When the gybe is complete, the boat is steered onto the new course.

1

● **Helmsman** Before the gybe, steer onto a broad reach. Check that the area to leeward and astern is clear, then warn the crew by calling "Stand by to gybe".

● **Crew** Prepare to pull in the mainsheet before the gybe and to sheet the jib across to the new side during the gybe. Ensure that the gybe preventer is removed, if you have been using one.

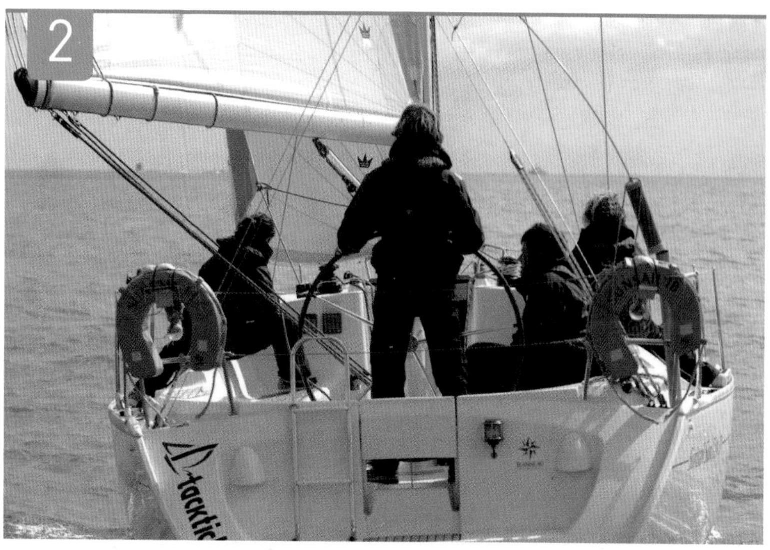

- **Helmsman** Steer onto a run but be careful not to gybe too soon.

- **Crew** Prepare to release the old jib sheet and pull in the new one.

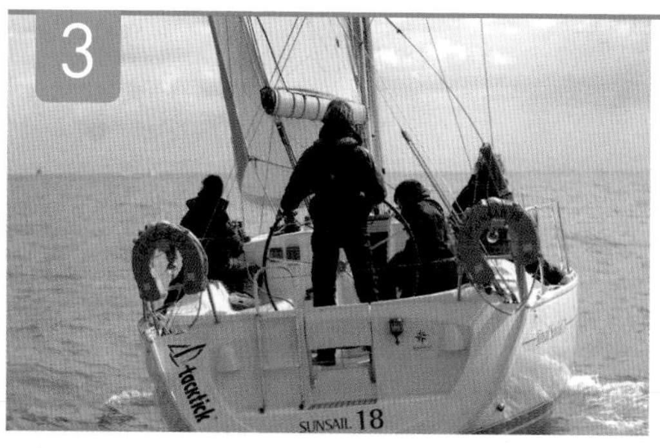

- **Crew** Pull the mainsheet in to bring the boom in to the middle of the boat and cleat it. This limits the distance it can swing in the gybe.

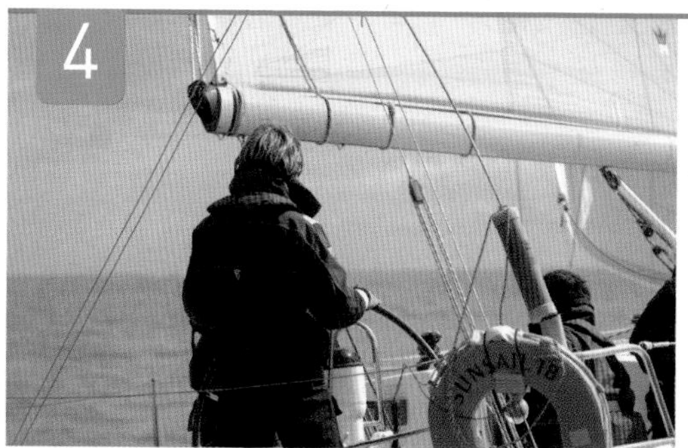

- **Crew** Tell the helmsman "Ready".

- **Helmsman** Check that the area you will gybe into is still clear and call "Gybe-oh".

5

• **Helmsman** Turn the wheel to bear away into the gybe.

6

• **Crew** Ease the old jib sheet and, as the jib blows across to the new side, pull in the new jib sheet to trim it for a run or broad reach.

7

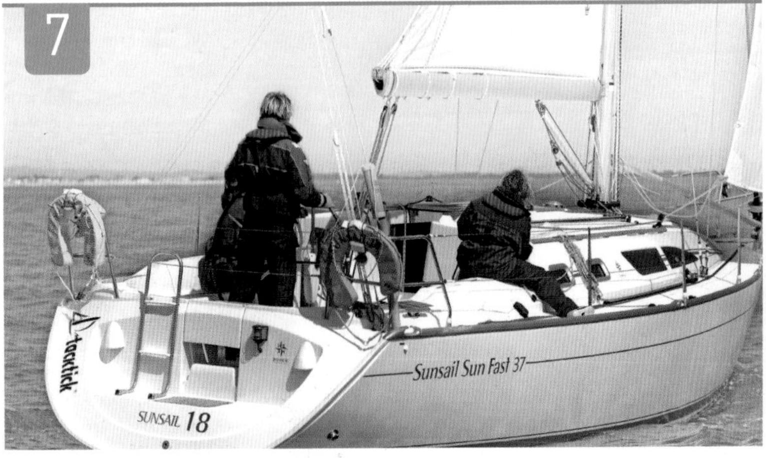

• **Helmsman** As the mainsail fills on the new side, straighten the rudder to prevent the boat turning further to windward.

• **Crew** When the mainsail fills on the new side, ease the mainsheet to let the boom out to the correct position.

8

• **Helmsman** Settle the boat on its new course and tell the crew when the boat is on the desired course.

• **Crew** Trim both mainsail and jib to suit the new course.

STAYING IN CONTROL

• **Avoid broaching** In breezy conditions the sheeted-in mainsail will try to turn the boat into the wind quite rapidly. If you are the helmsman, use the steering to correct this while the crew eases the mainsheet quickly.

Heaving-to

Heaving-to can be a very useful technique in a cruiser. You can heave-to to stop the boat in order to prepare and eat a meal in comfort, or to take in a reef if the wind strength increases. Heaving-to is also often a good tactic for riding out rough weather. If you have a choice, heave-to on starboard tack (see pp.186–87).

WHAT HAPPENS

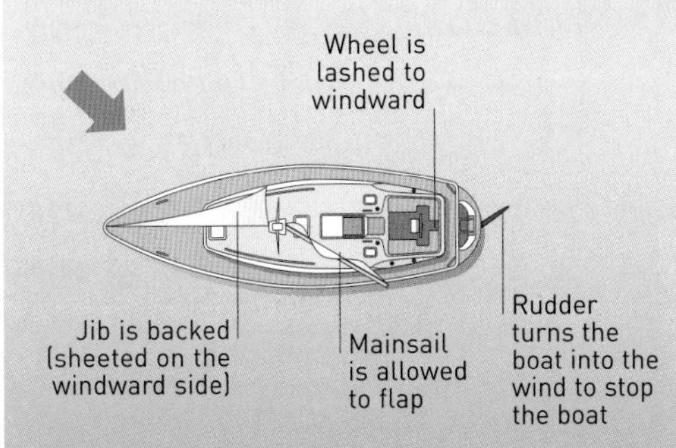

- **Balance of forces** When you are hove-to, there is a balance between the jib, mainsail, and rudder that results in the boat lying nearly stopped between 60° and 80° off the wind.

WHEN TO HEAVE-TO

- **To cook** Heave-to whenever you need to ease the motion of the boat, such as when cooking and eating a meal.

- **To reef** Slow the boat and keep it under control while reefing the mainsail by heaving-to.

- **To navigate** If you are uncertain of your position, you can slow the boat down by heaving-to while you confirm it.

- **Outside harbour** If you arrive at a harbour or bar before the tide is high enough, you can wait for the tide by heaving-to nearby.

- **In rough weather** When the wind or the sea get too bad to continue sailing, you can heave-to to wait for conditions to moderate.

- **To use the heads** In rough conditions, it will be more comfortable to visit the heads if the boat is hove-to for a short while.

- **To make repairs** If repairs are needed, it can be helpful to slow the boat and make it more stable by heaving-to.

HOW TO HEAVE-TO

1

- **Skipper** Explain to the crew that the boat is about to tack without adjusting the jib sheets.
- **Helmsman** From a close-hauled course, tack the boat by turning the wheel.
- **Helmsman** When the boat has tacked, use the wheel to turn the boat back towards the wind.
- **Crew** Ease the mainsheet to depower the mainsail.

2

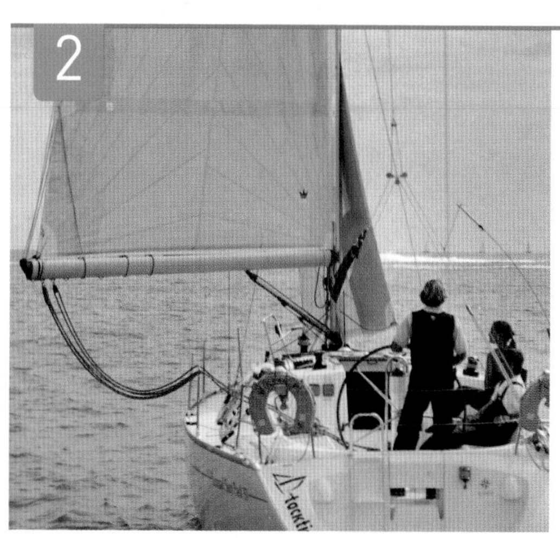

- **Helmsman and crew** Adjust the wheel angle and mainsheet until the boat lies steadily, moving forwards slowly.
- **Helmsman** Lash the wheel to windward (or the tiller to leeward) so that if the boat picks up speed, it will turn towards the wind and stop again.

Types of spinnaker

In light and moderate breezes, the typical cruiser with a Bermudan sloop rig is underpowered when sailing downwind. In these conditions, you can increase the sail area to improve performance by hoisting a downwind sail such as a conventional or asymmetric spinnaker, or a gennaker (sometimes called a cruising chute).

WHAT IS A SPINNAKER?

- **Spinnaker** This is a lightweight sail made of nylon that is used to increase sail area when sailing downwind. It requires a pole with uphaul and downhaul, and a sheet and a guy. The sheet controls the sail, the guy controls the pole. These may be duplicated on each side.

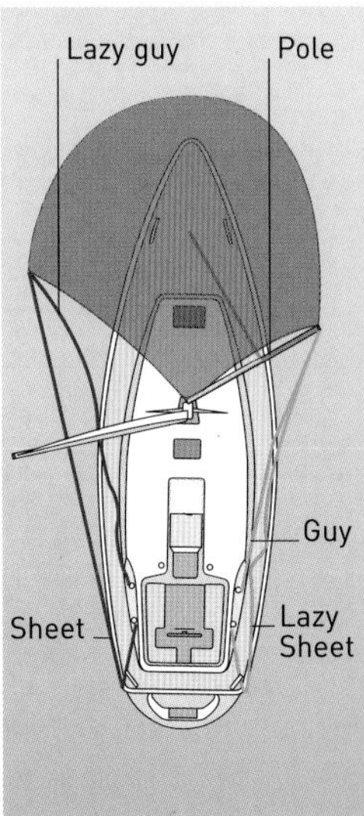

WHAT IS AN ASYMMETRIC SPINNAKER?

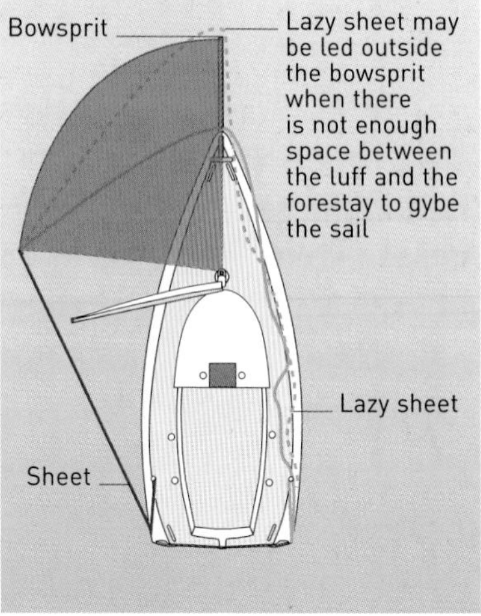

- **Fast cruisers** This type of boat may use an asymmetric spinnaker with a retractable bowsprit to hold the tack of the sail forward of the bow.

- **Sail control** The sail is controlled by two sheets that are led to winches in the cockpit. The lazy (non-working) sheet may be run in two ways, as described above.

WHAT IS A GENNAKER?

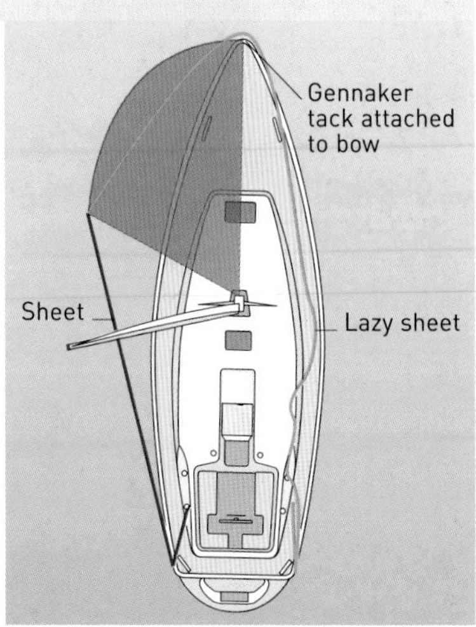

- **Cruising boats** These commonly have a gennaker, which is smaller than an asymmetric spinnaker and does not need a bowsprit or pole.

- **Sail control** Two sheets control the gennaker. The lazy sheet is run outside the gennaker luff.

Hoisting the spinnaker

Hoisting a spinnaker is best done on a very broad reach so that the mainsail will shield the spinnaker from the wind to stop it filling while it is being hoisted. For your first attempts at using a spinnaker, pick a light wind day and sail in an open area where you have plenty of room.

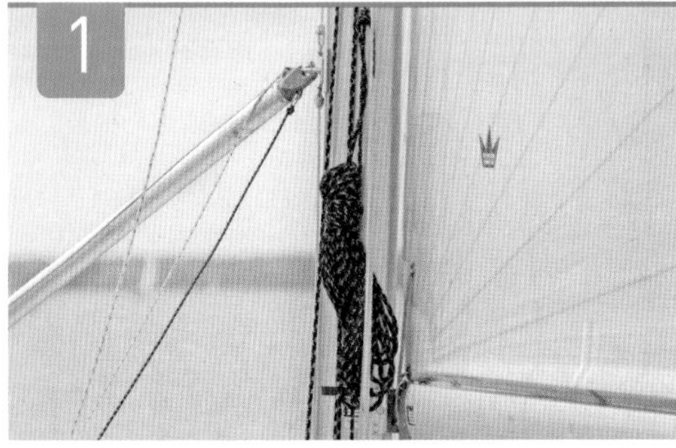

1

- **Foredeck crew** Attach the spinnaker pole to the mast and raise it to about head height on its track.
- **Cockpit crew** Use the uphaul and downhaul lines in the cockpit to control the angle of the pole.

2

- **Foredeck crew** Secure the spinnaker bag at both its ends to the guardrail to prevent it from going over the side.

3

- **Foredeck crew** Lead the sheets and guys on both sides of the boat from their winches through their sheet blocks, and attach them to the sail's clew and tack.
- Attach the halyard to the head of the sail.

4

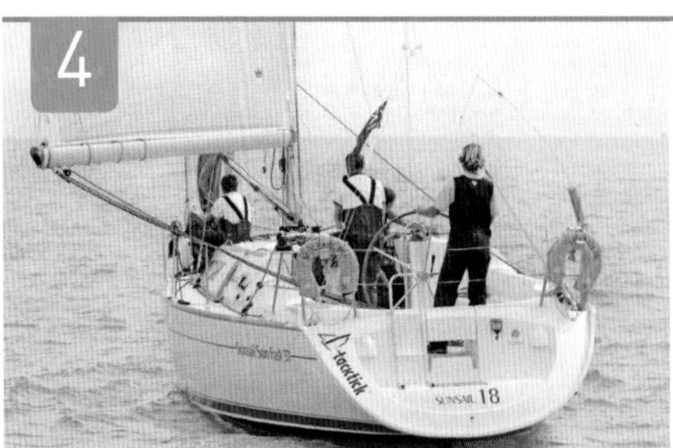

• **Helmsman** Steer on a broad reach so the spinnaker can be hoisted in the lee of the mainsail to ensure that it does not fill until you are ready to sheet it in.

5

• **Foredeck crew** Pull the halyard to hoist the sail in conjunction with the cockpit crew.

• **Cockpit crew** Tail the halyard on its winch to take up the slack. Pull on the guy to bring the clew to the end of the pole.

TIPS FOR SETTING THE SPINNAKER

• **Halyard** Make sure that the spinnaker is fully hoisted.

• **Pole angle** Use the guy to set the pole at a right angle to the wind.

• **Pole height** Set the pole height with the uphaul and downhaul so the clew and tack are level.

• **Sheet** Ease the sheet until the spinnaker begins to curl at the luff, then sheet in slightly.

Dropping the spinnaker

When lowering a downwind sail, it must be kept under control until it is in its bag or below deck. Always steer onto a run or broad reach before lowering the sail so that it can be lowered in the wind shadow behind the mainsail. A headsail is usually hoisted or unfurled before lowering the spinnaker as it prevents it from wrapping around the forestay.

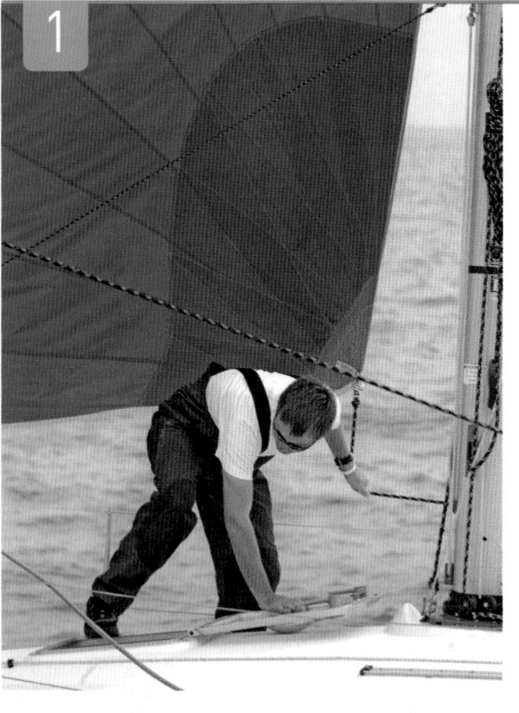

1

- **Helmsman** Steer onto a broad reach so that the spinnaker can be collapsed in the lee of the mainsail.
- **Cockpit crew** Ease the guy so the pole swings forwards to let the sail collapse behind the mainsail. Do not let the pole hit the forestay.
- **Foredeck crew** If dropping through the forehatch, open it before the drop. Then grasp the sheet, or the lazy guy – if a double sheet and guy system is in use – and move to the centre of the foredeck.

2

- **Foredeck crew** Sit on the deck by the hatch and, with the sail collapsed, pull the clew towards you.

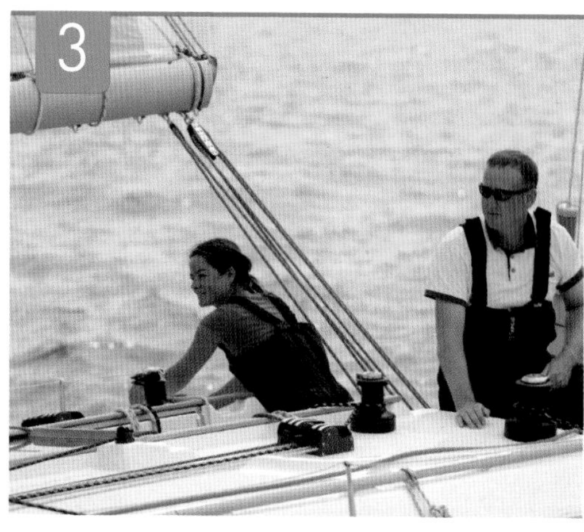
3

- **Cockpit crew** Prepare to ease the halyard and the guy, working in coordination with the foredeck crew.
- **Foredeck crew** Pull the foot (bottom edge) of the sail in. Then instruct the cockpit crew to lower the halyard.

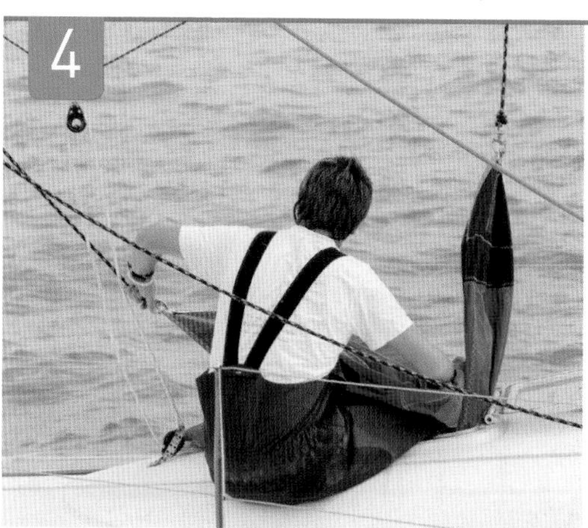
4

- **Cockpit crew** Lower the halyard under full control at the speed at which the foredeck crew can gather it into the boat. Make sure that the guy is free to run.
- **Foredeck crew** Bundle the sail down the hatch as quickly as possible and remove the sheet, guy, and halyard.

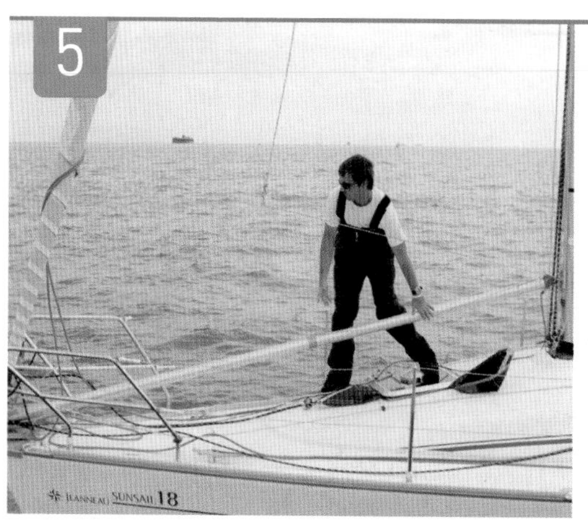

5

- **Cockpit crew** Ease the pole uphaul and tension the downhaul to lower the spinnaker pole under control onto the foredeck.
- **Foredeck crew** Tie the three corners of the sail together. Remove the pole from the mast and stow it.

End-for-end gybe

When you need to gybe, you must change the set of the spinnaker from one side to the other. The technique used to do this varies, depending on the type of downwind sail being used. When flying a symmetrical spinnaker, one common technique is the end-for-end gybe. It requires communication and cooperation between the cockpit and foredeck crews.

1

● **Foredeck crew** With the yacht sailing on a run, unclip the inner end of the spinnaker pole from the mast. This end of the pole will be the outer end once the spinnaker is gybed.

2

● **Foredeck crew** Take the leeward sheet, clip on the free end of the pole, and push the pole out to the new side. Then unclip the other end of the pole from the windward guy.

- **Helmsman** Bear away to gybe the mainsail.
- **Foredeck crew** Pull the unclipped end of the pole towards the mast.
- **Cockpit crew** Provide enough slack in the new guy.

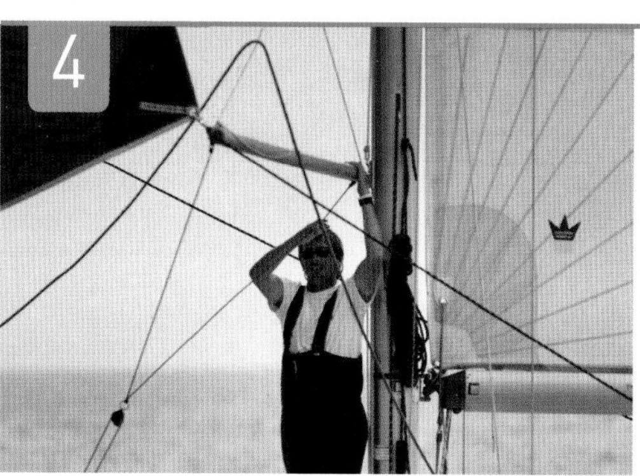

- **Foredeck crew** Clip the pole on to the mast while the spinnaker is blanketed by the mainsail and not fully powered.
- **Cockpit crew** Adjust the sheet and guy to set the spinnaker on the new tack.

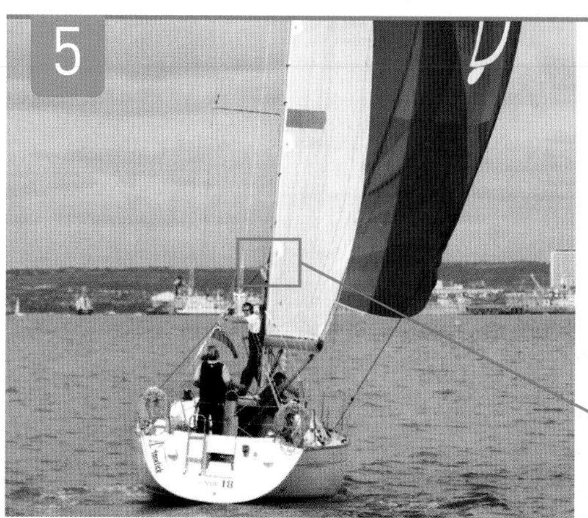

- **Cockpit crew** When beam-reaching under spinnaker, keep the pole well forward but ensure that it does not hit the forestay and break.

Dip-pole spinnaker gybe

When the boat needs to gybe, the crew must set downwind sails on the other side. The technique used to do this varies, depending on the type of downwind sail being used. Use a dip-pole gybe technique when you are flying a spinnaker with double sheets and guys.

1

- **Helmsman** Steer onto a run and give the order to gybe.
- **Foredeck crew** Pull the piston-release line to release the old guy from the outer end of the pole.
- **Cockpit crew** Raise the pole's inner end and ease the uphaul to drop the outer end of the pole inside the forestay.

2

- **Cockpit crew** Ensure the new guy has plenty of slack in it. Keep the sail full by trimming it with the guy and sheet.
- **Foredeck crew** Grasp the lazy guy, move forward to the bow and drop the guy into the jaws of the spinnaker pole.

- **Cockpit crew** Sheet in on the new guy to bring the clew to the pole end and move the pole aft.
- Keep the mainsail sheeted in near the centreline.
- **Foredeck crew** Adjust the inner end of the pole if the control is not led back to the cockpit for adjustment.

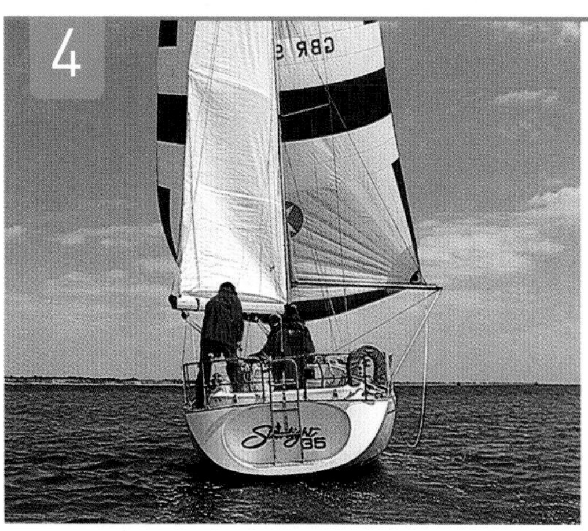

- **Cockpit crew** Gybe the mainsail onto the new tack.
- **Helmsman** Steer onto the new course.

- **Helmsman** Keep the boat on its new course.
- **Crew** Trim the mainsail and spinnaker to suit the course and tidy up the sheets.

Reducing sail

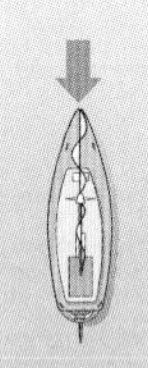

For all sailing boats, there is a certain wind strength in which the boat is fully powered. Beyond this optimum wind speed, the boat will be overpowered, will heel excessively, slow down, and be harder to steer. This moment will arrive sooner if the air is cold or the sea is rough.

WHEN TO REDUCE SAIL

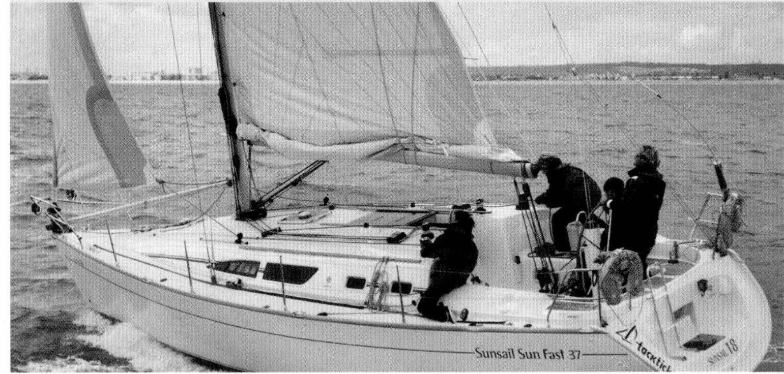

- **Consider reducing sail** When the boat starts to feel overpressed, heels excessively, and is hard to steer, consider reefing. In general, reef early as it will be easier. (See also pp.194–97.)
- **In rough seas** You may need to reef to slow the boat down because of the sea state. Sailing a boat fast in steep seas is uncomfortable and may result in a breakage.

REDUCING THE HEADSAIL

- **Furling headsail** Furl in some of the sail to balance the amount of reefed mainsail (see p.60).
- **Hanked headsail** When using a hanked headsail, lower the large headsail and replace it with a smaller one, stowing the first sail below or in a locker.

REEFING THE MAINSAIL

● **Ease the mainsheet** and boom vang, tighten the topping lift, open the clutch, and ease the halyard around the winch for the crew to pull the reefing point in the luff down the mast to the boom.

● **Wind the reefing point** in the leech down and out along the boom until the foot of the sail is taut.

● **Tension the main halyard**, then pull in the mainsheet and tension the boom vang.

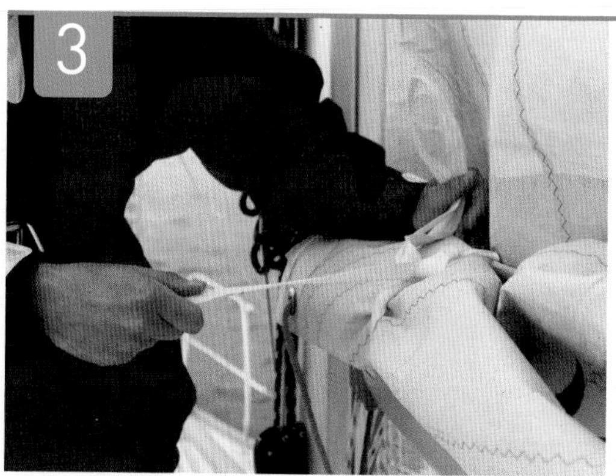

● **Roll up the excess** and secure with sail ties through the reefing eyes and under the sail's foot. Some yachts have lazy jacks (networks of lines between the boom and mast) to catch the sail.

A secure berth

At the start and end of every trip you will need to negotiate the exit and approach to your berth – in a marina or at a harbour quay. In this section, you will learn how to manoeuvre the boat safely and keep it secure.

Fenders

Plastic fenders are made in a variety of shapes and sizes. You should use at least four when lying alongside, and have some spare in case someone berths alongside without enough fenders to protect both craft. The movement of fenders can damage the gelcoat or paint on the hull. Prevent this by hanging a fender skirt between the hull and fenders.

WHERE TO PLACE FENDERS

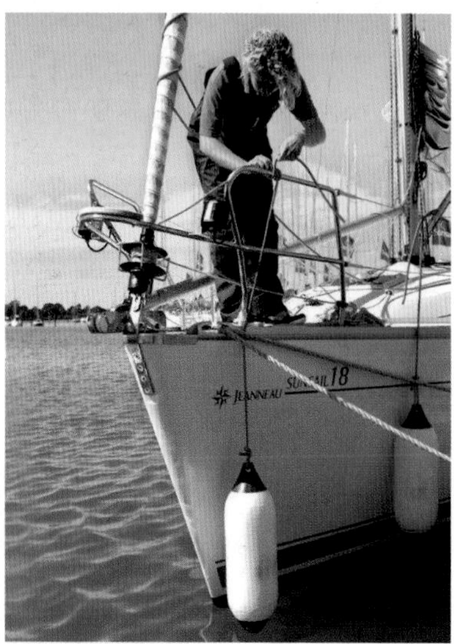

- **Protect the hull** Spread the fenders out along the widest part of the hull, where there is a possibility of contact with the quay or another boat.

- **Strong attachment points** Tie the fenders to strong points such as handrails or toerails.

- **Avoid the guardrails** Try not to attach the fenders to the guardrails or stanchions. If you have to use the rails, try to tie them next to a stanchion.

- **Roving fender** Have a fender ready to use where needed when manoeuvring into or out of a berth.

JUDGING THE RIGHT HEIGHT

- **Height** Adjust the height of the fender to protect the hull from the pontoon and to keep the bottom of the fender clear of the water.

- **Horizontal** Many fenders have an attachment point at top and bottom, and this can be used to hang the fender horizontally when needed – for example, at the bow or stern (see p.110).

WHICH KNOT TO USE

- **Clove hitch** Use this knot (see p.246) to tie a fender to an attachment point. It is quicker to undo if tied using a slip hitch.

- **Temporary** Use a quick-release clove hitch for short periods. However, it will work loose if left for a long time.

Mooring warps

Warps are mooring ropes used to tie a boat to a pontoon, quayside, mooring buoy, piles, or other boats. All warps should be strong enough to hold your boat and long enough to allow for rise and fall in tidal waters. Mooring lines are usually secured to cleats on the pontoon or quay, and knowing how to secure a warp to a cleat is a key skill.

USING MOORING WARPS

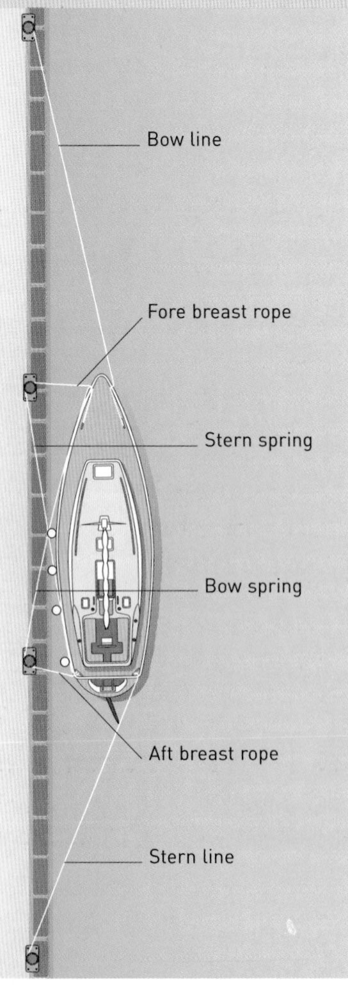

- **Bow and stern lines** The bow line and the stern line position the boat in a berth. The further away they are taken from the boat, the less adjustment is needed as the tide rises or falls.

- **Bow and stern springs** Springs prevent the boat from moving ahead or astern. They are not usually as long as the bow and stern lines, and will need to be adjusted as the tidal height changes. The bow spring is sometimes called the aft spring and the stern spring is also called the fore spring. See also pp.116–17.

- **Fore-and-aft breast ropes** Breast ropes are sometimes used in addition to the four main warps to hold the boat close alongside. Breast ropes and springs may be used alone when lying alongside a pontoon.

CLEATING A WARP

• **Lead the warp** around the back of the cleat.

• **Make a full round turn** around the base of the cleat.

• **Take the rope across** the top of the cleat and pass it behind the upper horn, and then bring it back across the front to form a figure of eight.

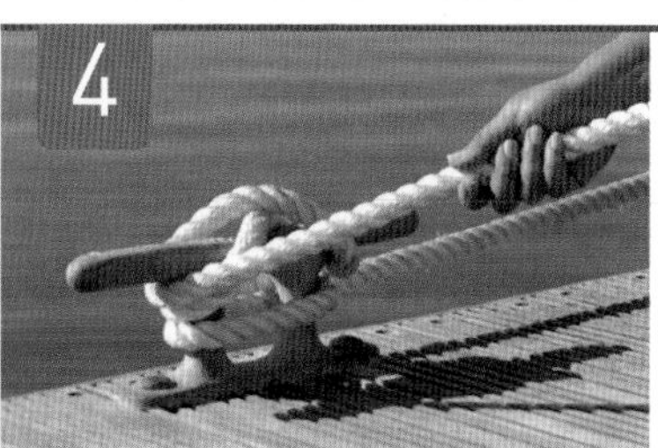

• **Add two or three** further figure-of-eight turns to ensure sufficient friction to keep the rope secure.

• **Finish off** by taking another full turn around the base of the cleat.

Choosing an approach

On arrival at a port or marina, you need to identify a suitable berth, then decide on your approach. Your choice of berth may be made for you by a marina dockmaster or harbourmaster, or you may be able to select your own. Once you have identified the berth you will need to decide on the best approach to it – bow first or stern first.

HOW TO APPROACH STERN FIRST

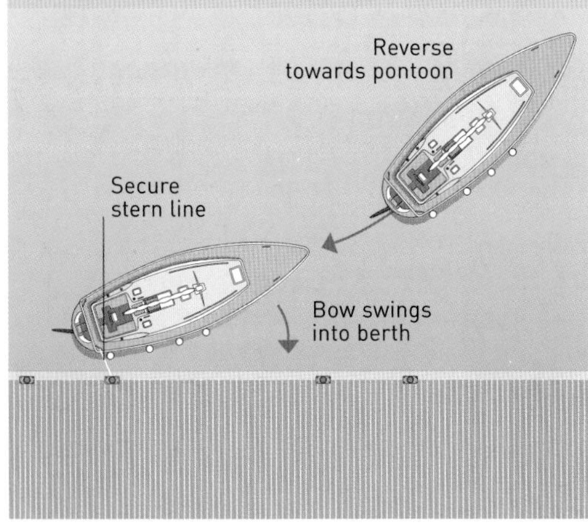

- **Approaching stern first** Many modern cruisers handle very well under astern power, unlike some older designs.
- **Reversing in** Approach stern first into wind or tide to help stop the boat and swing the bow into the berth.

HOW TO APPROACH BOW FIRST

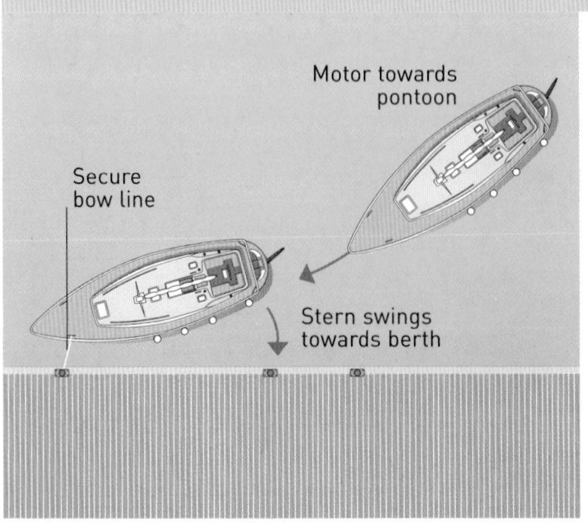

- **Approaching bow first** Many older designs do not handle well in reverse so you will usually have to approach bow first.
- **Visibility** If you are the crew, sit down if possible to make sure you are not blocking the helmsman's vision as the helmsman has less visibility than when reversing.

APPROACHING INTO THE TIDE

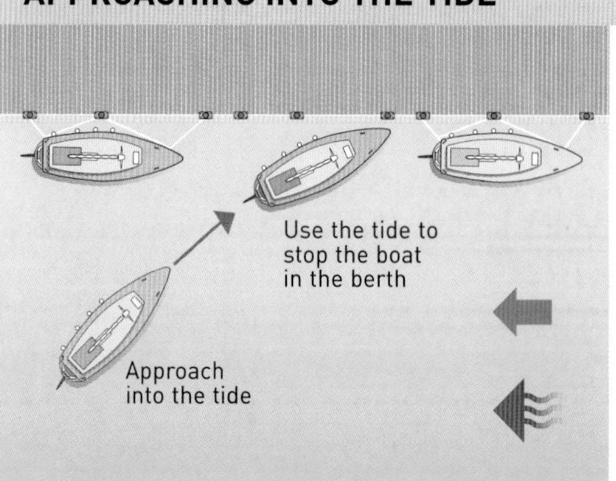

- **Speed** Where there is a tidal stream or current and the wind is either in the same direction or opposed, approach the berth into the tide as slowly as possible, while retaining necessary steerage way (see p.45).

APPROACHING WITH AN ONSHORE WIND

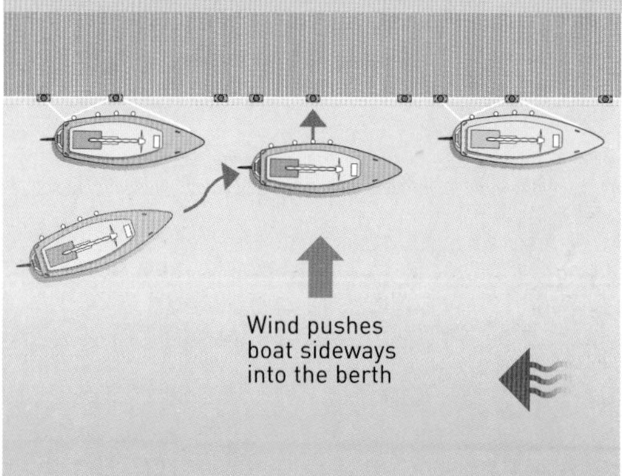

- **Positioning** Approach slowly and aim to stop the boat parallel to the berth about half a boat width to windward. Allow the boat to blow sideways into the berth.

APPROACHING WITH AN OFFSHORE WIND

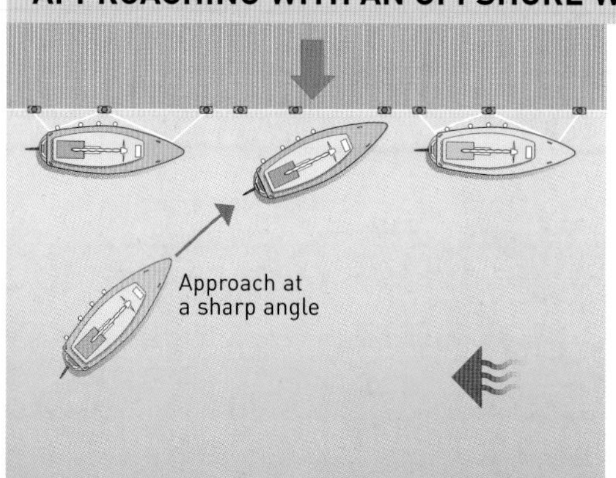

- **Angle** In a strong offshore wind the bow tends to blow downwind as the boat slows down. Counter this by leading the stern line further forward than usual and approach at a sharper angle. Get the lines ashore and secured quickly.

Mooring alongside

When mooring alongside, you must decide on your approach with reference to the wind and tide, and choose whether it is better to approach bow first or stern first. Modern cruisers often handle well under power astern, giving you the option of entering the berth stern first. This gives the helmsman a good view of the approach to the pontoon.

APPROACHING STERN FIRST

1

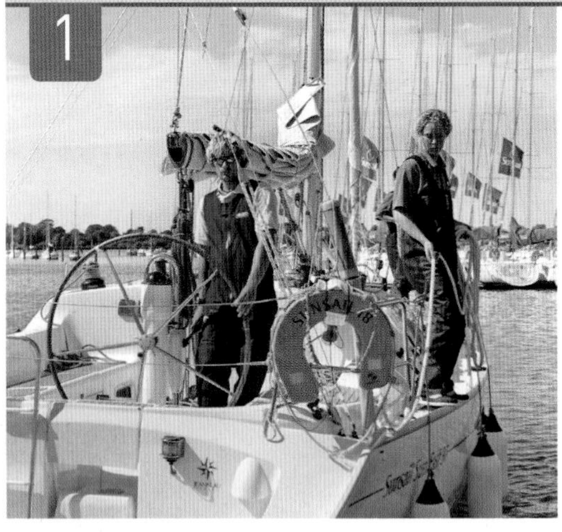

- **Helmsman** If the yacht has a wheel rather than a tiller, stand forward of the wheel, looking aft for a clear view.
- **Shore crew** Rig the stern line and be ready to step ashore with it. Take care not to interfere with the helmsman's view.

2

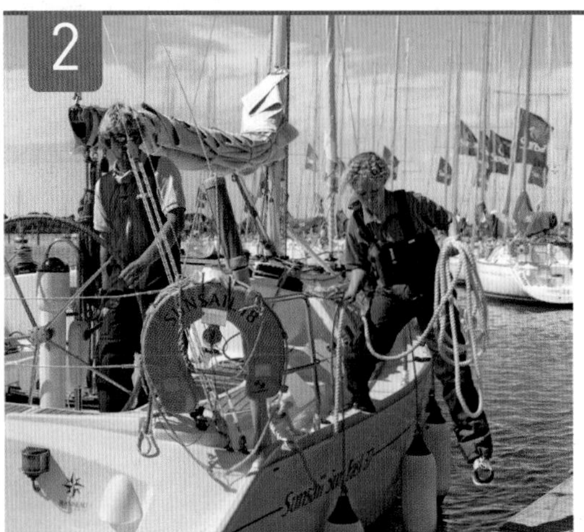

- **Helmsman** Approach slowly and allow for prop walk. Stop the boat alongside so that the crew can step off.
- **Shore crew** Step ashore with the coiled stern line.

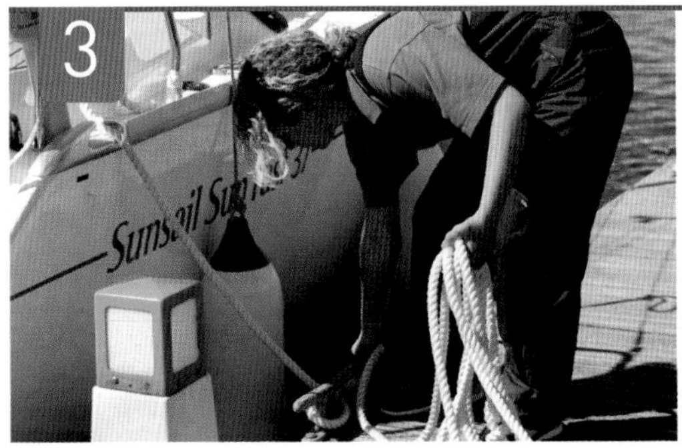

- **Shore crew** Make the stern line fast on a pontoon cleat. You can re-fasten it properly later, with the excess rope on board, when the boat is secured.

- **Deck crew** Pass the bow line to the shore crew.
- **Shore crew** Make the end fast on a pontoon cleat.
- **Deck crew** Pull the slack back on board and make the warp fast on a deck cleat.

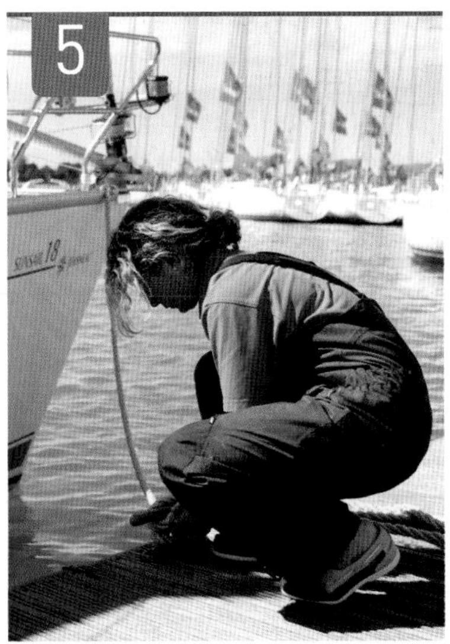

- **Shore crew** Secure and adjust the other warps to position the yacht in the berth.

- **Shore crew** Adjust the fenders to the correct height so they do not trail in the water.

APPROACHING BOW FIRST

- **Helmsman** After briefing the crew, approach the berth into the tide or wind to be able to slow the boat easily.
- **All crew** Rig bow and stern lines and prepare spring lines. Make sure you stand out of the helmsman's line of sight so he has a good view of the berth.
- As the distance closes, help the helmsman by estimating the remaining distance to the pontoon.

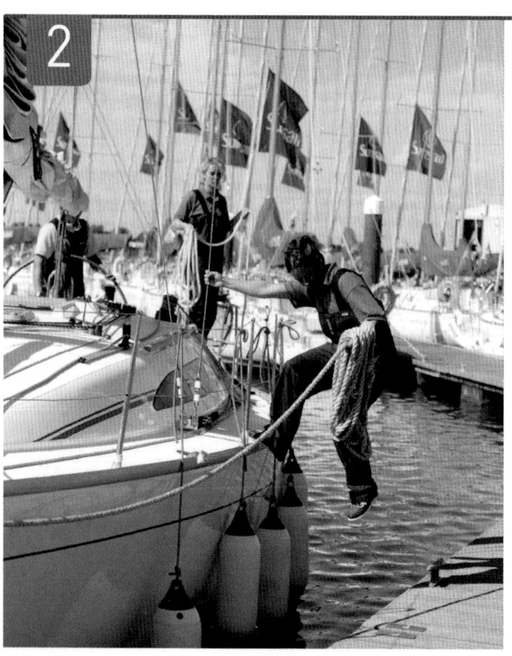

- **Shore crew** When close to the pontoon or shore, step ashore with the bow line. Beware of the gap between the boat and pontoon and try to step rather than jump.

• **Shore crew** Secure the bow line around a cleat or bollard to prevent the yacht drifting back on the wind or tide.

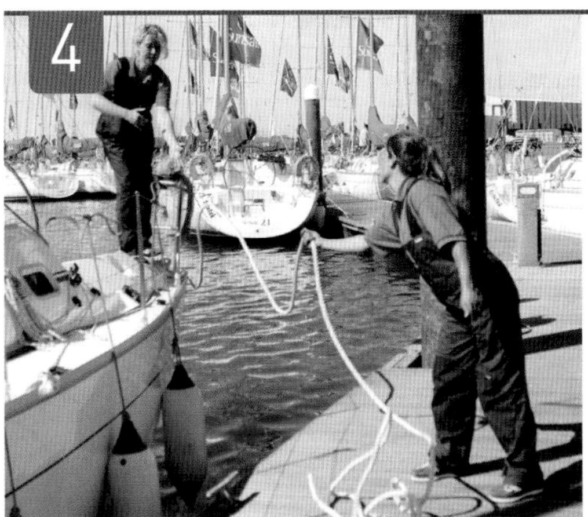

• **Deck crew** Pass the stern line to the shore crew, who secures it on a cleat.

• **Shore crew** If the boat does not have separate springs, take the end of the stern line forward as a bow spring, but only use this method for a short stop. Otherwise, it is much better to use a dedicated warp for each job.

Stern-to or bow-to

Mooring stern-to or bow-to a pontoon or quay is standard practice in areas such as the Mediterranean. Both allow yachts to pack more tightly into harbours than mooring alongside. Berthing stern-to provides easy shore access, but there is less privacy and you need to check that the water is deep enough alongside for the rudder and propeller.

BERTHING STERN-TO

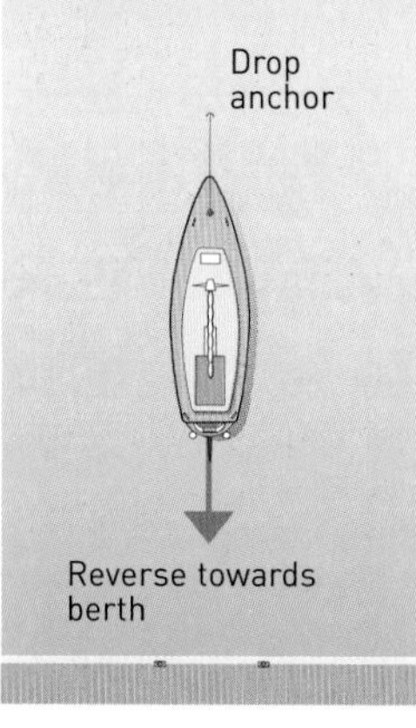

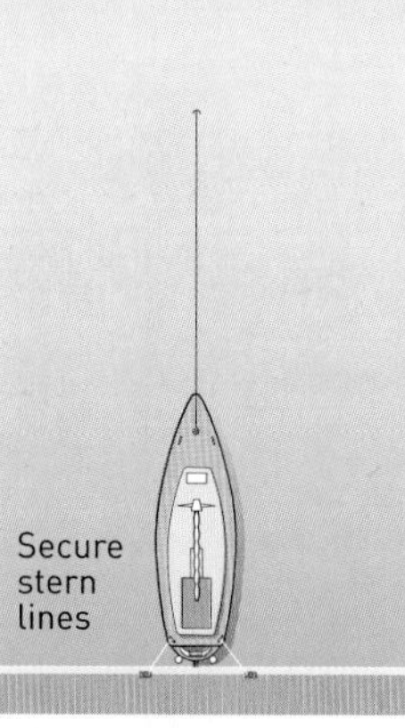

- **Positioning** Reverse towards your chosen spot and drop the anchor from the bow a few boat lengths from the berth.
- **Anchoring** To slow the boat, set the anchor as you approach the berth.

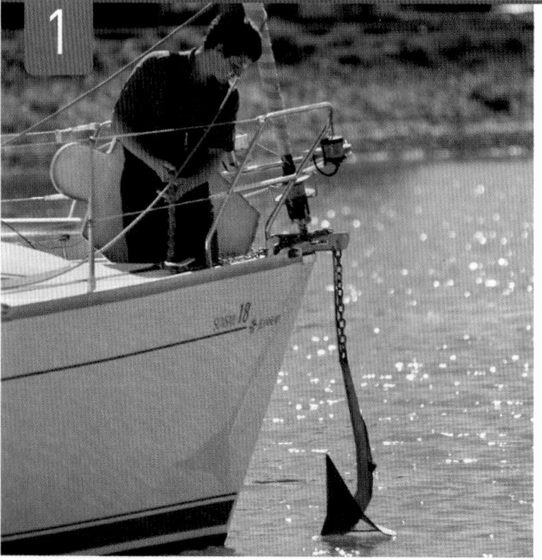

- **Deck crew** Prepare the anchor and have it ready to drop.
- **Foredeck crew** At the skipper's command, lower the anchor and pay out the anchor cable.
- **Skipper** When the boat approaches the dock, order the anchor cable to be secured to set the anchor and to slow the boat's approach.

- **Helmsman** Stand in front of the wheel for best control and a good view of the berth.
- **Crew** Tie off and coil two stern lines and stand out of the helmsman's line of vision.

- **Helmsman** Stop the boat just short of the pontoon with a short burst ahead.
- **Crew** Step ashore with the stern lines.

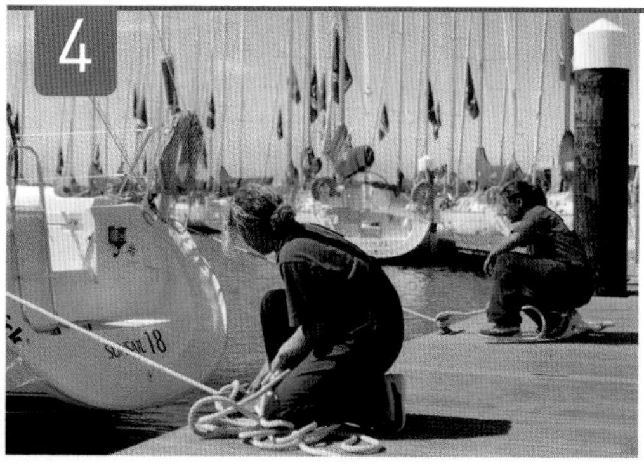

- **Crew** Secure the stern lines to cleats, which should ideally be far enough apart to prevent the stern moving sideways.
- You can also cross the stern lines, so that the port warp runs to starboard and vice versa.

BERTHING BOW-TO

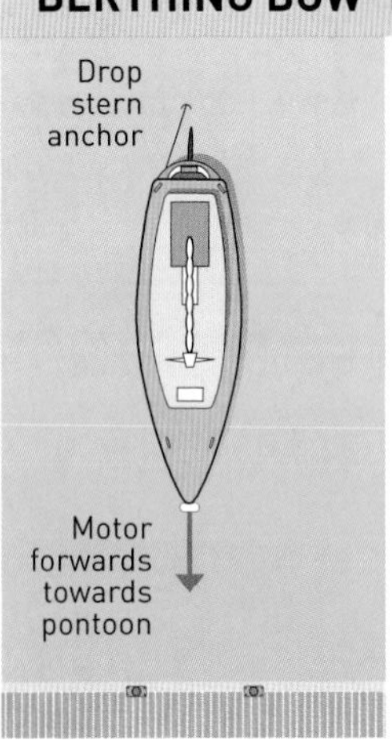

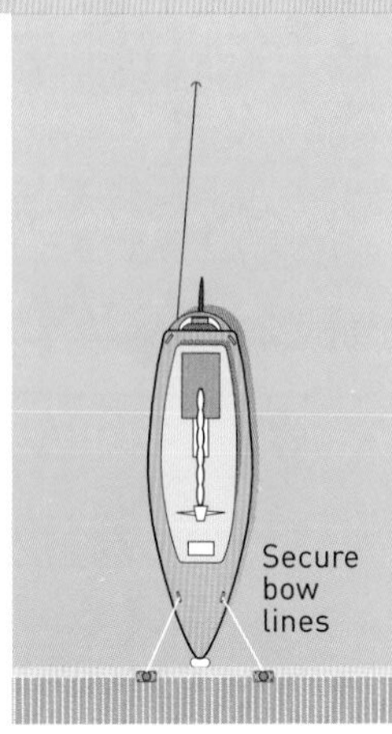

- **Drop anchor** As you approach the berth bow-to, drop the stern or kedge anchor. If necessary, use the anchor cable to help slow the boat.

- **Keep bow away** Rig and secure two bow lines, and tighten the anchor cable to hold the bow away from the pontoon.

- **Permanent moorings** Some bow-to berths have a permanently laid mooring for the stern line with a pick-up line that runs to the pontoon. This makes it easy to pick up the line as you approach the berth.

- **Protect the hull** Hang a fender under the bow to protect the hull.

USING PILE AND PONTOON BERTHS

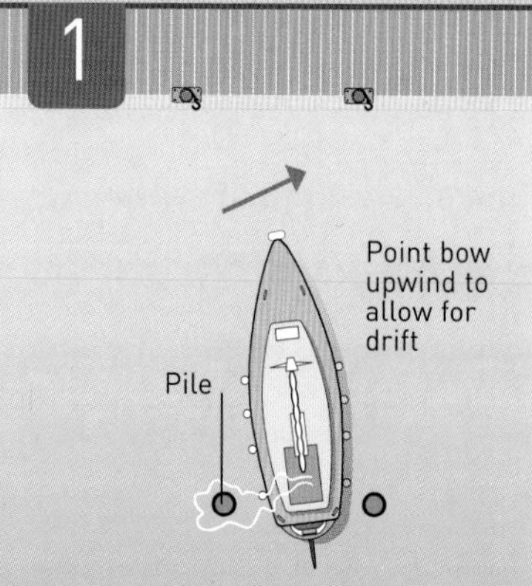

- **Approach bow-to** in most cases where there is a mix of piles and pontoons used to create bow- or stern-to berths.
- **Approach the upwind pile** first under power. If there is a cross wind, lasso the pile with a loop of the stern line and leave slack.

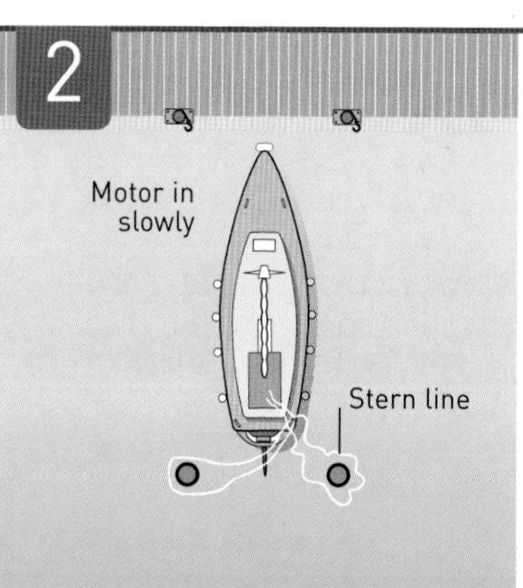

- **Lasso the second pile** with the other stern line.
- **Motor in**, taking care to keep the stern lines clear of the propeller.

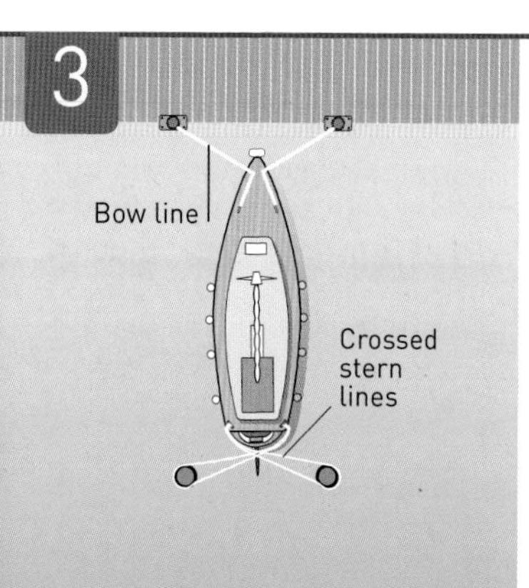

- **Stop the boat** just clear of the pontoon and make fast ashore using two bow lines.
- **Position the boat** just clear of the pontoon and hang a fender under the bow to protect it.

Arriving at a marina

Marinas can provide safe berths and useful facilities, such as fuel, fresh water, showers, shops, restaurants, pubs, repair yards, and chandlers. However, marinas can be crowded and noisy and charges can be quite high. Communicate with the marina using VHF before you arrive and ask for assistance berthing if you need it. Ask for another berth if the one you are directed to is too difficult to enter. Make sure that you brief your crew and have your warps and fenders rigged before you start the approach.

BOW-IN, LEEWARD BERTH

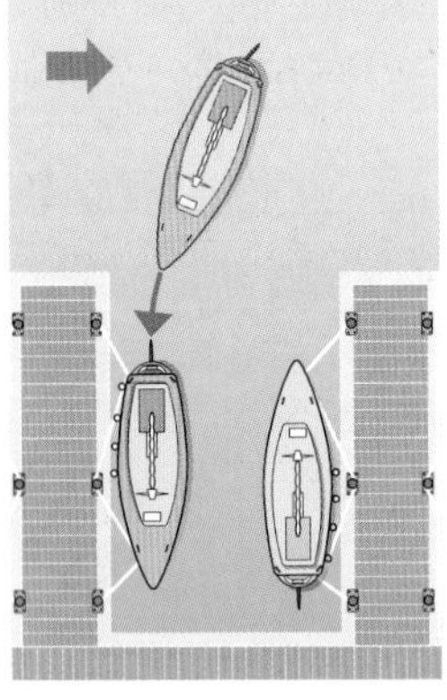

- **Approach the berth** with enough speed to be certain that the boat will not slow down or stop before reaching the pontoon.
- **Maintain sufficient speed** to avoid drifting downwind into the neighbouring boat. The stronger the wind, the more important it is to have enough speed.
- **Be ready to use** reverse gear, or a stopping spring, to bring the boat to a stop in its berth.

STERN-IN, LEEWARD BERTH

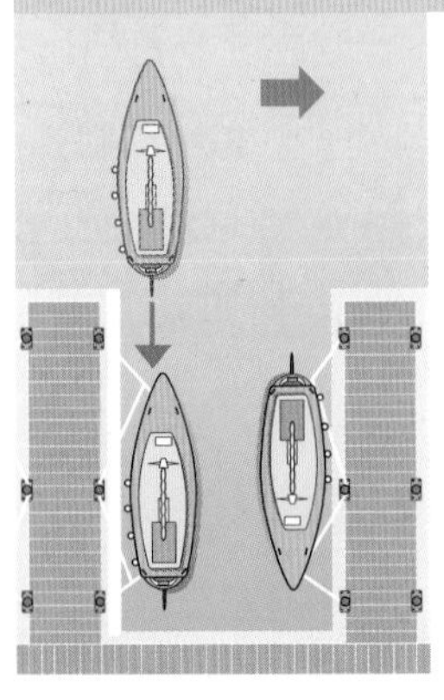

- **Reverse in**, if you have good control and little prop walk. Maintain sufficient speed to avoid being blown away from the pontoon.
- **Use a strong burst** of power in forward gear to stop the boat, and get the warps ashore quickly.
- **Come in at an angle** from the leeward of the berth and swing into it if the boat will not reverse straight in a beam wind. Avoid other boats and have a roving fender ready.

BOW-IN, WINDWARD BERTH

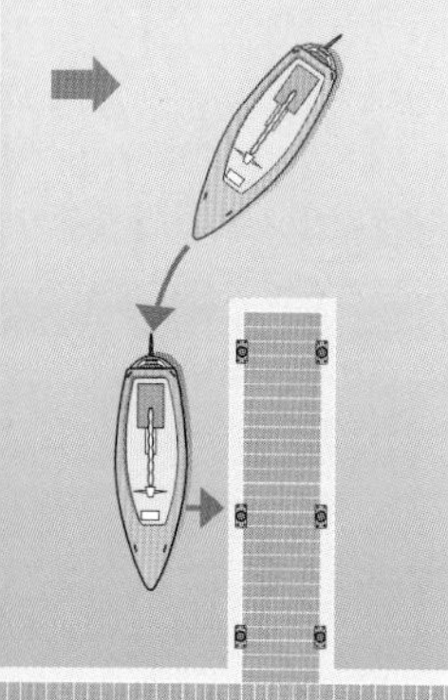

- **Motor fairly slowly** into the berth bow first, aiming to windward of the pontoon.
- **When the boat is to windward** of the berth, put the engine into neutral or engage reverse briefly to stop the boat, and let the boat drift sideways into the berth.
- **Wait for the wind** to push the boat alongside the pontoon before stepping ashore with the warps.

BOW-IN, WIND ASTERN

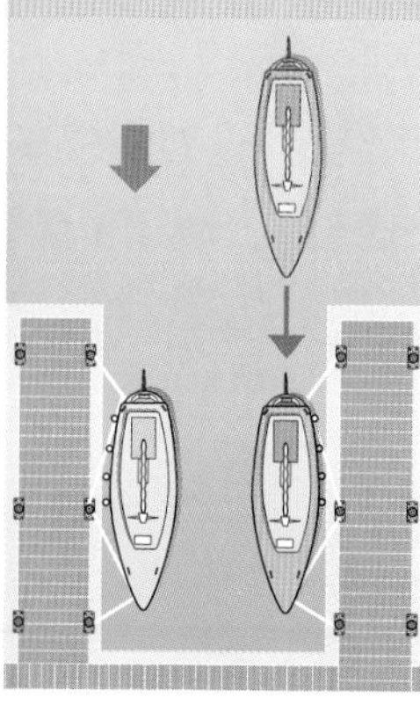

- **Enter a wind astern berth slowly**, bow first, if your boat does not handle well in reverse.
- **Take the stern line** and bow spring ashore to stop the boat, and put the engine into reverse.
- **Beware of prop walk** pushing the stern away from the pontoon. A stopping spring, rigged from the middle of the boat, can be used on its own if you are short-handed.

STERN-IN, WIND AHEAD

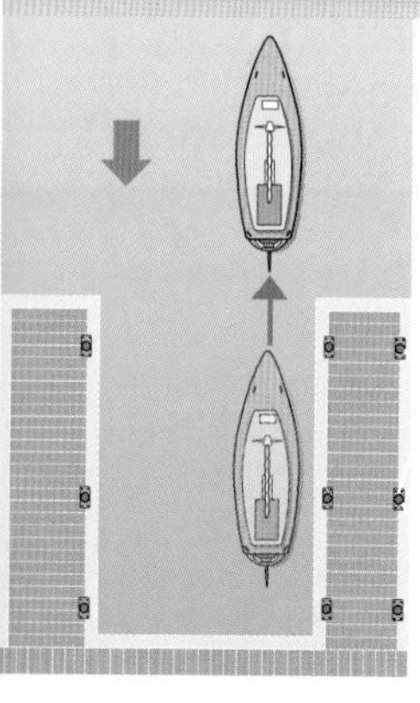

- **Reverse into the berth**, if you have good control when motoring astern. This position is the best choice when possible as it reduces draughts in the cabin.
- **Use a burst of forward power** to stop the boat when you are alongside and quickly rig the warps starting with the stern spring and bow line.

Leaving a marina berth

As the skipper, consider how the wind and tide will affect the boat as you leave the berth and as you exit the marina. While you plan the exit, start the engine and allow it to warm up in neutral. Brief the crew on your plan and make sure they know which lines you want released in which order. Once clear of the berth, remove all warps and fenders, and stow them away.

WINDWARD BERTH, STERN FIRST

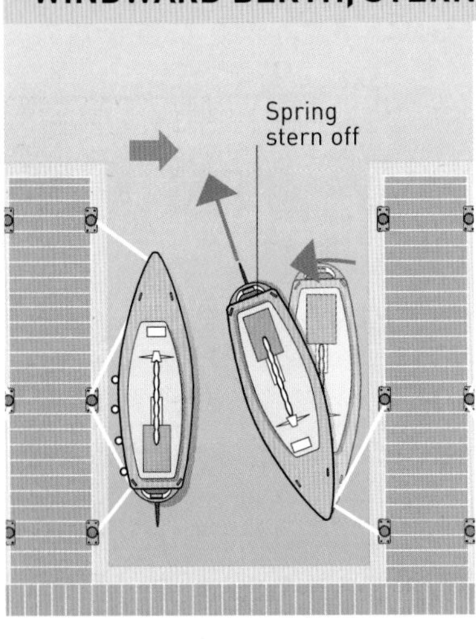

- **Spring the stern out** if your boat has good control under power in reverse, and if there is sufficient space.
- **Rig a spring** from the bow to a pontoon cleat near the middle of the boat. Have a fender at the bow. Cast off other warps.
- **Motor gently ahead** When the stern has swung out, engage neutral, slip the spring, then motor out astern.

WINDWARD BERTH, STERN FIRST, RESTRICTED SPACE

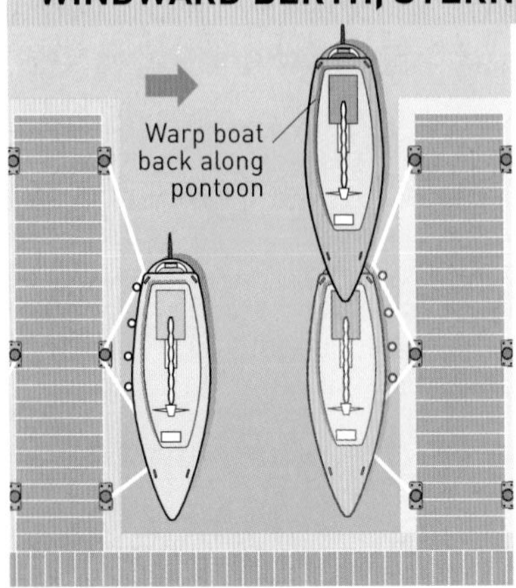

- **Pull the boat** back along the pontoon first if you do not have the room to spring the stern out, or if your boat handles poorly astern.
- **Cast off** the other warps and pull the boat back using the bow spring and stern line.
- **Motor out astern** when the boat has reached the end of the pontoon and the crew are back on board with the warps.

LEEWARD BERTH, BOW FIRST

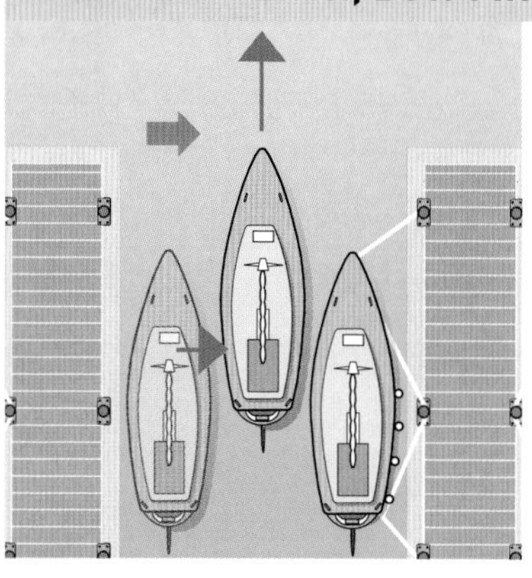

- **Use the wind** on the beam to push you off the berth.
- **Recover the warps** and the boat will blow away from the pontoon, allowing you to motor straight out.
- **Be careful of other boats** moored on your leeward side on the opposite pontoon and have a roving fender ready in case you get too close.

STERN-TO-WIND BERTH, STERN FIRST

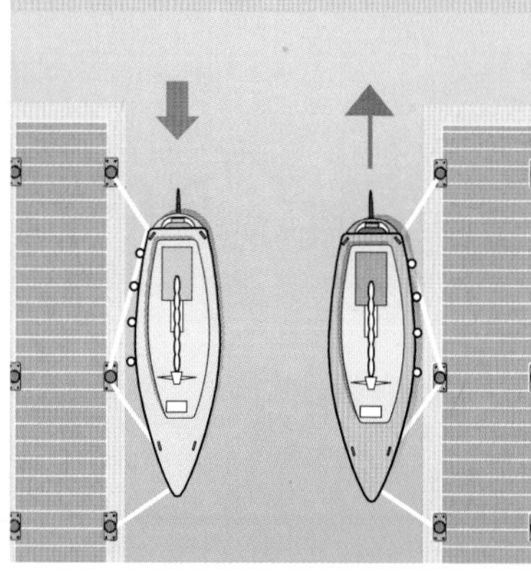

- **Try using prop walk** to pull the stern clear of the pontoon as you motor astern if you are lying bow-in.
- **If prop walk fails** and pushes the stern onto the pontoon, spring the stern out then reverse out.
- **With a weak engine**, the crew can help by walking the boat back along the pontoon using a stern line and bow spring.

HEAD-TO-WIND BERTH, BOW FIRST

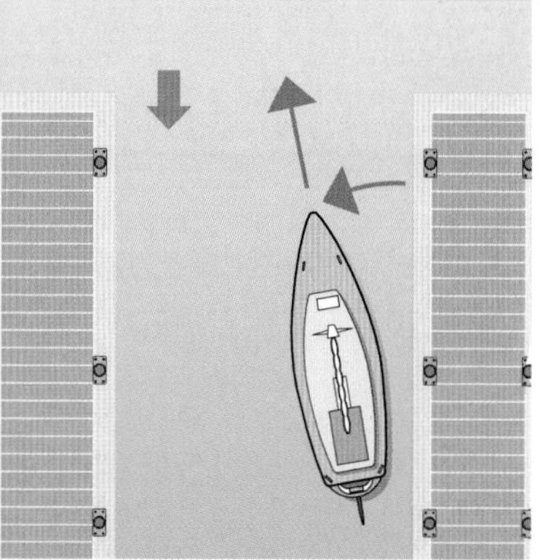

- **Start the engine**, release the warps, and push the bow off, before motoring straight out. This is the easiest exit route.

Using springs and warps

When mooring alongside a pontoon or quay, or when rafting alongside another boat, it is important to stop the boat moving fore and aft under the influence of wind, tide, or wash. So it is important to rig bow and stern springs to stop this movement. Springs are also very useful when you need to turn the boat using its warps.

WHAT DO I NEED TO KNOW ABOUT RAFTING?

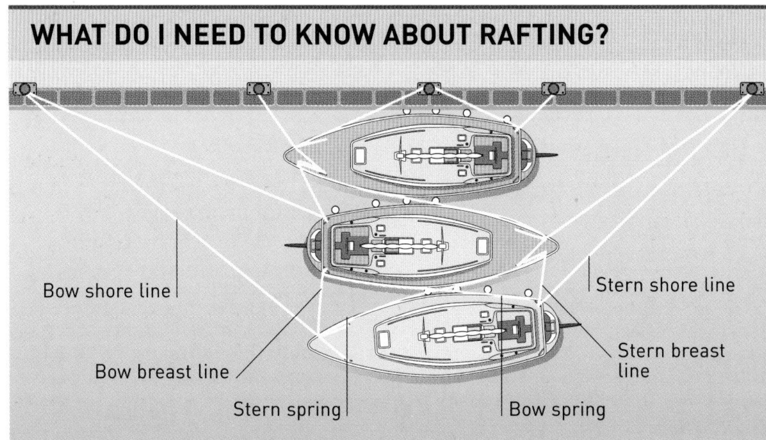

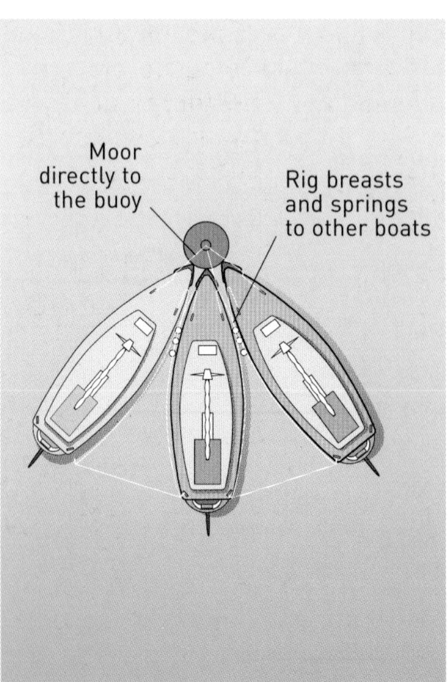

- **Rafting** When boats are stacked one outside the other beside a pontoon or around a buoy, it is known as rafting.
- **Use your own lines** Always secure your own lines to the shore or to the buoy.
- **Springs** Use springs to secure the boat to the neighbouring boat.
- **Mast alignment** Position your boat so that the mast is not in line with that of the next boat in case of clashing if the boats roll.
- **When not to raft** Try not to raft on the outside of a smaller boat.

TURNING USING WARPS AND TIDES

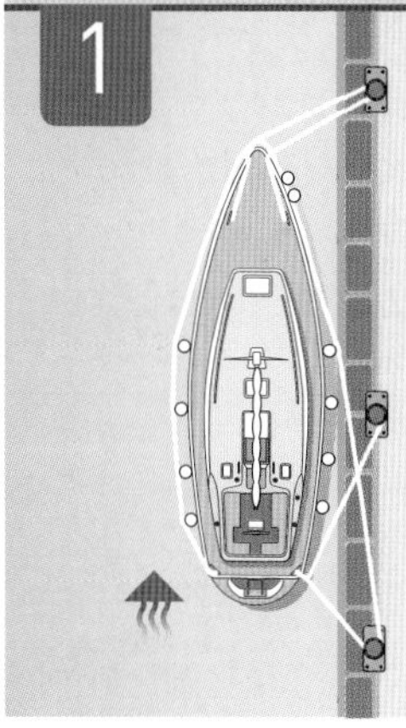

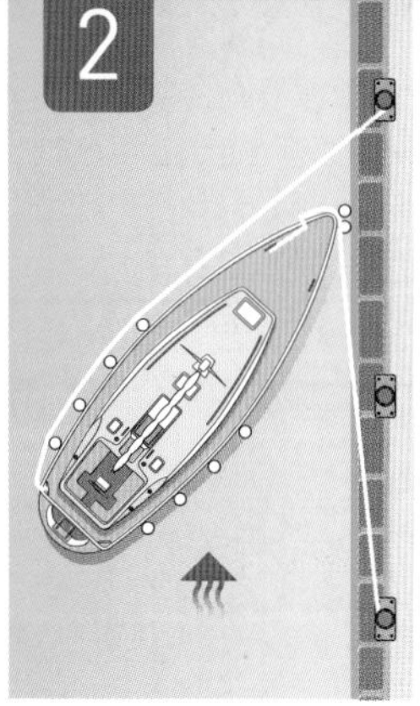

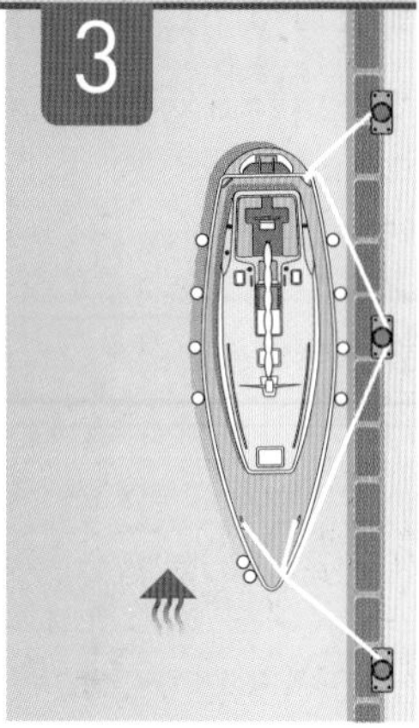

- **Rig a stern line** outside all rigging on the outboard side. Move the bow spring to a cleat on the outboard side and the shore end to a cleat aft of the boat.
- **Release** the bow line, stern spring, and stern line and push the stern out. Let the tide swing the stern out. Take up the slack on the new stern line.
- **The turn** will slow down as the boat lines up with the tide. Make fast the new lines.

USING SLIP LINES

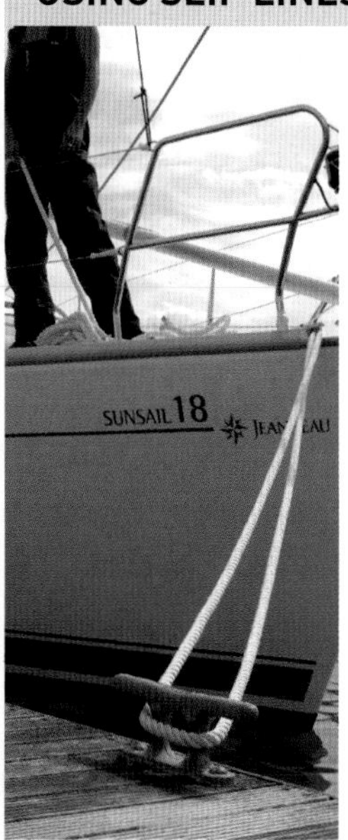

- **Slip line** This is a warp passing through a ring or around a cleat or bollard ashore with both ends fastened on board. It allows the crew to release the warp from on board.
- **How to lead a slip line** Lead a slip line up through a horizontal ring and down through a vertical ring. This will stop the line jamming when you release and pull it aboard.
- **Short-term holding** Never rig a line permanently as a slip, as this will chafe the middle of the warp.

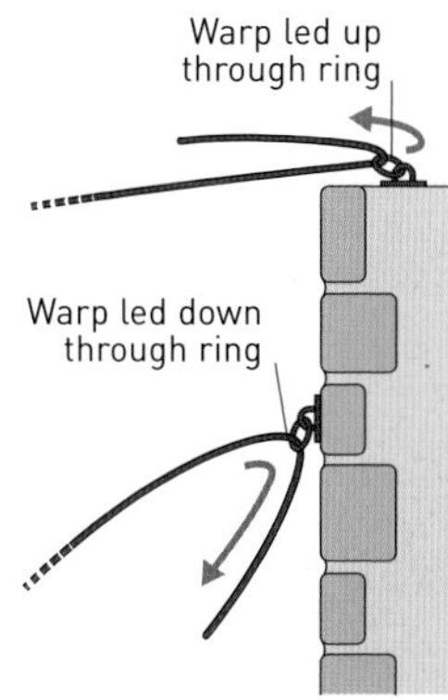

Leaving bow first

To leave bow first, the bow must be pushed away from the pontoon to allow for the tendency of the stern to pivot against the dock as you steer away. The tide or a strong wind on the bow will help push the bow out. Alternatively, you can reverse against a stern spring for the same effect.

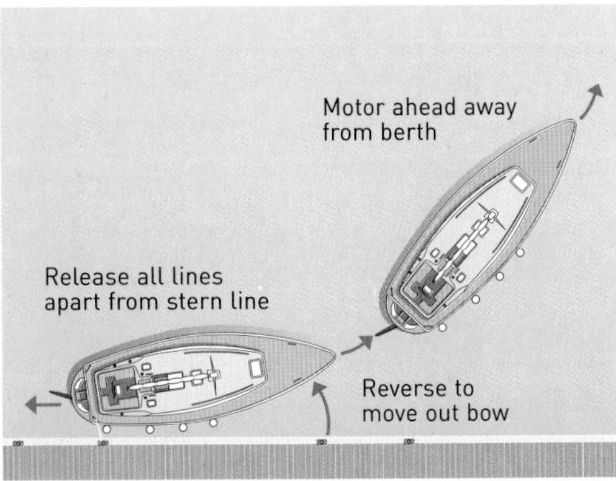

- **Move the bow** The key to leaving a berth bow first is to move the bow away from the berth before you motor away.
- **Use a stern spring** You can move the bow of a small boat by pushing it away. Otherwise, reverse against a stern spring (see p.100).

- **Shore crew** Position a fender near the stern to protect the hull as the stern swings in when you reverse against the stern line.

- **Shore crew** Cast off (release) the bow line and all other warps except the stern line, which you will reverse against.

● **Shore crew** Tie a bowline in the stern line so it can be looped over a cleat for quick release. As the boat reverses, the stern line will act as a spring.

● **Helmsman** Reverse slowly against the stern line until the bow swings out sufficiently.

● Engage neutral so that the shore crew can release the spring.

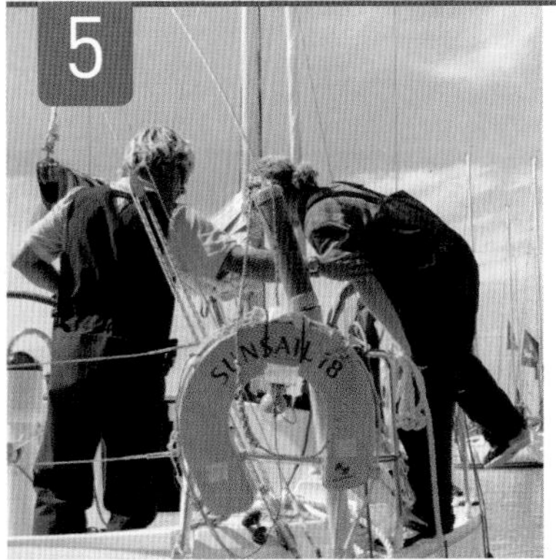

● **Shore crew** Board the boat.

● **Helmsman** Engage forward gear and motor away from the berth.

Leaving stern first

If the tide or a strong wind are on the stern, you will need to leave stern first. The stern must be pushed away from the pontoon in order to motor out without rubbing the bow on the pontoon. Rig a bow spring to motor against to force the stern to swing out. If there is a strong tide on the stern, it will push the stern out against the spring.

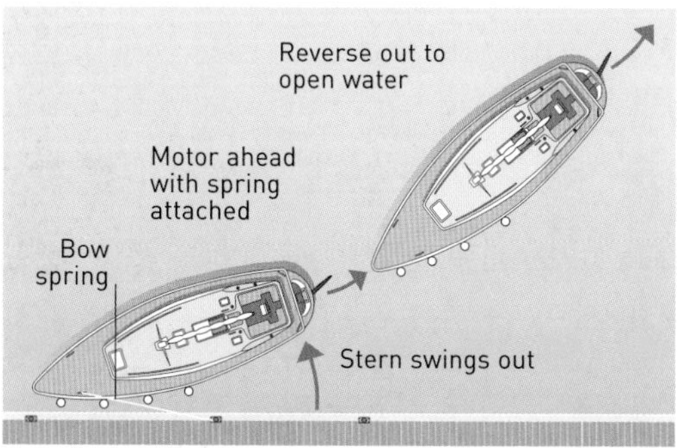

- **Move the stern out** To leave a berth stern first, move the stern clear of the berth before motoring away.

- **Use a spring** Move the stern of a small boat by pushing it away. Otherwise, use a spring line to motor ahead against.

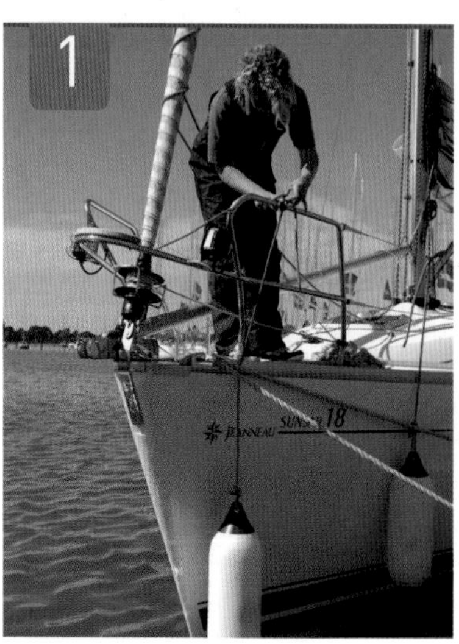

- **Crew** Tie a fender near the bow at the correct height to protect the hull when it swings in towards the pontoon.

- **Shore crew** Cast off the stern line and stern spring and pass them back on board for a crew member on the boat to coil.

- **Shore crew** Cast off the bow line and signal the helmsman to motor forward against the bow spring.

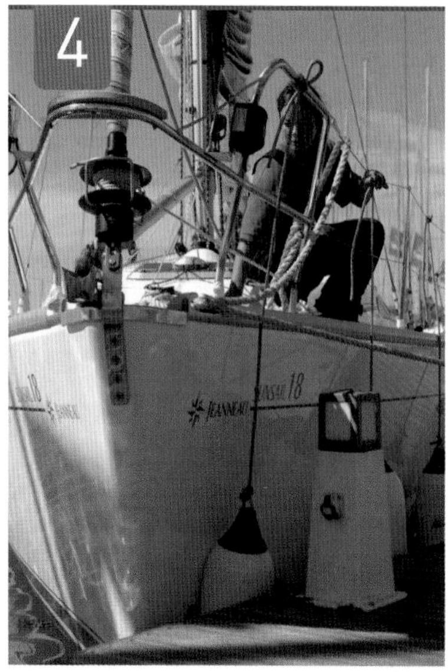

- **Helmsman** As you motor slowly ahead, the bow swings in, protected by the fender, and the stern swings out.

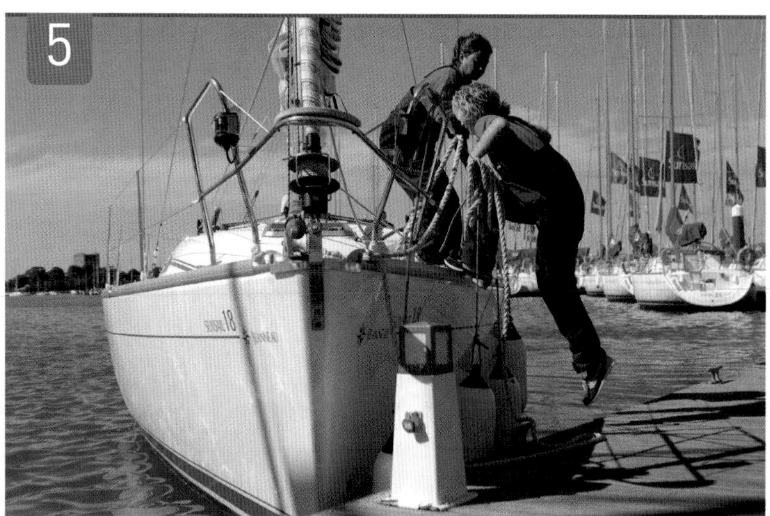

- **Helmsman** When the stern has swung out sufficiently, engage neutral.

- **Shore crew** Release the spring and step aboard.

- **Helmsman** Reverse out of the berth.

Anchoring and mooring

Although marina berths are now the most common mooring option in many sailing areas, all sailors need the skills and equipment to anchor or pick up a mooring buoy when necessary, especially if you are sailing in an area without marinas.

Judging an anchorage

When choosing an anchorage, consider the amount of shelter from wind, swell, and waves, depth of water throughout your stay, type of seabed, swinging room, ease of approach and departure under sail or power, and access to the shore. Check the weather forecast before you anchor and look for any predicted changes that may affect you.

WHAT MAKES A GOOD ANCHORAGE?

- **Seabed** If possible, choose to anchor in sand or firm mud, which provide the best holding.
- **Avoid rock and soft mud** Be careful when anchoring on rock, weed, or coral covered by thin sand, as these provide poor holding for most anchors. Very soft mud also offers poor holding.
- **Depth** Make sure that there will be sufficient depth of water even at low tide.
- **Shelter** Choose a sheltered spot in which the wind and sea conditions are unlikely to change for the duration of your stay. A bay surrounded by high hills usually gives excellent protection.

HOW MUCH SPACE DO I NEED?

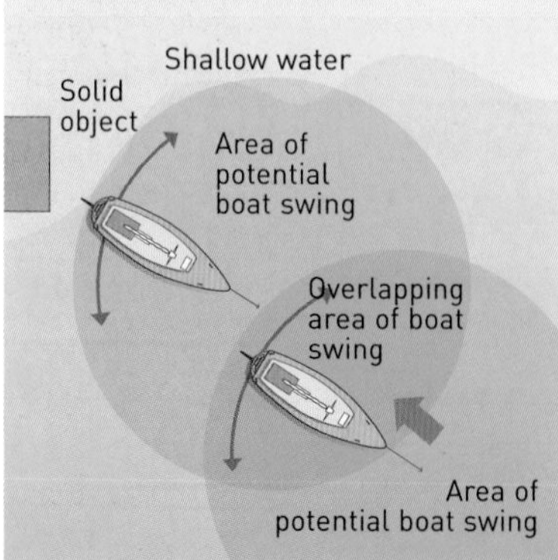

- **Swinging room** Allow sufficient space for your yacht to swing as the wind or tide changes direction, without getting too close to other boats, solid, fixed objects, or to shallow water.
- **Similar types** Yachts that are of similar types tend to swing in unison, which makes it possible to anchor them relatively close together.
- **Different types** Motorboats, which do not have rigs or deep keels, tend to have different swing characteristics.
- **Leave additional space** If you are mooring in the same area as other types of boat, be sure to leave extra space.

WHAT TO LOOK OUT FOR

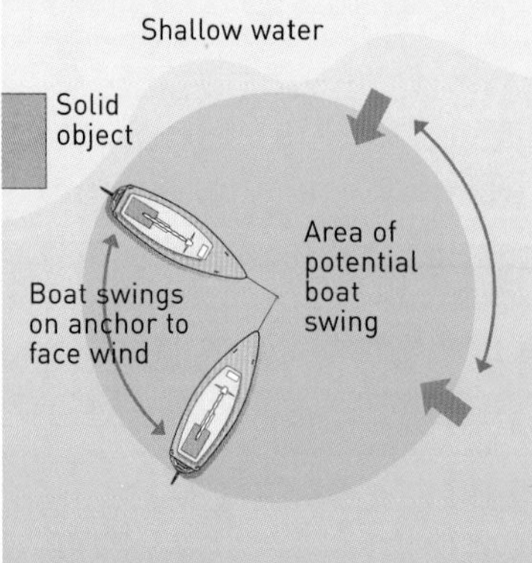

- **Space** Avoid anchoring close to other boats that are of a different type or have a different cable or scope to yours.
- **Fouling** If your boat fouls another that was anchored before you arrived, it will be your responsibility to move.
- **Dragging** Beware of your boat or others dragging in strong winds or gusts. Boats anchored on short scopes or with rope are at particular risk.
- **Weather** Check the weather forecast for likely changes in wind direction.
- **Tide** Know the time of high water and whether the tide is coming in or going out.

HOW TO PREVENT SWINGING

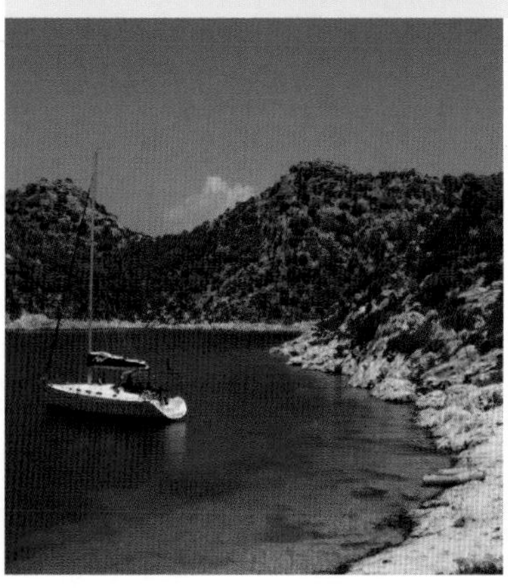

- **Rope ashore** It may be possible to prevent the yacht swinging at anchor by securing a stern line ashore, as shown on the left. This works well in a non-tidal area with deep water close to shore.
- **Use a tender** You may need to carry the line to the shore in a tender and secure it to a large rock or other fixed object if no purpose-made mooring point is available.

Anchors and chains

All cruisers should carry at least two anchors and more will be required for long-distance cruising. Anchors vary from the classic Fisherman's anchor that has several parts and which can be dismantled, to single, one-piece anchors such as the Spade. All anchors have one or more flukes designed to bury themselves into the seabed or hook onto rocks.

WHAT TYPE OF ANCHOR SHOULD I CHOOSE?

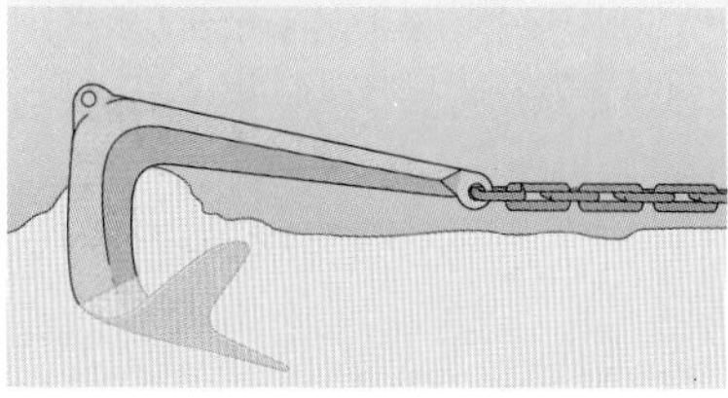

• **The Bruce** This is a solid anchor with large flukes and no moving parts. It is a good choice as a main anchor and stows well on a bow roller.

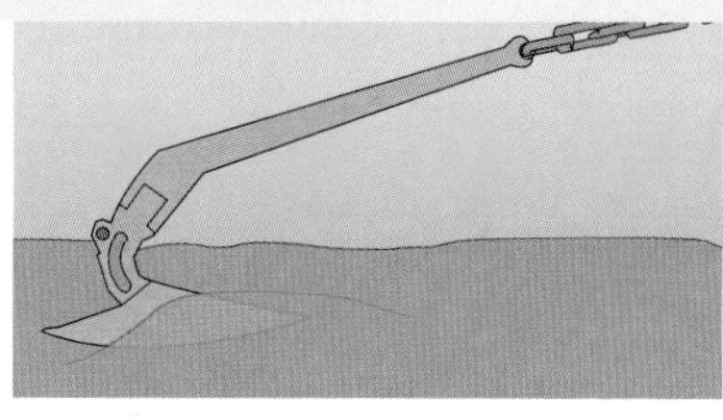

• **Plough-type** This type of anchor is very popular. Most plough anchors have a hinged shank but some have a solid construction.

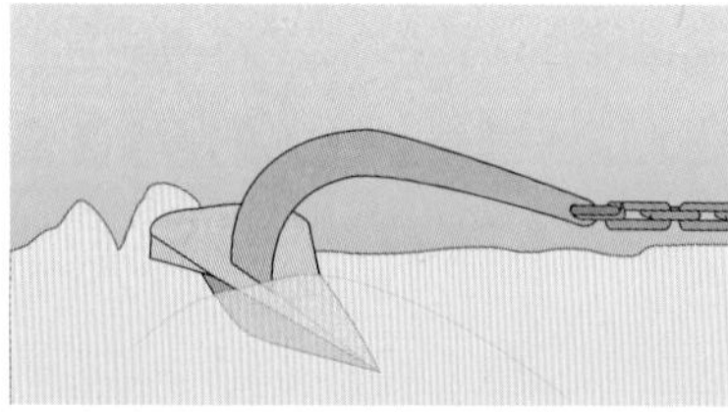

• **The Spade** A high-performance anchor, the Spade is often carried by cruisers. It is available in aluminium, galvanized steel, or stainless steel.

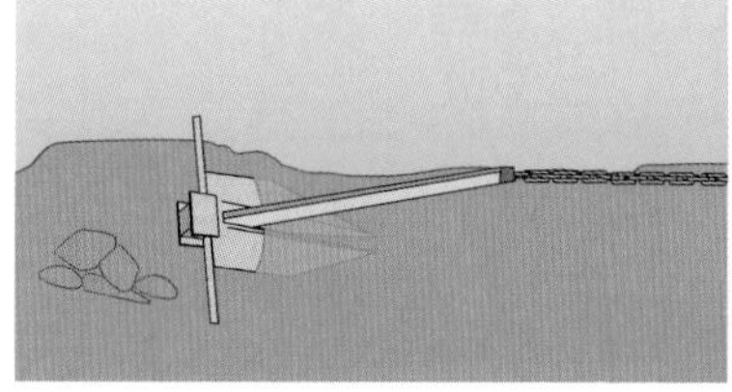

• **The Danforth** This anchor uses a hinged plate to form the flukes and a stock to prevent it rolling over. It is easy to stow on deck because it lies flat.

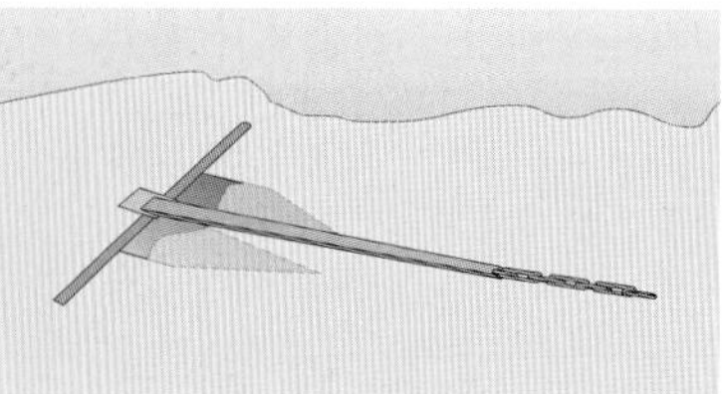

• **The Fortress** This lightweight anchor is made from aluminium. It has wide flat flukes, but their hinge angle can be adjusted to suit sand or mud bottoms. The Fortress can be dismantled.

WHERE IS THE ANCHOR STOWED?

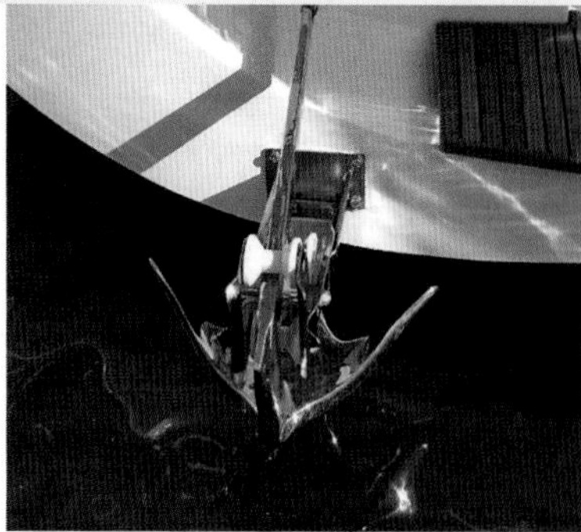

- **Bow roller** Most cruisers carry their main anchor on a bow roller. On some boats the anchor is stowed in an anchor well in the foredeck.

- **Stern anchor** Some cruisers carry a secondary anchor at the stern. It can be useful to use a stern anchor when mooring bow-to in a marina berth.

WHAT KIND OF ANCHOR CABLE DO I NEED?

- **Chain** Stronger than rope, chain is much more resistant to chafe on the seabed while its weight helps prevent the boat snubbing against its anchor.

- **Rope** If a rope cable is used, it should be nylon, which has good stretch properties. There should be a short length of chain about 2m (6.5ft) between the rope and the anchor to resist chafe on the seabed.

HOW TO CALCULATE THE LENGTH OF CABLE

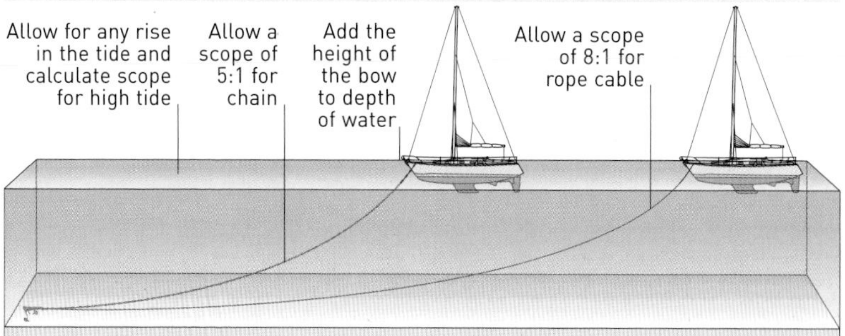

- **Chain** The minimum scope when using chain is 3:1 but you should aim for 5:1, that is, five times the depth of water.

- **Rope** The minimum scope when using rope cable is 5:1 but you should aim for 8:1, that is, eight times the depth of water.

Anchoring routines

Dropping and weighing anchor relies on good communication between the skipper and foredeck crew, who control the weight of anchor and chain. For safety, keep children away from the foredeck, and have a crew member in the middle of the boat if it helps communication.

DROPPING ANCHOR

• **Crew** If the anchor and chain are stowed in an on-deck anchor well, open and secure the lid and lift out the anchor.

• **Crew** Carefully put the anchor in position on the bow roller.

• **Crew** With one person holding a retaining line to the anchor, lay out the chain.

• **Crew** Take a turn of the chain around a deck cleat to help control the anchor's release.

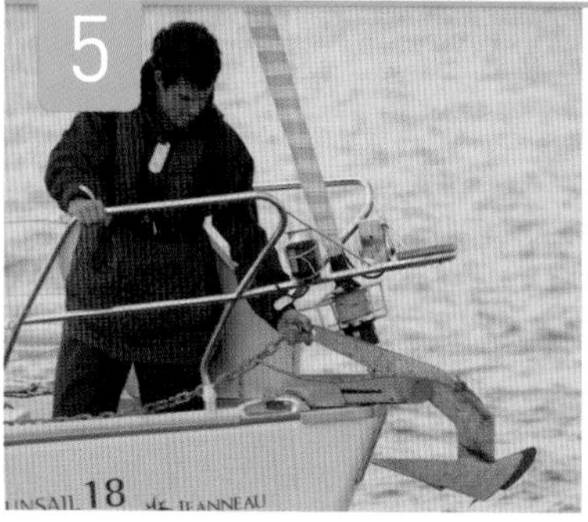

- **Helmsman** Approach the anchoring spot slowly, head-to-wind or tide.

- **Crew** If the anchor is not self-launching, carefully lift the back of the anchor and slide it forward in the bow roller.

- **Crew** Keep tension on the retaining line to ensure that the anchor is not launched prematurely. Inform the skipper that the anchor is ready to go.

- **Helmsman** Stop the boat over the anchoring spot and wait until it starts to move astern. Instruct the crew to lower the anchor.

- **Crew** Lower the anchor under control to the seabed, then pay out chain hand over hand until a sufficient length has been let out for the depth of water, as instructed by the skipper. Some boats have an electric windlass to assist in lowering and raising the anchor.

- **Crew** When sufficient chain is out, secure the chain on the deck cleat.

- **Helmsman** Motor gently astern to set the anchor and to check that it is not dragging. Then stop the engine and take anchor bearings.

CHECKING FOR DRAG

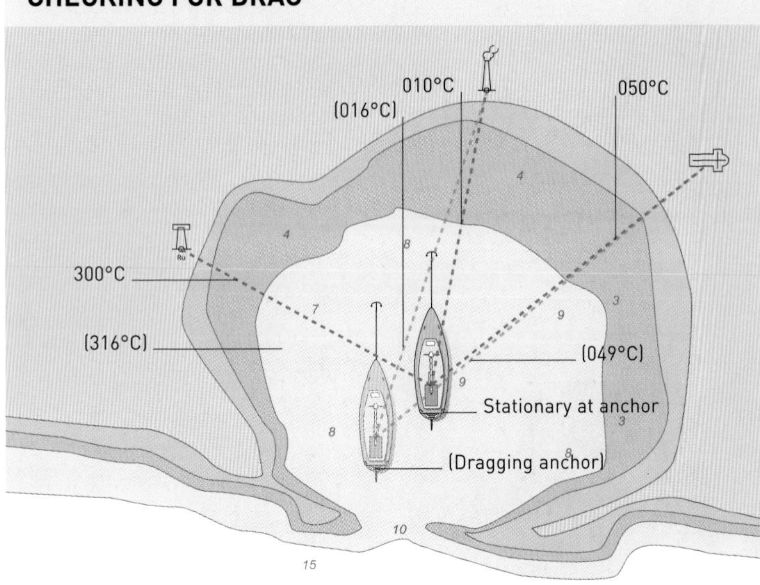

● **Anchor bearings** Once the boat is anchored, take at least two and preferably three or more bearings on prominent shore features. Check these bearings periodically to ensure that the boat is not dragging its anchor.

● **Dragging** If the boat begins to drag, let out more anchor chain or warp and, if the anchor bites again, take new anchor bearings.

● **Reposition** If the boat continues to drag, raise the anchor and try re-anchoring in a different spot.

WEIGHING ANCHOR

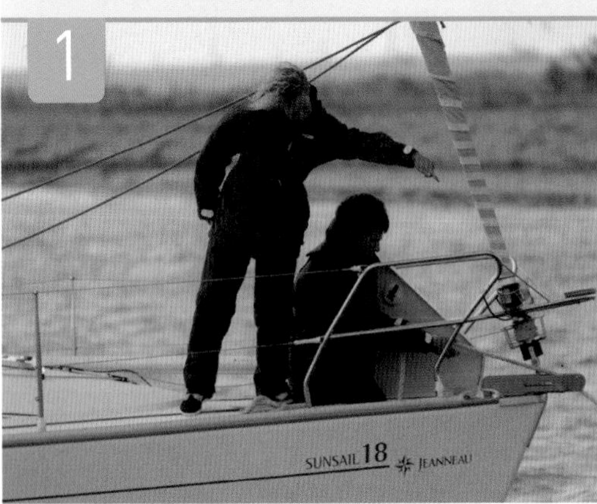

● **Crew** Point in the direction of the anchor so that the helmsman can motor slowly towards it.

● Pull in the slack chain or rope as the boat moves forwards.

- **Crew** When the chain is vertical, signal to the helmsman.
- **Helmsman** Put the engine in neutral.

- **Crew** Break the anchor free from the bottom and pull it to the surface. One or two people can usually do it.
- When the anchor has released from the bottom, tell the helmsman.

- **Crew** Clean off mud and weed before bringing the anchor on board and stowing it in its well. If the anchor stows on the bow roller, pull it into place before cleaning off the mud.
- Wherever the anchor is stowed, make sure it is well secured.

Using a mooring

When you visit a harbour with visitors' mooring buoys, choose a mooring suitable for your boat. Ensure that the mooring is strong enough, that the water is sufficiently deep for your boat at low tide, and that there is enough room to swing around the buoy with the wind and tide. Avoid picking up a permanent mooring as its owner may return to claim it.

WHAT ARE THE PARTS OF A MOORING?

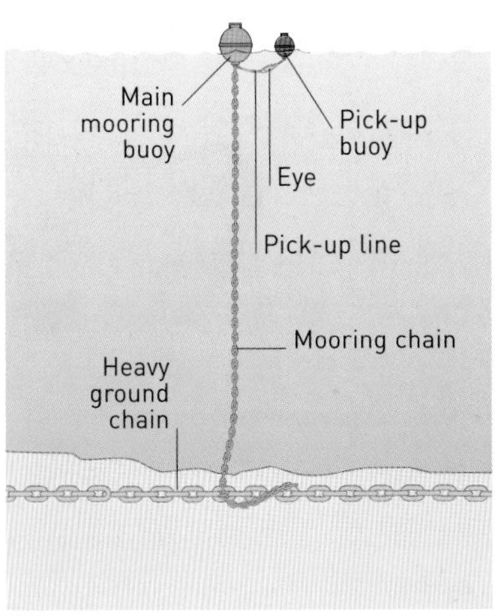

- **Mooring buoy** This is attached by a mooring chain to a heavy ground chain.
- **Pick-up buoy** A lightweight pick-up buoy is sometimes attached to the main mooring buoy.

WHAT ARE FORE-AND-AFT MOORINGS?

- **Fore-and-aft moorings** These are laid at the edges of narrow channels to stop the boat swinging.
- **Shoal-draft cruisers** Some boats can dry out comfortably on fore-and-aft moorings at low tide.

PICKING UP A MOORING

1

- **Head into the tide**, or the wind if there is no tide, keeping your speed as slow as possible while maintaining steerage way.
- **Aim to stop the boat** with the bow alongside the buoy, if possible. Use a boathook to pull the pick-up buoy aboard.

2

- **Pull in the pick-up line** until the eye in the line can be placed over a cleat on the boat.

3

- **Use one of your own warps** if the pick-up line looks suspect in any way. Tie it to the eye on the top of the main mooring buoy using a bowline.
- **Make the mooring line fast** to a deck cleat and let the skipper know that all is secure.

SLIPPING A MOORING

- **Helmsman** Start the engine while briefing the crew. Plan a route away from the mooring.
- **Foredeck crew** Prepare to cast off the mooring when the helmsman is ready.
- **Helmsman** When you are ready, say "Let go".
- **Foredeck crew** Cast off the mooring. Once it is released, call "All gone".

Tenders

The most popular type of tender is an inflatable dinghy. It is compact enough to be stowed on deck, at the stern, or, deflated, in a locker. It can be rowed or powered by an outboard motor and is light and easy to carry ashore. Rigid dinghies are easier to row and more practical for long-term cruising, but are often harder to stow and heavier to lift.

KNOWING YOUR TENDER

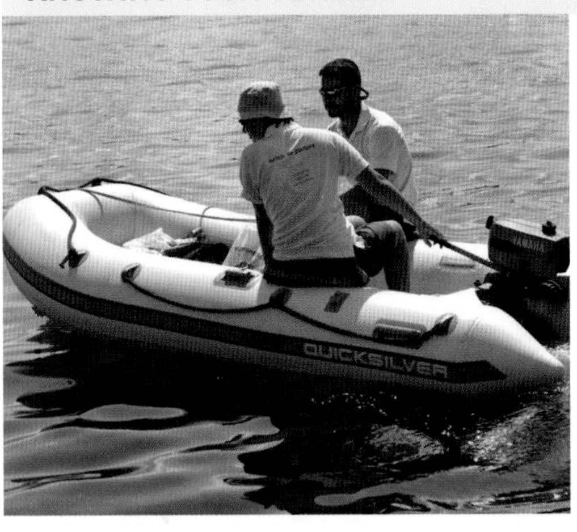

- **A small inflatable dinghy** This is the most popular type of tender for use on cruising yachts.
- **Floor options** A rigid floor improves the performance of an inflatable tender. This type of floor is usually removable. An inflatable floor is another option.

POWERING A TENDER

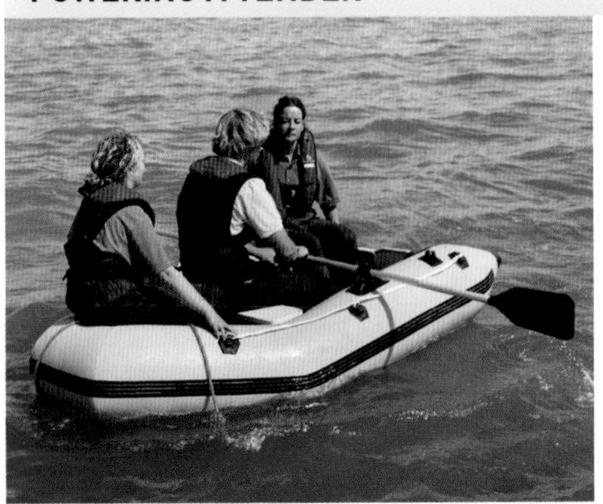

- **Rowing** It can be difficult to row an inflatable as it tends to scoot around on top of the water. Practise until you become proficient.
- **Outboard motor** A small outboard makes propulsion easier, but you should always be able to row the tender.

TOWING A TENDER

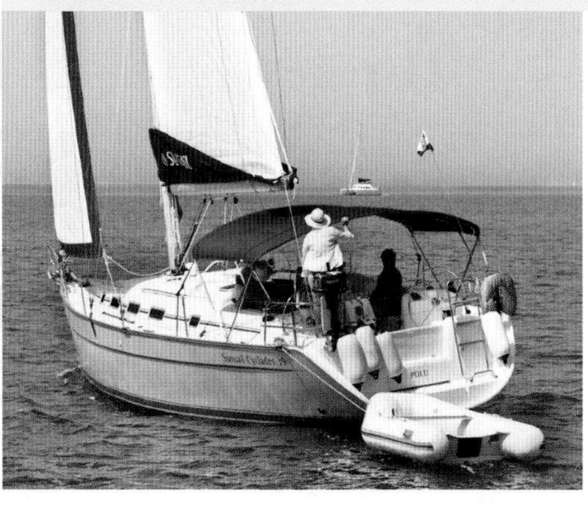

- **Tow behind** The tender can be towed behind for short trips in calm conditions.
- **Gear** Remove the outboard, oars, and other equipment, and tie the painter so that the tender's bow is tight against the yacht's stern.

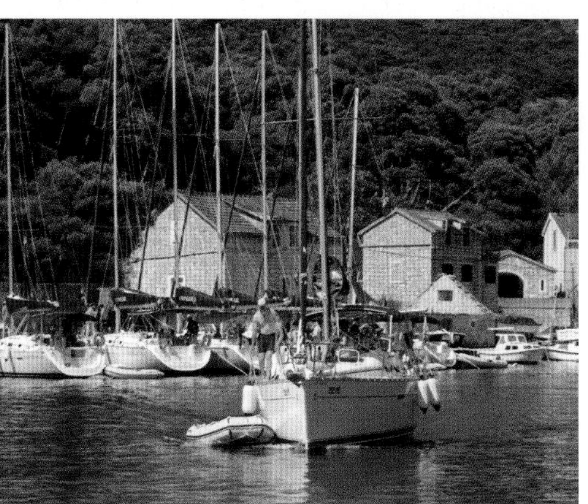

- **Alongside** In congested areas it may be necessary to tow the tender alongside while manoeuvring.
- **Secure** Use bow and stern lines and a stern spring on the tender to hold it close to the side of the yacht.

STOWING A TENDER

- **On deck** An inflatable dinghy can be stowed on deck but must be well lashed down. It is usually best to stow it upside down.
- **Locker** A small inflatable can be fully deflated for stowing in a locker.

Getting into a tender

Accidents can happen when using a tender so be careful, always wear a lifejacket, and never overload the dinghy; if necessary, make two trips to transport the crew and their gear. Ensure you have everything you need for safety, even if it is a short trip. If you are using an outboard, check that you have sufficient fuel and always carry oars.

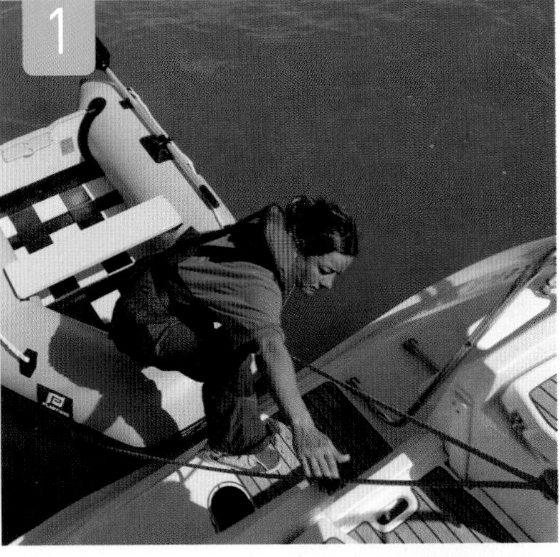

- **Crew** Use the painter (mooring rope) to pull the dinghy close alongside the most convenient boarding spot on your boat and hold it tight.
- **First person** Climb aboard, keeping your weight low, then move to the stern to make room for the next person.

- **Rower** Once the first person is sitting down, climb aboard, keeping your weight low, and sit down as soon as possible.

• **Rower** Once you are aboard and sitting down, prepare the oars for rowing. In many small inflatable tenders, the oars are stowed along the tubes.

• **Third person** When the rower is ready, board the dinghy and sit in the bow.

• When the rower is ready to go, cast off from the yacht and pull in the painter.

• **Rower** If you need to balance the boat, ask the passengers to move their weight. The person at the stern may have to sit to one side to provide room for the rower's legs.

Getting out of a tender

The procedure for disembarking from a tender is the reverse of that for getting in (see p.136). It is important to keep the boat balanced; as each person gets out, those remaining should adjust their positions to compensate. When everyone has disembarked, secure the tender by its painter or bring it on board. Stow or remove the oars when you disembark.

1

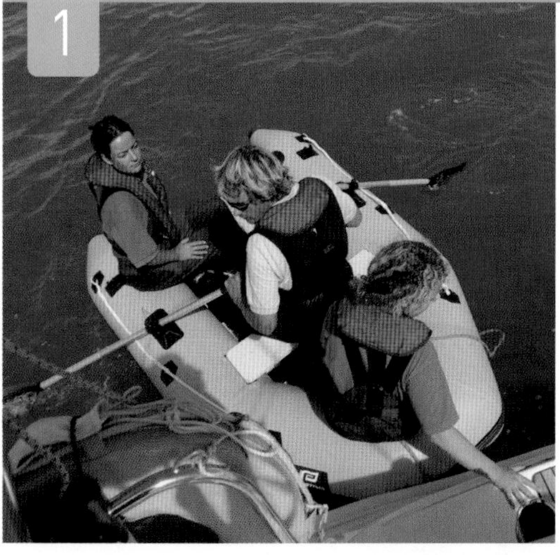

- **All passengers** Keep the rower informed about his course and proximity to the cruiser as he is rowing facing aft.
- **Bow person** Grab hold of the cruiser and prepare to secure the dinghy with the painter (mooring rope).

2

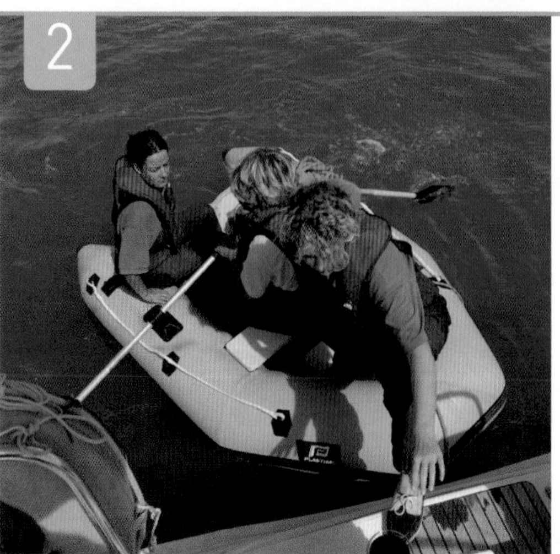

- **Rower** Use the oars to hold the tender close to the yacht as the bow person disembarks.
- **Bow person** Keep your weight low as you climb out.

- **Bow person** Disembark, taking the painter with you.
- **Crew** Make the painter fast to a cleat or other strong point.

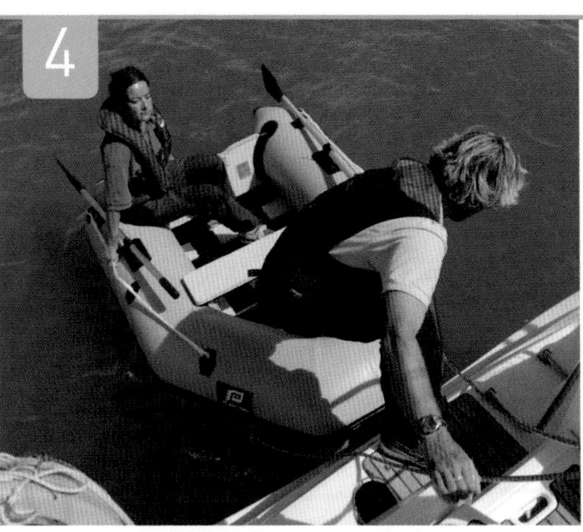

- **Rower** Stow the oars or pass them on deck. Disembark carefully, keeping your weight low.
- **Stern person** Prepare to move forward to balance the tender as the rower gets out.

- **Stern person** Pass out any gear that needs stowing before disembarking.
- If an outboard has been used, bring it aboard the cruiser and stow it. Do not leave it on the tender for any length of time.

Living on board

Cruising on a small yacht involves living in a confined space with the other crew members for the duration of the trip. Make it a great experience by learning to live and work as part of a team, and adapting to the limitations of the onboard facilities.

Sharing space

When four or more crew are living on board, space on yachts can be limited, so the skipper must explain to the crew the importance of being tidy, stowing gear when not in use, and keeping the boat clean and dry. Nothing reduces morale faster than living in a damp, dirty boat with personal items scattered about the small space.

KEEPING THE CABIN CLEAR

- **Personal gear** Stow all personal items in the lockers allocated to you, and do not leave anything lying around on tables or seats as it may end up on the cabin floor when the boat heels.

- **Keeping tidy** Do not clutter working spaces such as the chart table or galley with your personal gear.

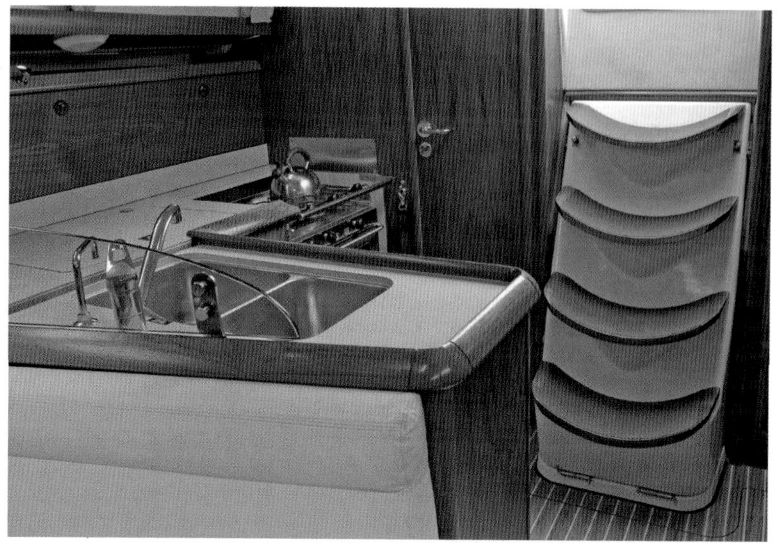

● **Cleaning schedule** Clean the galley, heads, and cabins regularly, depending on the size of the crew and boat, and weather conditions.

● **Keeping record** Note down where equipment and supplies are stored, so you can find things easily without searching the boat.

WORKING TOGETHER

● **Team work** Cooperation is important for all jobs on the boat, not just sailing tasks. Organize a rota for chores to ensure that everyone participates in all the sailing and domestic jobs.

● **Consideration** Help crew members get good quality rest when off watch by respecting their personal space. Limit bright lights in cabins at night, and keep unnecessary noise to a minimum.

Berths and stowage

On a cruiser for offshore passages, there should be a sea berth for every off-watch crew member and enough stowage space for personal gear. Most boats are designed to provide as much stowage space as possible in a limited area. There is usually stowage space under each berth, inside the saloon table, under the cabin floor, and in cupboards at the hull sides.

HOW TO STOW GEAR

- **Label and hang** Hang lifejackets and safety harnesses in a dedicated, easy to access locker that is ventilated and drains to the bilge to allow wet gear to dry.

- **Dedicated lockers** There should be a dedicated locker space for as much equipment as possible. Store crockery in lockers where it cannot be thrown or tipped out of its stowage when the boat heels.

- **Personal kit** Keep all your personal kit neatly stowed in the locker(s) assigned to you, and do not leave the kit loose in the main cabin (saloon).

USING LEE-CLOTHS

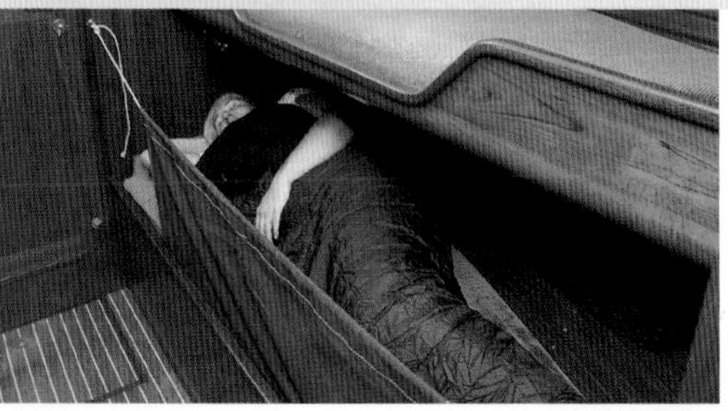

- **Comfort under way** All sea berths should be fitted with lee-cloths or leeboards, which retain a sleeping person in the berth when the boat heels.

FORECABIN BERTH

- **V-berth** Many yachts have a V-berth built into the forecabin.
- **Best in port** Berths in the forecabin are really only usable in harbour as the motion is usually too great in the bow to allow sleeping at sea.

SALOON BERTH

- **Extra berths** In most boats the saloon settees also double as berths.
- **Pros and cons** Berths in the saloon are usually near the middle of the boat where the motion is least, but they are in a busy part of the boat and can be noisy.

AFT CABIN BERTH

- **Less motion** An aft cabin berth can provide a good sea berth as the motion is usually much less than in the bow.
- **Double or split** Double berths are often fitted in the aft cabin. They can be difficult to sleep in at sea, unless they are split with a lee-cloth.

Cooking on board

Appetites generally increase while sailing, so it is very important to provide sustaining food. It is essential that meals are prepared to suit the watch system and that the galley is kept clean and tidy. Cooking is usually on gas, so the skipper must brief the crew on safety precautions.

FEEDING THE CREW

- **Plan ahead** Have a menu plan for your trip and provision the boat accordingly.
- **Cook in advance** If the boat has a fridge or freezer, prepare meals ashore for a short cruise.
- **Ready-meals** Have a stock of these in case of bad weather and keep a container of chocolate, biscuits, fruit, raisins, and other snacks for the on-watch crew.

HOW IS THE GALLEY ARRANGED?

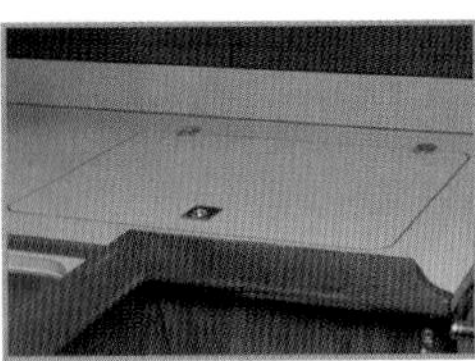

- **Fridge** A top-opening fridge is fitted under the galley worktop.

- **Sink** Single or twin sinks are usually located near the cooker close to the companionway.

- **Fiddles** High fiddles on counters hold pots, pans, and utensils in place and prevent spillages when the boat heels.

USING GAS SAFELY

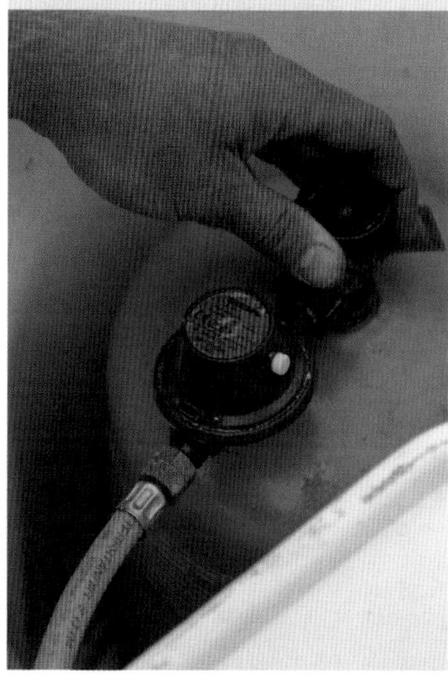

- **Stowage** Stow the gas bottle in a self-draining deck locker.
- **When not in use** Turn off the supply at the bottle, and at the cabin valve if fitted, when the gas is not being used.
- **Gas alarm** Fit and maintain a gas alarm and pump the bilges frequently to expel leaked gas.
- **Ventilation** Open hatches if appropriate to let in fresh air when cooking.

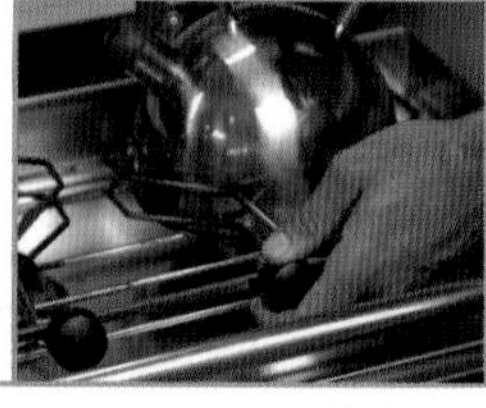

- **Pan clamps** These hold pots and pans securely on the gimballed stove.

- **Gimbals** These fittings permit the cooker to swing when the boat heels, allowing pans on top to remain horizontal.

- **Crash bar** Fitted in the front of the cooker, a crash bar provides an important handhold for the cook.

Heads and plumbing

Most heads contain a marine toilet, a small washbasin, and lockers for personal items. Some also have a shower with hot and cold water. The skipper should make sure that all crew and visitors understand how to operate these facilities, especially the toilet. Mistakes here can make things very unpleasant. Put clear instructions for use by the toilet.

USING THE TOILET AND SHOWER

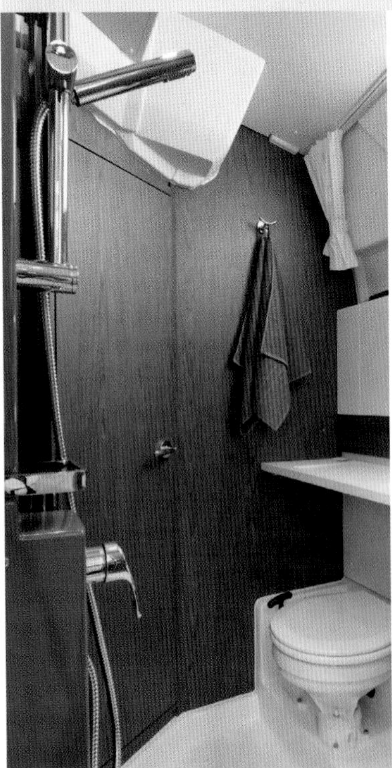

- **Compact arrangement** The toilet and shower are usually fitted into a small compartment with minimum storage space.
- **Cleanliness** Always keep the heads clean or the compartment will quickly start to smell.

- **Shower** Some heads have a shower facility with hot and cold pressurized water.
- **Water use** If a pressure shower is fitted, make sure all the crew know the limitation on the amount of water carried.
- **Pressure system** It is best to turn the pressure system off at sea and use a fitted hand-pump to conserve water. There should always be a manual fresh water pump in both galley and heads.

UNDERSTANDING THE PUMPS

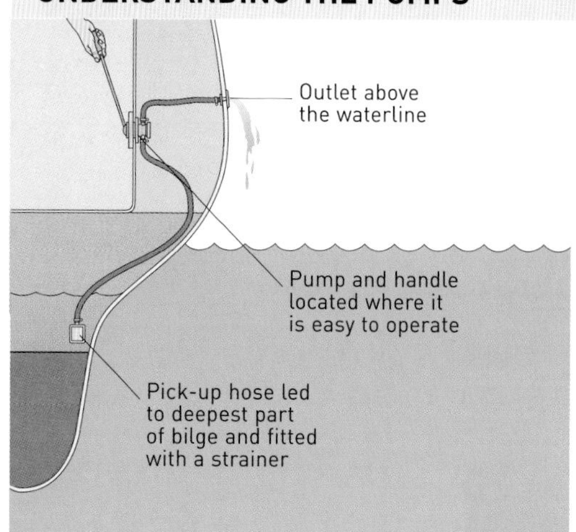

- **Bilge pump** A yacht should have at least one high-capacity manual bilge pump to pump out water that collects in the bottom of the hull.

- **Usability** The pump must be fitted in a place where it is easy and comfortable to use for long periods, with the handle stowed close by.

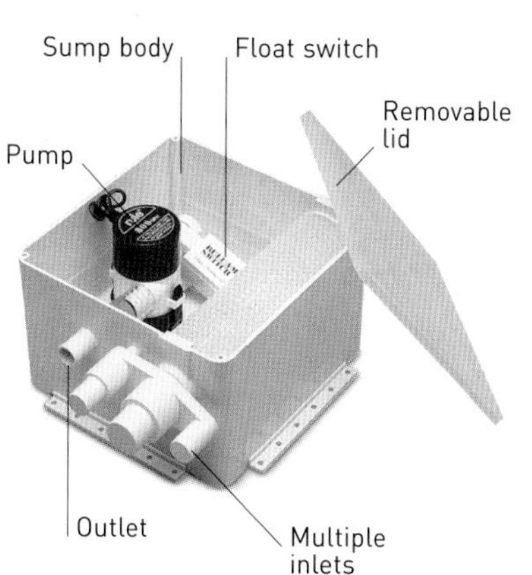

- **Sump pumps** A shower tray is often emptied by an electric pump, which may be mounted in its own sump along with a float switch.

- **Maintenance** Clean shower sump pumps regularly to prevent the build up of hair, which can cause a blockage. Check the float switch for free movement. Tighten stainless-steel clips on the hoses to ensure water-tightness.

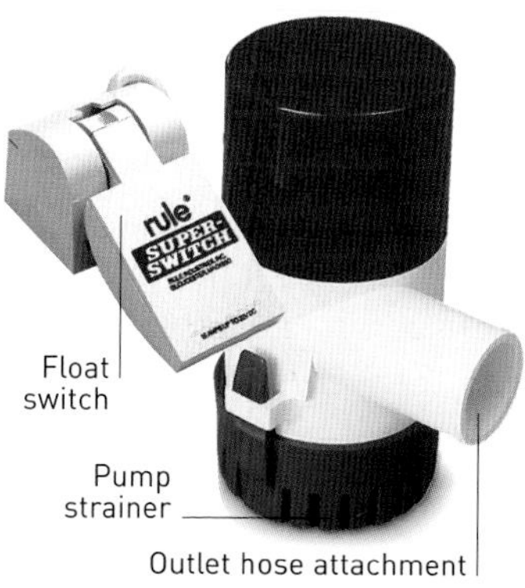

- **Electric bilge pump** Clean the pump strainer, and test the float switch and the in-use alarm regularly to prevent failure.

- **Manual bilge pump** Always have a high-capacity manual bilge pump fitted to cope with any serious ingress of water, such as after a collision.

Electric power sources

Most cruising yachts rely heavily on their electrical system. 12-volt power is used to run navigation and communications equipment, lighting, entertainment systems, and a fridge. 240-volt power is also used on many boats for domestic needs. Consequently, there is a need to generate and store sufficient power, and to be frugal in its use.

WHAT DO I NEED TO KNOW ABOUT BATTERY POWER?

Domestic battery bank

Engine start battery

- **Storage** Power is stored onboard in batteries, usually at 12 volts DC. This is used when the engine is not running to power all the yacht's electrical systems.

- **Domestic batteries** Traction batteries, often wired in series, in a battery bank, are the most suitable type for domestic power needs on board.

- **Engine start battery** There should be a separate battery used solely to start the engine.

- **Engine-charging** An alternator on the engine provides power to the starter and domestic batteries whenever the engine is running.

- **"Smart" regulator** This regulator increases the charging efficiency and reduces the amount of time you have to run the engine to charge the batteries.

- **AC battery charger** Many cruisers have a battery charger that can be powered from an onshore AC power source.

WHAT ARE THE ALTERNATIVE SOURCES OF POWER?

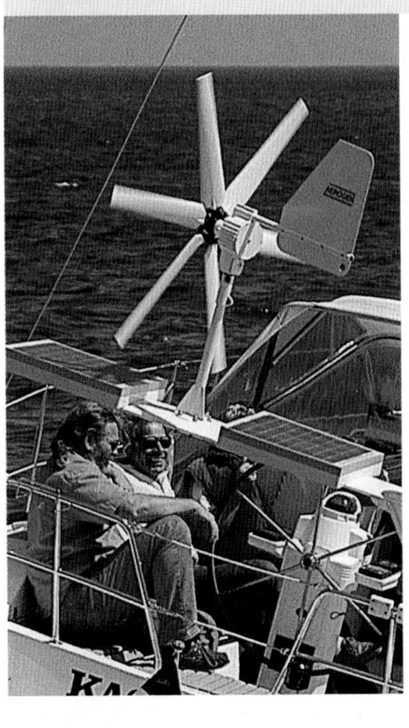

- **Wind power** A wind generator can deliver useful power to the batteries. The equipment should be mounted high enough so that the blades are well clear of head height to avoid injury.
- **Solar panels** Useful in sunny climates, rigid, semi-flexible, and flexible designs are available.
- **Combined power** Wind and solar power together can provide enough power to run all the necessary systems and minimize the need for engine-charging.
- **Water-driven generators** Efficient power generation can also be provided by a generator attached to the stern and driven by water flow.

USING AC POWER

- **Shore power** Most marinas have shore power stations on the pontoon that deliver AC power.
- **Safety** If the boat has an AC system, it should be kept isolated from the 12-volt domestic system and should be professionally installed and maintained.
- **Generator** Larger yachts often have a dedicated generator for charging the batteries and generating AC current for domestic equipment.

Power usage

Unless you spend a lot of time living aboard, it is easy to forget to conserve electrical power, with the result that you have to run the engine for many hours to replenish the batteries. Your time spent cruising will be less noisy, cheaper, and simpler if you minimize your use of electrical equipment and have efficient systems.

HOW TO CONTROL POWER DISTRIBUTION

- **12-volt system** Most boats use this system to power their DC equipment, including instruments, lights, and fridge.
- **240-volt system** Some boats use a 240-volt system to power domestic AC equipment such as a kettle or a microwave oven. The AC system must have a separate switch panel.
- **Electrical circuit** Equipment such as fridges and lights are controlled at a distribution panel with switches and fuses or circuit breakers.
- **Battery monitoring** A battery-monitoring system is very useful for checking the amount of charge or discharge in the system.
- **Battery charge** Never let the batteries run completely flat as it may damage them. Monitor their state and recharge them before they get down to 20 per cent of charge.
- **Isolating switch** Know where to find the battery isolating switch in case of a problem in the electrical system. There should be a switch on each battery bank.

HOW TO CONSERVE POWER

- **Use engine power** Turn off any equipment not needed when the engine is not running. Charge phones and run other equipment when the engine is running.

- **Limit usage** Restrict your use of electrical items.

- **Keep the fridge door closed** Avoid opening the fridge door too often, as this allows cold air to escape, which wastes energy.

- **LED bulb** Replace conventional or halogen bulbs with LED ones to reduce your energy usage.

How much power?

Calculate the size of battery bank needed by working out the total daily power usage (multiply current in amps by the length of time for which you expect to use each item), using the table on the right as a guide. Assuming you charge batteries once a day and do not want to discharge them beyond 50 per cent of total capacity, your battery bank should be at least twice the size of your estimated daily power usage. Do not skimp on the size of batteries and charging systems. Batteries that are regularly run nearly flat because they are too small for the task may fail in the first year or two.

ITEM	TYPICAL CURRENT DRAW
Anchor light	1 amp
Tricolour light	2 amp
Interior lights (each)	1 amp
Log/depth sounder	0.5 amp
GPS	<0.5 amp
VHF	<0.5 amp
CD player	1–5 amp
Autopilot	4–10 amp
Warm air heater fan	1–2 amp
Refrigerator	4 amp

MAKING USE OF AC POWER

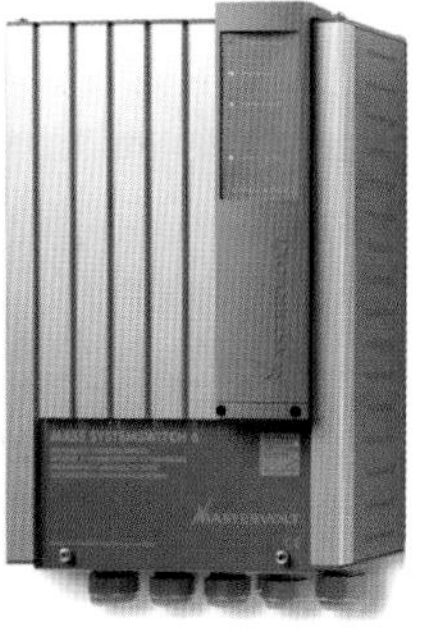

INVERTER

- **Shore power** Plugging in to shore power is a convenient way to get AC power on board when in a marina. It will run a battery charger and power domestic 240-volt equipment.

- **Inverter** An inverter converts DC power to AC and allows you to run AC appliances such as a computer, phone charger, or kettle from your 12-volt system.

- **Generator** Larger yachts can use a stand-alone AC generator to provide AC power.

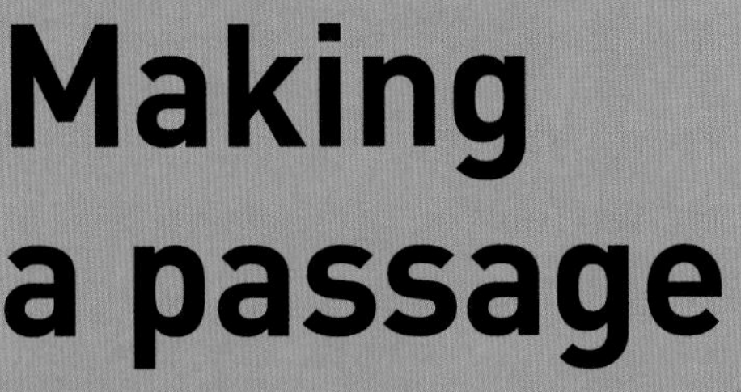

Making a passage

Once you have mastered essential boat-handling techniques, you will be eager to try out your new skills by taking your boat safely from one port to another. In this section, you will find a helpful introduction to the skills of navigation and passage-making.

Ujorasugssuk
Flakkerhuk
Gule Ryg
Skorstensfjeldet
Iviangernat
Kulmine
Skansen
Nunguaq
Kulmine
Per Dam

Preparing a passage

Before you go sailing, even for a short trip, the skipper and crew should check that the boat is ready for sea, that all its equipment is in place and in working order, and that all the crew understand its use. It is crucial that the safety gear is fully functional and that the crew know when and how to use it. Remember to inform someone ashore of your itinerary.

BEFORE YOU SET OFF

- **The plan** If you are the skipper, allow time to brief the crew on the plan for the passage.
- **New crew** Give a tour of all the key equipment to any crew who are new to the boat so that they understand its use.
- **Safety** Explain to the crew the safety equipment that is carried on board, its location, and when it is to be used.
- **Navigation** Prepare a passage plan, noting details of weather, tides, and other key information.
- **Clothing** Make sure that all crew on board are equipped with the right clothing and personal safety gear.
- **Notify** Let a responsible person ashore know what your plans are and the time you expect to return or reach your destination.

Equipment checklist

Make sure you have all the basic equipment on board that you need for the trip, and check that it is in working order before you set sail. Take the time needed to do a visual check of all systems.

ENGINE

- Check fuel, oil, and water systems, and the tightness of drive belts, seawater intake, impellor, and filter.
- Run the engine to warm it up before you cast off. Check that cooling water is being discharged.
- Check the propeller shaft's stern gland and greaser, if fitted.
- Check that the batteries are fully charged.
- Be sure that a suitable toolkit is on board, with sufficient engine spares, and other equipment.

BOAT EQUIPMENT

- Check the condition of the anchor chain. Know how much is available. Check that the end of the chain is secured on board to a strong point that is easily reached.
- Know your bilges – is she a dry or wet boat? Make sure that you know what level of water is normal in your bilge.
- Check gas bottle fittings and piping, and test the gas alarm is working.
- Operate all seacocks. Ensure you have bungs of the correct size available.
- Have a waterproof torch with spare batteries and bulbs.
- Check that your navigation lights and VHF radio are in working order.
- Close all hatches and ventilators that may let in water.

SAFETY EQUIPMENT

- Check that your first-aid kit is complete and up to date. Brief the crew on its location and composition.
- Check that you have safety harnesses and lifejackets in working order for all of the crew.
- Confirm that the liferaft has been serviced recently and that its lashings are secure.
- Ensure that there are sufficient usable flares and a foghorn on board.
- Check that fire extinguishers are serviceable and in date.

RIG AND SAILS

- Check masts and spars – look for broken strands in standing rigging, cracks in fittings, loose pins or joints, damage, and metal fatigue.
- Check running rigging for fraying and chaffing.
- Check sails: seams, stress points, cringles, strengthening patches, battens, and earlier repairs.

NAVIGATION EQUIPMENT

- Be sure to have an up-to-date chart on board for your sailing area.
- Have local tide tables, tidal atlas, and local sailing instructions on board.
- Check that all the navigation instruments are in working order.

GENERAL CHECKS

- Check there are sufficient provisions and water on board, with enough to allow for an unexpectedly long trip.
- Make sure your deck hardware is working.
- Check all hatch seals for signs of leaks.
- Complete all necessary repair jobs.

Communication

Traditional means of communication, such as flags, lights, and sound signals, are still used at sea, but most communications from a cruiser are carried out using a VHF (Very High Frequency) radio or mobile phone. While a phone is useful for general communications, VHF is more reliable for essential safety information and distress signals.

WHAT ARE THE COMMUNICATIONS OPTIONS?

- **VHF** A VHF radio provides broadcast communication between yachts, other boats such as rescue craft or commercial shipping, and marine shore and safety services.

- **Hand-held VHF radio** This is commonly used as a backup and for use on deck or for communication when away from the yacht. Most yachts carry it in addition to a fixed VHF set with an external aerial.

- **Mobile phone** Do not rely on your mobile phone for distress and safety calls. It is designed for use on land and may not prove reliable in an emergency (see p.161).

- **Other methods of communication** These include sound signals using a foghorn and specialized means of sending a distress signal such as by emergency position indicating radio beacon (EPIRB) (see p.161).

USING VHF

Fixed VHF radio

- **VHF features** A modern VHF set incorporates Digital Selective Calling (DSC). This sends a signal that includes the yacht's Maritime Mobile Service Identity (MMSI) number that works with the Global Maritime Distress and Safety System (GMDSS) (see p.284).

- **Alerts** DSC VHF radios allow you to send a distress alert simply by pushing a red emergency button.

- **Talking** Think what you need to say, then speak slowly and clearly. Use the phonetic alphabet to spell out key words (see p.160).

- **Talk button** Remember to push the button in order to talk, and release it to listen to the other side of the conversation.

HOW DO I SEND A DISTRESS MESSAGE?

● **Degrees of urgency** A "SÉCURITÉ" signal is used for an important safety, navigational, or weather warning. Use a "PAN PAN" signal for a serious situation for which you require help – for example, if the boat has been disabled, but is not in imminent danger of sinking. Send a "MAYDAY" message if a vessel or a person is in grave and imminent danger.

How to send a PAN PAN message

"PAN PAN, PAN PAN, PAN PAN.

This is Yacht *Dream, Dream, Dream*.

PAN PAN Yacht *Dream*.

Marine Mobile Service Identity (MMSI) if known.

My position is (latitude and longitude, or bearing and distance from a landmark).

Yacht dismasted and engine disabled by rope around propeller.

I have three crew.

I require a tow.

Over."

How to send a MAYDAY message

"MAYDAY, MAYDAY, MAYDAY.

This is Yacht *Dream, Dream, Dream*.

Mayday Yacht *Dream*.

Marine Mobile Service Identity (MMSI) if known.

My position is (latitude and longitude, or bearing and distance from a landmark).

Yacht holed by a rock and in danger of sinking.

I have three crew.

I require immediate assistance.

Over."

Phonetic alphabet

A	Alpha
B	Bravo
C	Charlie
D	Delta
E	Echo
F	Foxtrot
G	Golf
H	Hotel
I	India
J	Juliet
K	Kilo
L	Lima
M	Mike
N	November
O	Oscar
P	Papa
Q	Quebec
R	Romeo
S	Sierra
T	Tango
U	Uniform
V	Victor
W	Whiskey
X	X-ray
Y	Yankee
Z	Zulu

How to say numbers

Use the following pronunciation:

zero, wun, too, tree, fow-er, fife, six, sev-en, ait, nin-er; 10 as wun zero; 22 as too too; 537 as fife tree sev-en.

SENDING DISTRESS SIGNALS USING EPIRB

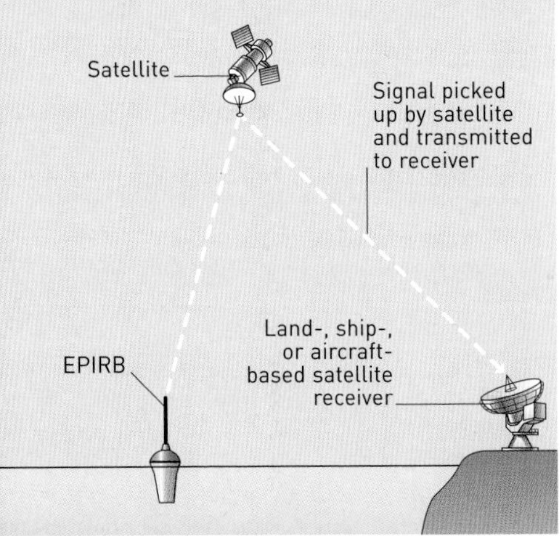

- **Emergency position indicating radio beacons (EPIRBs)** These beacons automatically send a distress signal via the GMDSS network if the receiver gets immersed – for example, if the boat sinks.

WHEN SHOULD I USE A MOBILE PHONE?

- **Casual communication** A mobile phone is useful for coastal sailing, but its main role is for non-essential messages, such as booking into a marina, or calling up friends on shore.

- **Distress communication** Do not use a mobile phone if a DSC VHF is available. It may be unreliable at sea and it cannot be used by the rescue services to determine your position.

USING A FOGHORN

- **Foghorn** This device is essential in fog (see p.192), but it can also be used when you need to make your intentions clear when manoeuvring in close situations.

- **Mouth-blown horn** This is the minimum requirement, but an aerosol or electric horn requires less effort.

Buoyage and pilotage

Although navigation marks can be found well offshore, they are mostly encountered near land, around shipping lanes, or in coastal waters where they are used to identify dangers and safe channels. Buoyage is regulated by the International Association of Lighthouse Authorities (IALA). There are two systems: IALA A and B (see pp.164–65).

HOW TO RECOGNIZE DIFFERENT TYPES OF MARK

● **Colour** Cardinal marks have different combinations of yellow and black according to the mark's sector (see opposite).

● **Lateral marks** These are positioned on channel edges. Their colour and shape indicates on which side to pass depending on the IALA system in use (see p.164).

● **Cardinal marks** These warn of hazards, such as wrecks. They are named North, South, East, and West. Stay to the north of a north cardinal, and so on.

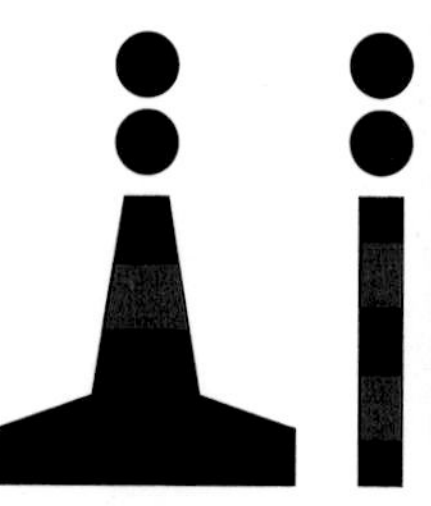

● **Isolated danger marks** These marks are used to indicate isolated dangers with safe water all around.

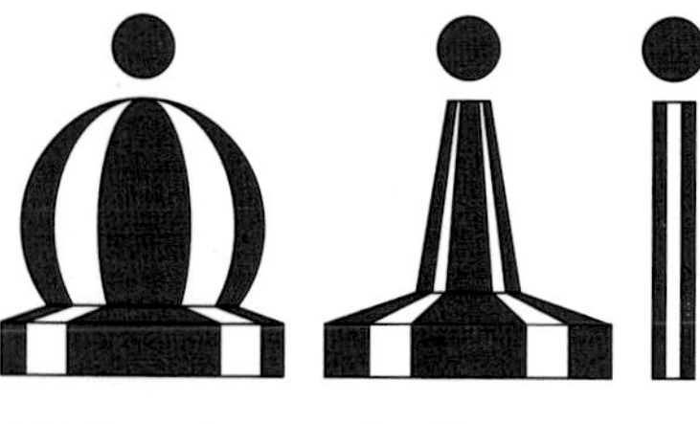

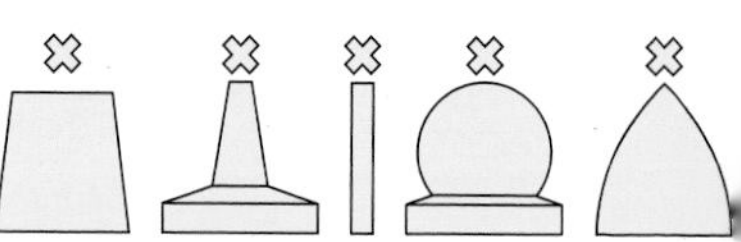

● **Safe water marks** These indicate safe water around their position and are used for mid-channel or landfall marks.

● **Special marks** These indicate a special area or feature, but are not primarily intended to assist in navigation.

UNDERSTANDING CARDINAL MARKS

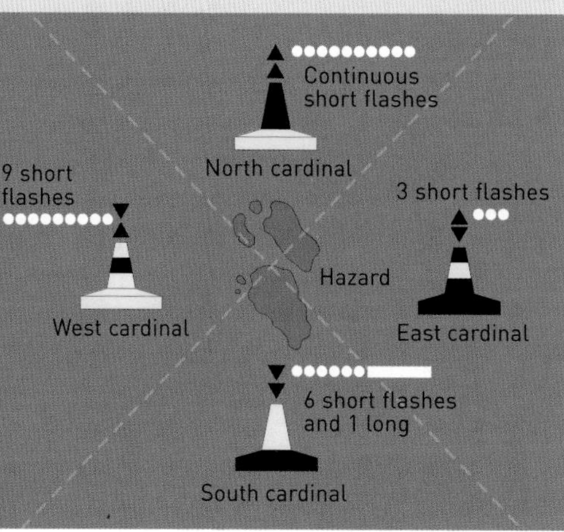

- **Sector** A north cardinal is placed in the 90° sector north of the hazard. The E, S, and W cardinals are similarly placed in their sectors.
- **Topmarks and lights** Each mark is topped by two black cones according to its sector. At night, the marks have different light characteristics.

WHAT DO I NEED TO KNOW ABOUT LIGHTHOUSES?

- **Light** Due to its height and power, the light on a lighthouse is visible from a long distance.
- **Range** A light's range is marked on the chart and in pilot books. If a light appears over the horizon as you approach, you can use a Rising and Dipping table in a nautical almanac to find its distance.

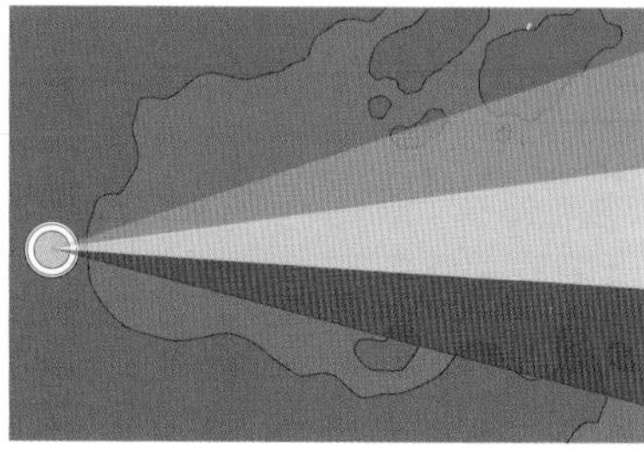

- **Light sectors** Lighthouses and some other beacons often use coloured sectors (angles) to indicate safe and dangerous areas.

WHICH IALA SYSTEM APPLIES?

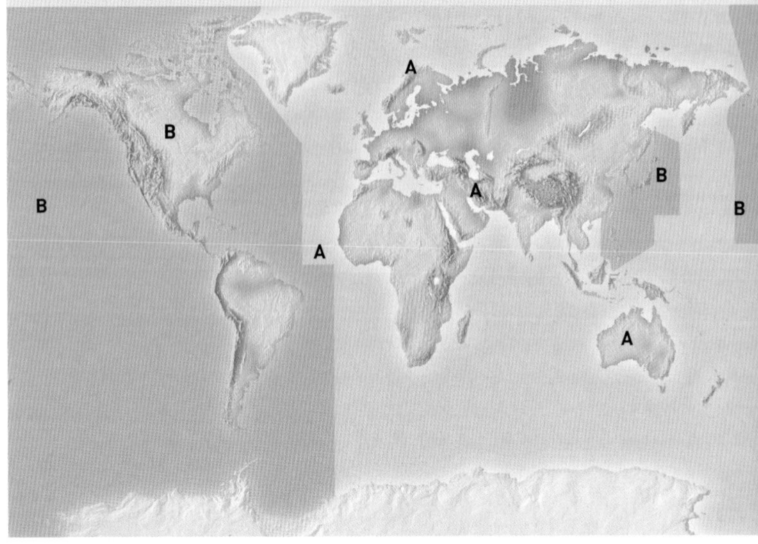

- **IALA system A** This system is used in Europe, Africa, Australia, India, and most of Asia.
- **IALA system B** This is used in North, Central, and South America, Japan, Korea, and the Philippines.

WHAT ARE THE DIFFERENCES?

- **Colour** The key difference between the two systems is in the colour used for lateral marks. Cardinal marks are not affected.
- **Buoyage direction** This is usually from the seaward direction and is usually obvious. Check your chart if the direction of buoyage is not obvious; it will be marked using an arrow with two dots.

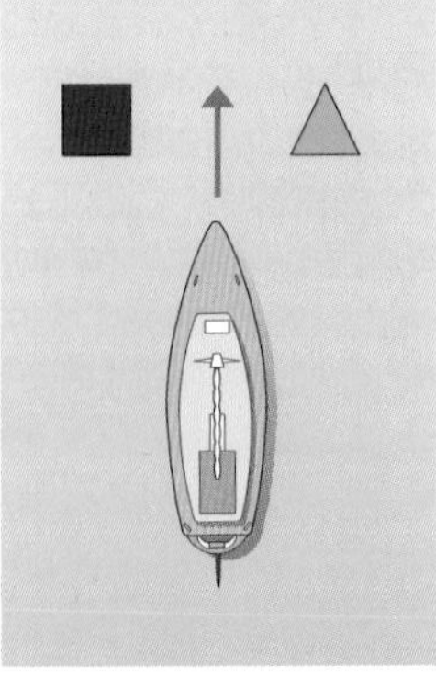

- **IALA A regions** Red cans are left to port and green cones to starboard when entering harbour.

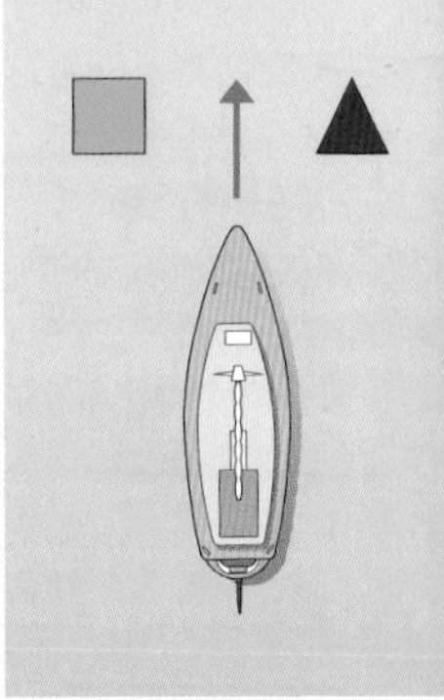

- **IALA B regions** Green cans are left to port and red cones to starboard when entering harbour.

FOLLOWING CHANNEL MARKINGS – IALA A

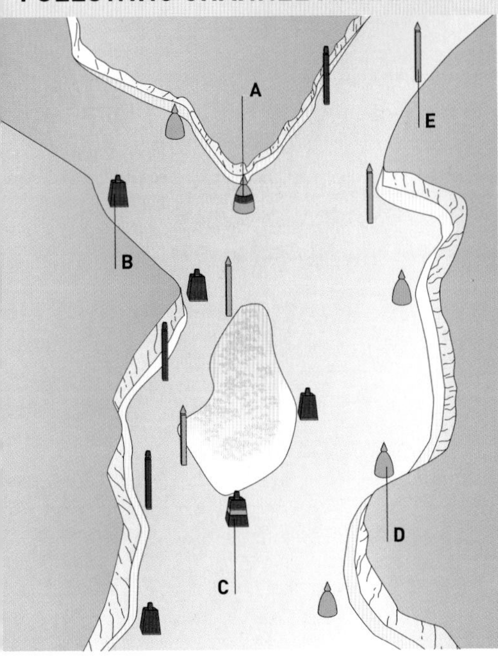

- **A** Preferred channel mark – here the channel is to port.
- **B** Port-hand mark – red can.
- **C** Preferred channel mark – here the channel is to starboard.
- **D** Starboard-hand mark – green cone.
- **E** Posts use colour and topmark to indicate the correct side to leave them.

FOLLOWING CHANNEL MARKINGS – IALA B

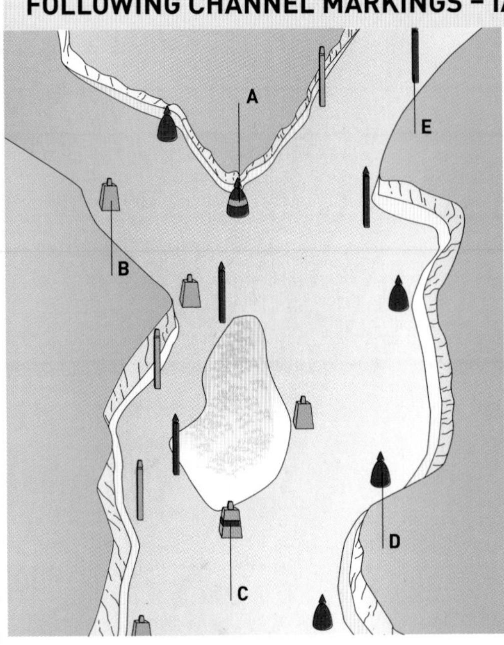

- **A** Preferred channel mark – here the channel is to port.
- **B** Port-hand mark – green can.
- **C** Preferred channel mark – here the channel is to starboard.
- **D** Starboard-hand mark – red cone.
- **E** Posts use colour and topmark to indicate the correct side to leave them.

Position and direction

The prime requirement of navigation is to know exactly where you are on a chart and be able to relate it to the surrounding water and nearby land. Your position can be plotted on a paper or electronic chart using lines of latitude and longitude as coordinates. Understanding direction allows you to confirm a position and to plot a course.

UNDERSTANDING LATITUDE AND LONGITUDE

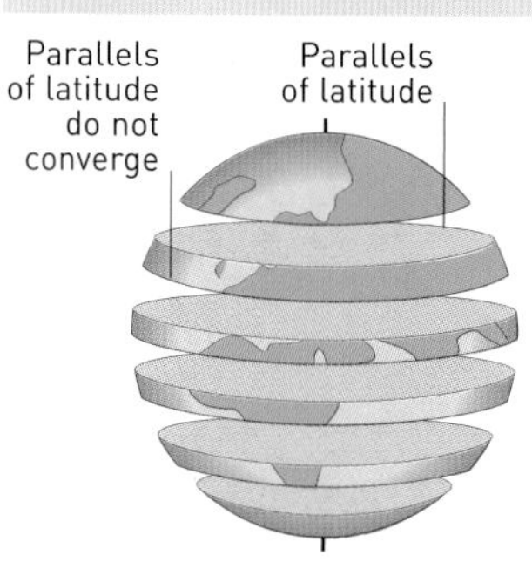

Parallels of latitude These "slice" the Earth laterally and the slices are largest at the Equator and smallest near the poles.

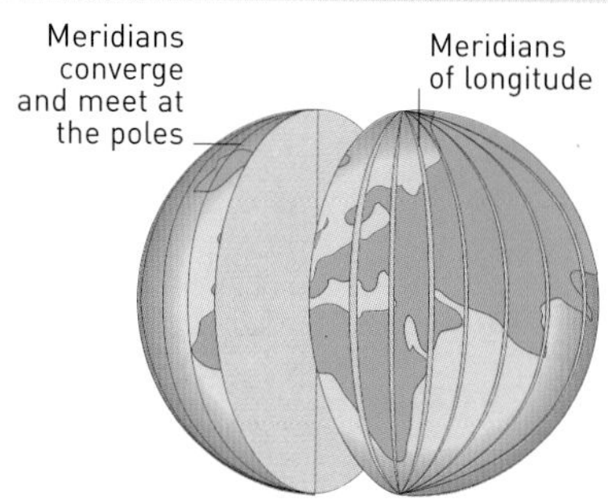

Meridians of longitude These "cut" the Earth from pole to pole. All meridians of longitude converge at the poles.

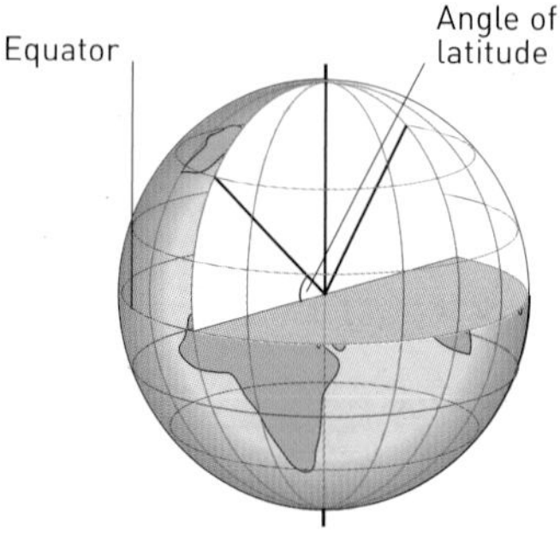

Latitude This is measured at the centre of the Earth along the prime (Greenwich) meridian from the Equator, and ranges from 0°–90° north and south.

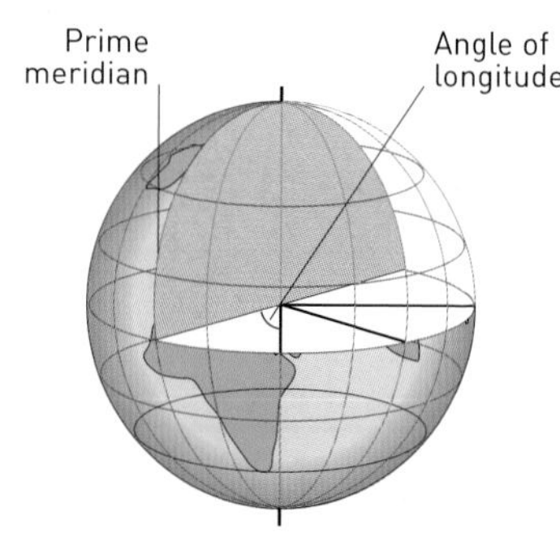

Longitude This is measured at the Earth's centre along the Equator from the prime meridian, and ranges from 0°–180° east or west.

HOW CAN GPS HELP?

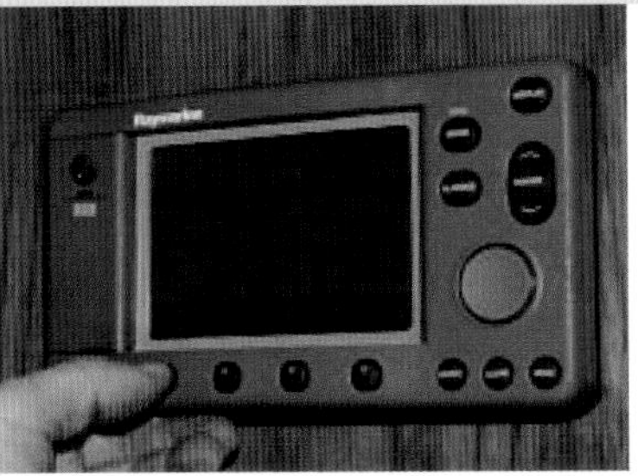

- **Finding out your location** A GPS set will tell you your position in terms of latitude and longitude coordinates. You can then plot these coordinates onto a paper chart to find the position, or show them on an electronic chart displayed by a chartplotter.

Using navigational terms and symbols

A variety of terms and symbols are used to record information on charts and to write down bearings, headings, and other important navigational data. The symbols are recognized universally, eliminating (as far as possible) the risk of misunderstandings and enabling all navigators to understand the calculations. You need to know and understand these symbols to be able to navigate successfully.

SYMBOL	MEASUREMENT	DEFINITION
°T	Degrees true	Suffix attached to a direction measured relative to true north, e.g., 095°T.
°M	Degrees magnetic	Suffix attached to a direction measured relative to magnetic north, e.g., 135°M.
°C	Degrees compass	Suffix attached to a direction measured by the compass and not converted to °T or °M, e.g., 110°C.
M	Nautical mile	The unit of distance at sea. A nautical mile is equal to one minute of latitude (standardized at 1,852m/6,076ft). It is divided into 10 cables (ca) or tenths of a nautical mile. Each cable is 185m (600ft).
kn	Knot	The unit of speed used at sea. One knot is one nautical mile per hour.
m	Metre	The standard metre is used to display depth and height on charts. Metres are divided into decimetres; 7.1m is shown on charts as 7_1.
fm	Fathom	The old unit of depth, equal to 6ft (1.8m), sometimes found on older charts. Parts of a fathom are shown in feet, e.g., 38ft is shown as 6_2.

HOW TO MEASURE DIRECTION

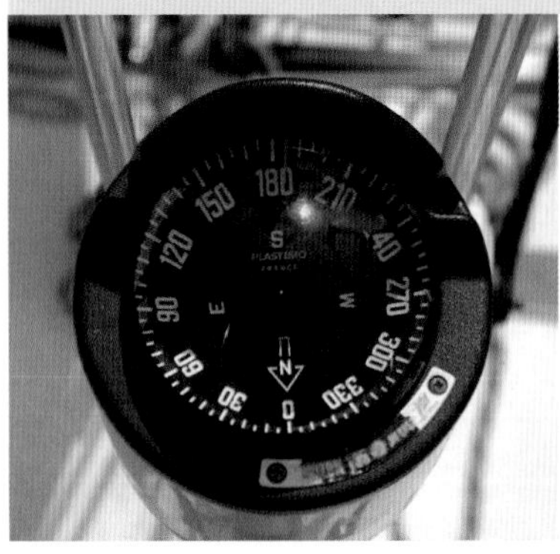

- **Compass** This is the primary means of establishing direction. It shows direction relative to compass north. This differs from magnetic north and true north. The steering compass is usually mounted near the wheel.

- **Variation** The magnetic north pole changes position annually and the difference from true north is called variation.

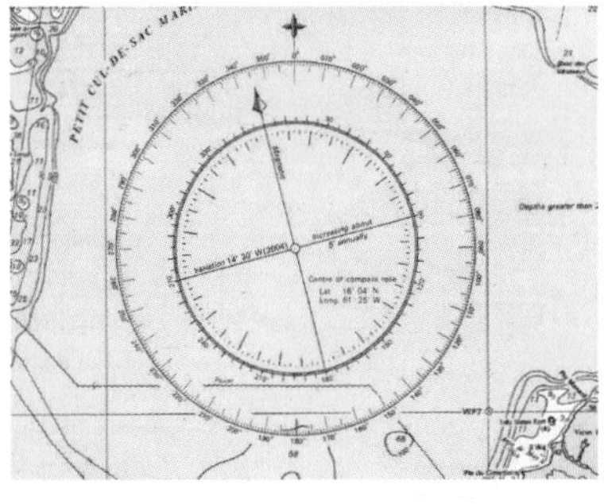

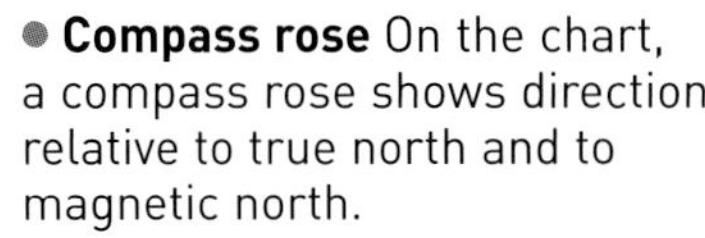

- **Compass rose** On the chart, a compass rose shows direction relative to true north and to magnetic north.

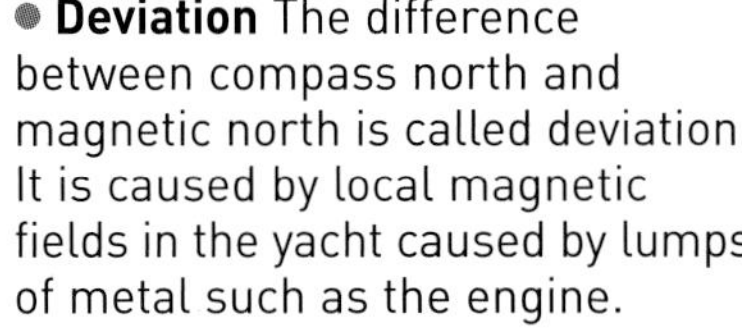

- **Deviation** The difference between compass north and magnetic north is called deviation. It is caused by local magnetic fields in the yacht caused by lumps of metal such as the engine.

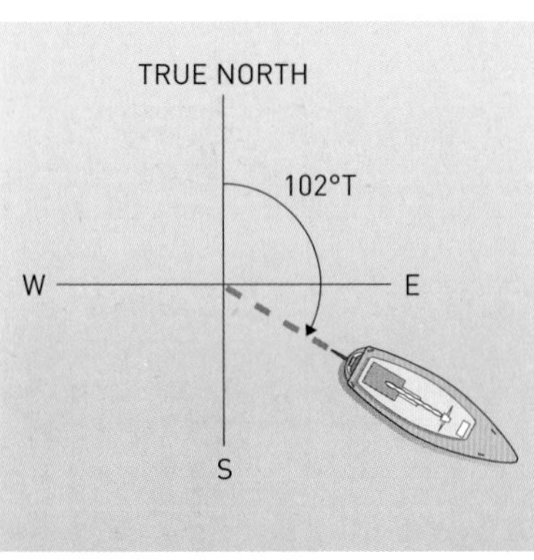

- **Heading** This is the direction in which you steer the boat. It is measured clockwise from north – either true, magnetic, or compass north. In this case the boat's heading is 120°T.

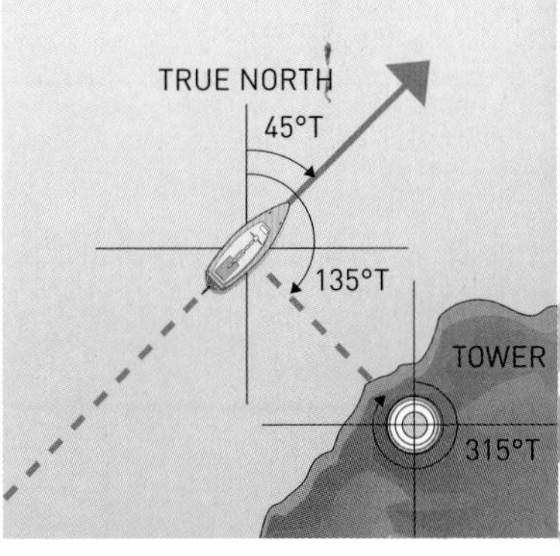

- **Bearing** This is the direction of an object from your position, or between two objects. Here the tower is on a bearing of 135°T from the boat. From the tower, the boat bears 315°T.

LOGGING YOUR POSITION

- **Record** Keep a note of your course and speed. It may be easiest to do this in the cockpit. Transfer this information later to the main logbook kept below.

- **Logbook** This is used for recording position, course, distance run, and other crucial information. You are required by maritime law to keep a logbook. Sample entries are shown below.

Time Make log entries at regular intervals

Course Detail course required and course actually steered

Remarks Include any useful observations

TIME	LOG	COURSE REQUIRED	COURSE STEERED	WIND	BARO	REMARKS
2230	574	060°C	065°C	SW2	1005	Extremely misty and damp
0000	582	060°C	060°C	SW2	1005	Six knots regularly
0045	588	060°C	060°C	SW4	1005	Yacht in sight starboard bow
0200	594	060°C	060°C	SW4	1005	Watch change

Log Use the log reading to measure progress

Wind Record wind strength and direction

Barometric pressure Can be used to forecast weather

Understanding charts

Vital to navigating at sea, charts convey key data using symbols, colours, and contour lines. They record potential dangers, locate navigation lights, buoys, and features on shore, and give depths and lines of longitude and latitude to help fix position and measure distance. Charts are updated regularly as critical features change.

WHAT'S ON A CHART?

- **Scale** Refer to your largest-scale chart of the area as it will provide you with the most detailed information.

- **Symbols** Learn the most common symbols and carry a reference guide to the full list. Some examples of symbols are shown opposite.

- **Hazards** Symbols are used on charts to indicate dangers and areas of particular importance.

- **Compass rose** You will find several compass roses on the chart that act as an aid to establishing direction.

- **Water depth** On a chart, depths shown are related to chart datum and are the lowest depths to which the water can be expected to drop. Different charts may show different soundings for the same area as various standards for chart datum are used. Check near the chart title for the datum used on your chart.

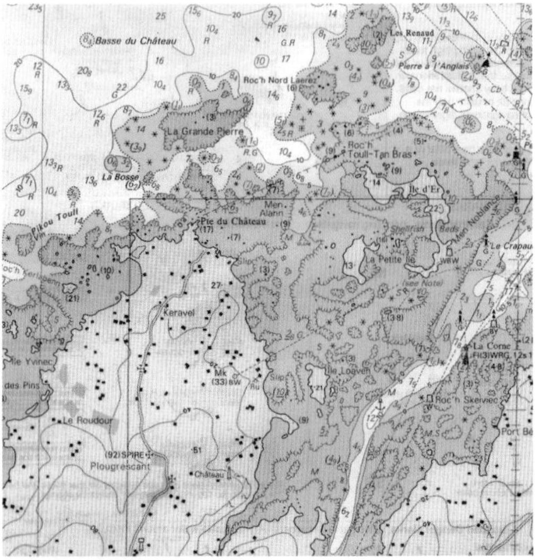

- **Units** Depths may be shown in metric or imperial units. Check the chart title to find out which is used on a particular chart.

- **Contour lines** These lines join points of equal depth on the chart and are extremely useful.

READING A CHART

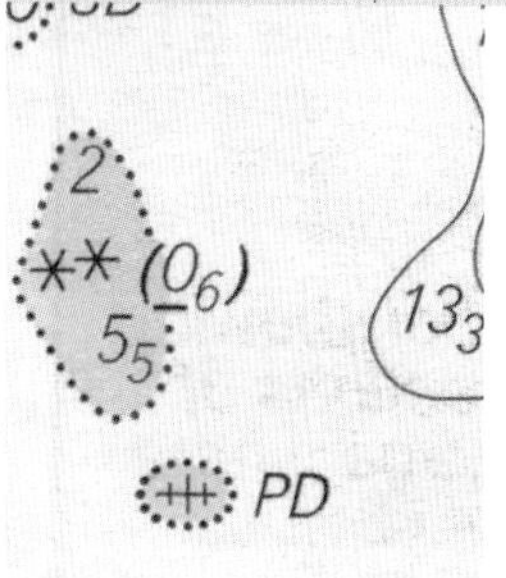

Rocks and wrecks The upper symbol indicates that rocks are awash above water at chart datum. The lower one warns of a dangerous wreck nearby, of which the masts may be visible.

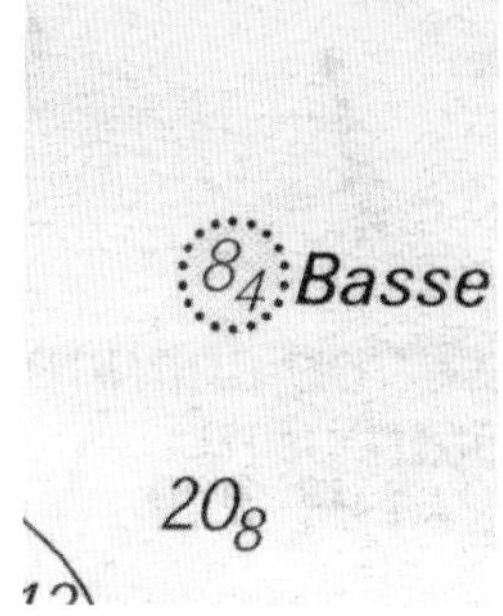

Shoal The figure in the circle (above) shows the depth of shoal (area of shallow water) at chart datum – in this case 8.4m (27½ft). Shoals may cause rough water in strong winds.

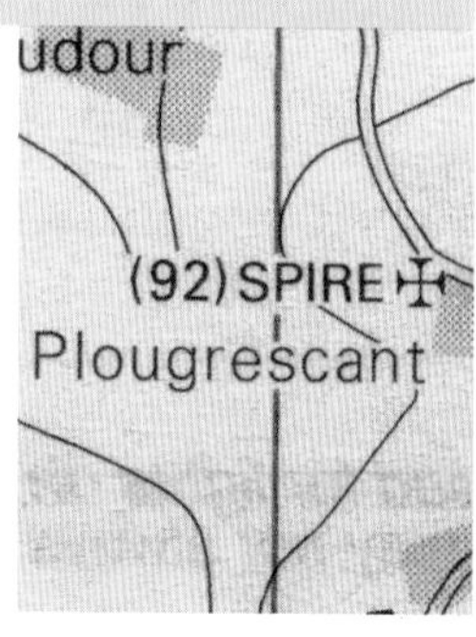

Landmarks Some of these are ideal for fixing position at sea. The church spire shown above is 92m (302ft) above Mean High Water Springs (MHWS), the average height of a spring tide's high waters.

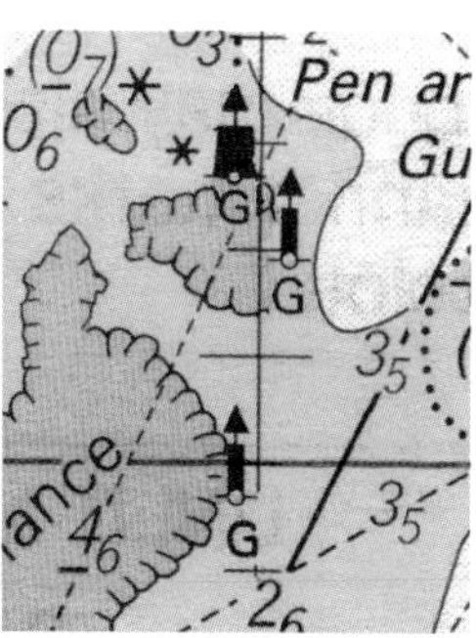

Buoyage Charts show the position and type of buoys. The beacon tower (top) and two beacons (below) are accompanied by the letter G, indicating they are green.

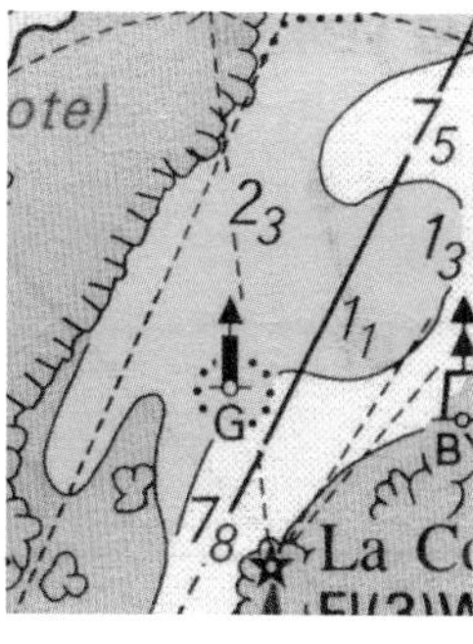

Low-water depths On this chart, low-water depths are colour-coded: dry areas are shown in green; 0–5m (0–16ft) depths in blue; 5–10m (15–33ft) depths in pale blue; and deeper areas in white.

Anchorage The symbol of the anchor (above) is accompanied by the figure 12, indicating that the water has a minimum depth of 12m (39ft). The letter M indicates a muddy seabed or river bed.

Working on paper charts

In spite of the sophisticated navigation systems available for yachts, navigating using a paper chart remains a vital skill for sailors. You must be able to plot your position and shape a course to be safe in the fairly common event that your electronic systems fail, so learn to be proficient when working on a chart using the basic plotting instruments.

WHAT INSTRUMENTS DO I NEED?

- **Parallel rule** The traditional ruler used for chart work is a parallel rule, which allows you to establish direction with reference to the chart's compass rose.
- **Plastic plotter** Consider using a plotting instrument, which is easier to use than a parallel rule.
- **Pencils** Use soft pencils, such as 2B, on charts to avoid permanently marking them. Pick hexagonal ones as they are less likely to roll off the chart table.
- **Pencil sharpener and rubber** Keep your pencils sharpened and a rubber handy to erase unwanted pencil marks on the chart.
- **Drawing compass** A drawing compass is used to draw arcs or circles on the chart.
- **Magnifying glass** This is useful for examining the fine details on a chart.
- **Dividers** One-handed dividers, with a curved top, are easier to use than straight ones.

USING DIVIDERS

- **Dividers** Use a pair of dividers to span the distance on the chart you want to measure. Then transfer the open dividers to latitude scale at the side of the chart to read off the distance.
- **Scales** Use the scale at the sides of the chart, NOT at the top or bottom edges.

USING A PLOTTER

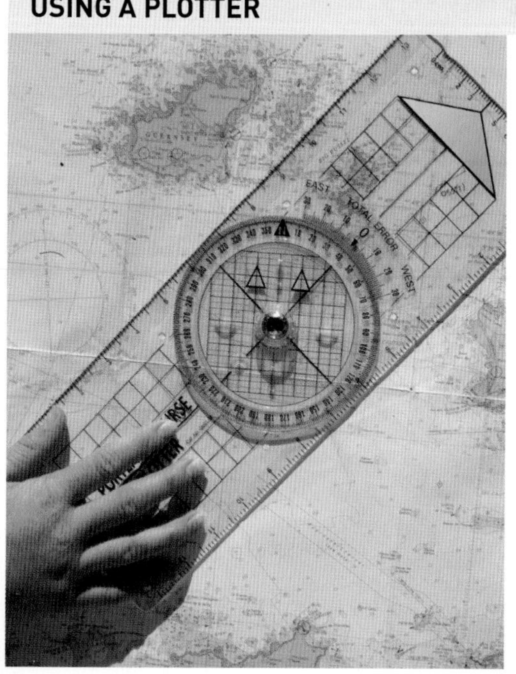

- **Plotter** A rectangular ruler with a rotating compass rose fixed in the centre is used for plotting and establishing direction on nautical charts.
- **Direction** Align one edge of the plotter with the line to be measured, then align the grid on the circular dial with the vertical or horizontal lines on the chart. Now read off the direction given against the bearing line on the rectangular ruler.

Navigation instruments

Navigation instruments include the compass to indicate direction steered, performance instruments that measure speed, distance, depth, wind speed and direction, position-finding instruments – GPS and chartplotter – and collision avoidance instruments – radar and AIS (see p.176). Information from all of them can be combined in many ways.

WHAT ARE THE TYPES OF COMPASS?

- **Steering compass** This is the most important instrument on the yacht. It is fixed in a position in the cockpit where the helmsman can see it easily. The compass is lit for use at night.

- **Hand-bearing compass** Use a hand-bearing compass for taking bearings on other vessels, sea, or shore marks, and for estimating leeway (see pp.182–83).

DO I NEED A HAND-HELD GPS?

- **Portable device** A hand-held GPS provides backup for the main unit and is useful in the cockpit or in a tender. Some hand-held units can display an electronic chart and function as a small chartplotter (see p.176).

MEASURING PERFORMANCE

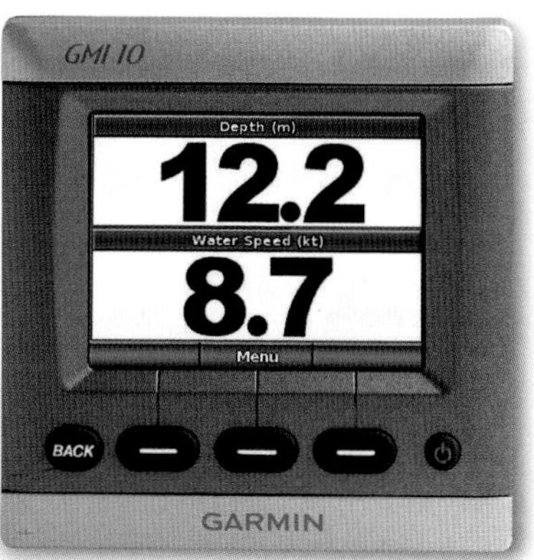

- **Electronic instruments** Most yachts are fitted with electronic instruments to measure distance travelled, speed, depth, and wind strength and direction. These instruments are usually fitted within sight of the helm with additional synchronized display heads by the chart table.

- **Depth and speed** Information such as speed, distance, and depth can be shown on separate or combined displays.

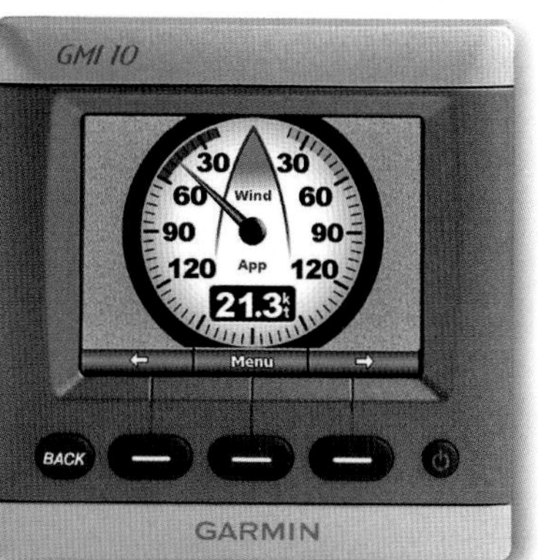

- **Wind** The direction of apparent or true wind is shown using a direction arrow with a digital wind speed display.

- **Combining information** When data from compass heading, boat speed and direction, and apparent wind speed and direction are all available, the instruments can calculate true wind speed and direction.

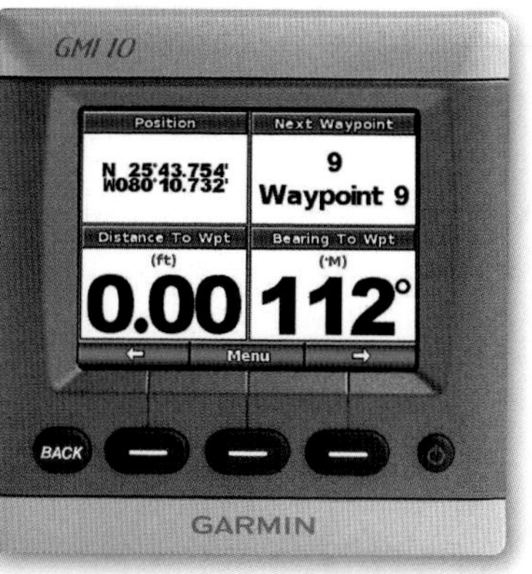

- **Multidisplay instruments** These can show a variety of information in a single display head. This is useful if space for displays is limited, if cost is an issue, or for use as an additional display at the chart table synchronized with individual instruments in the cockpit.

WHAT IS A CHARTPLOTTER?

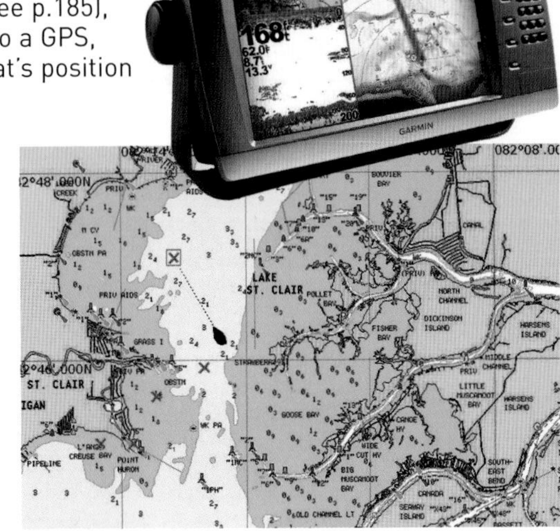

- **Digital plotting** A chartplotter displays an electronic version of a paper chart on screen. It can show waypoints (see p.185), and, when connected to a GPS, it will indicate your boat's position and track.

- **Electronic chart** Linked to a GPS, these charts provide real-time information on the boat's track. You can watch your boat's progress directly on the chart and monitor factors such as cross-track error (see p.185).

HOW CAN A RADAR HELP?

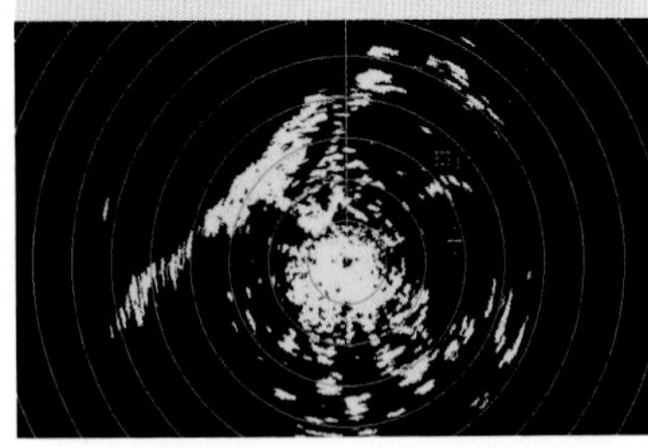

- **Radar display** This presents its information in picture form. Some displays can overlay the radar plot on an electronic chart. The radar displays a picture of features within range, including land, buoys, and other vessels.

WHAT DOES AIS DO?

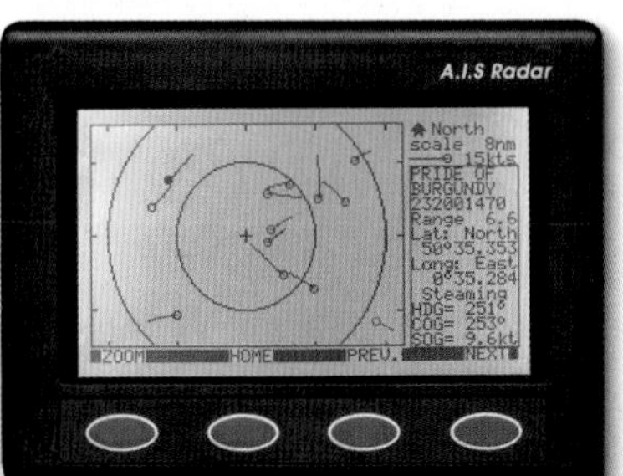

- **Automatic Identification System (AIS)** Information from the AIS shows details of vessels in your vicinity, including their course and speed.

USING A MULTIFUNCTION DISPLAY

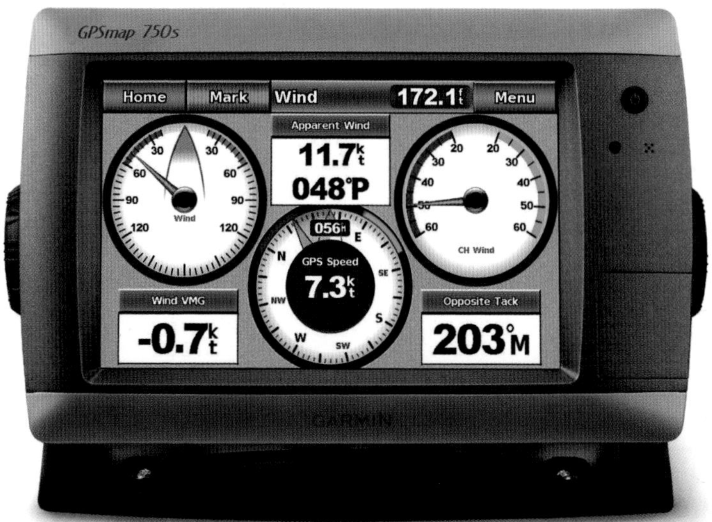

● **Choice** A multifunction display allows you to choose which information you want displayed, such as the multiple performance information shown here.

● **Calculate** By combining information from several instruments, the multifunction display can calculate and display additional useful information.

● **Overlays** A multifunction display can take in radar, AIS, and chartplotter information to overlay one on the other or combine and display them with performance information.

DO I NEED A LAPTOP?

● **Laptop computer** This is a popular choice for running navigation and chartplotting software. It can be set up to interface with other electronic instruments on board using their National Marine Electronics Association (NMEA) outputs.

Tides

When you sail in tidal waters, knowing the height of the tide and the direction and speed of the tidal stream is important for safe and accurate navigation. Areas with large tidal ranges may seem daunting, but they are not difficult to cope with once you know the relatively simple procedures for calculating tidal heights and streams.

HOW TIDE AFFECTS NAVIGATION

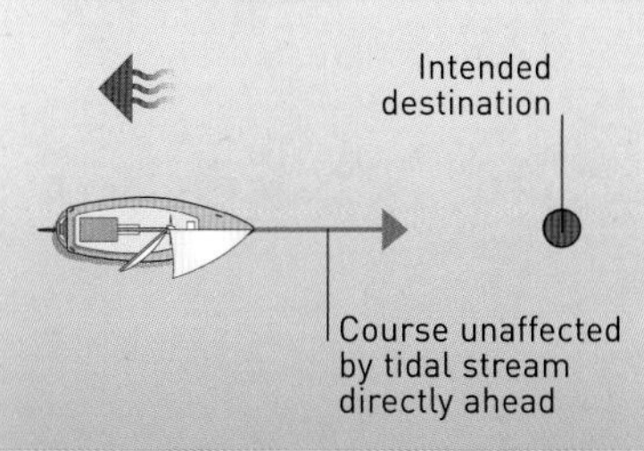

- **Same direction** If the direction (set) of the tidal stream is either directly ahead or astern, the boat's course will not be affected.
- **Tide at an angle** In this situation the strength of the tidal stream (drift) will determine how far the yacht is pushed off course.

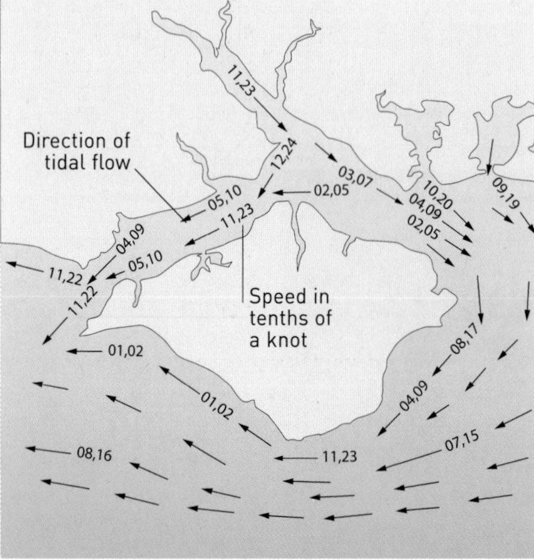

- **Tidal atlas** You can use a tidal atlas for your area to find the strength and direction of the tidal stream.
- **Time** Each page in the atlas relates to an hour before or after high water (HW) at the standard port to which it refers.
- **Other sources** You can also get tidal stream and height information from many chartplotters and smartphone apps.

CALCULATING TIDAL HEIGHT

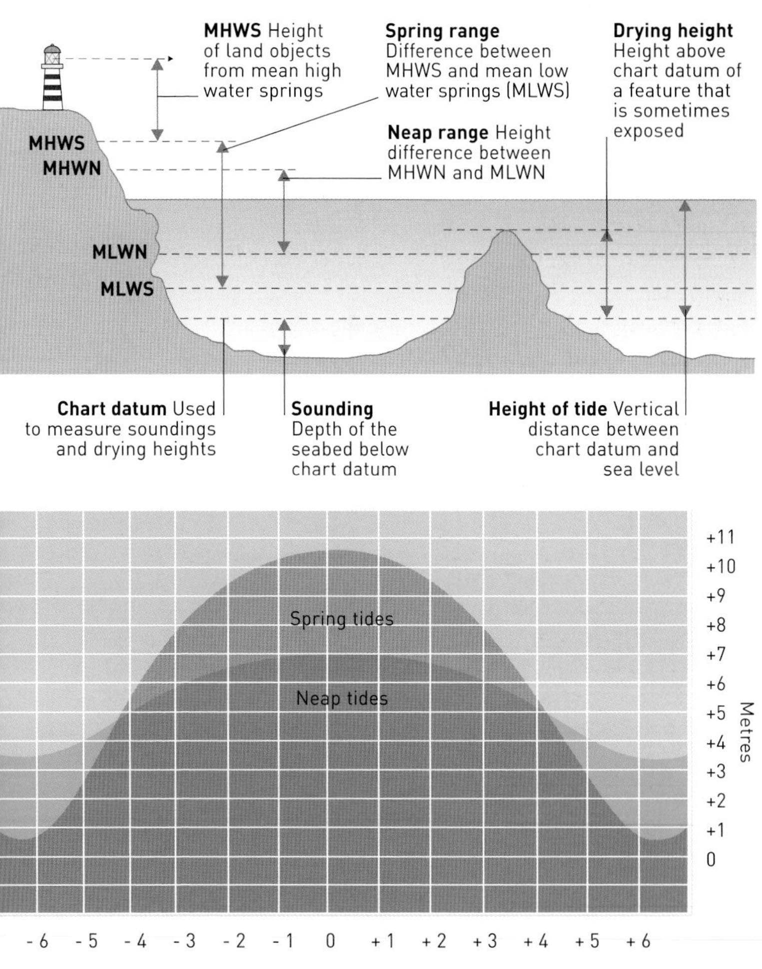

- **Tidal curves** These illustrate a cycle of spring or neap tides.
- **Use** They are used to calculate the depth between high and low water at any specific time.

HOW TIDE AFFECTS SEA STATE

- **Wind with tide** When the wind is blowing with the tide, the friction between wind and water is low and the sea remains fairly calm.
- **Wind against tide** With wind against tide, the friction between wind and water is increased and waves are formed.

Finding your position

The navigator must record the course steered, distance run, number of times course altered, and the leeway experienced. These records are used to plot the Dead Reckoning (DR) and Estimated Position (EP). A DR position is calculated using distance sailed from a known point on a known heading. An EP adds in the effect of the tide.

HOW TO PLOT THE DR AND EP

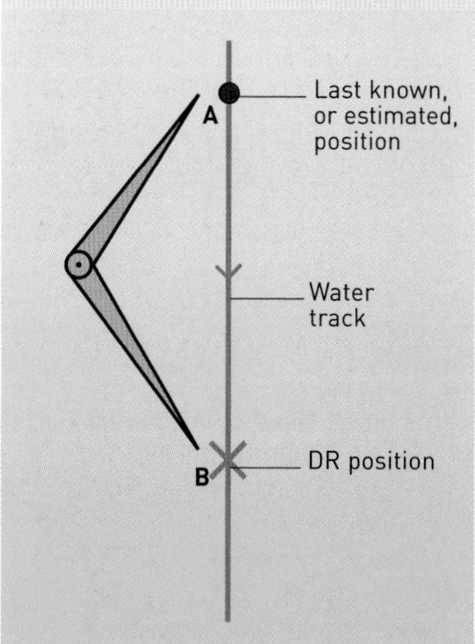

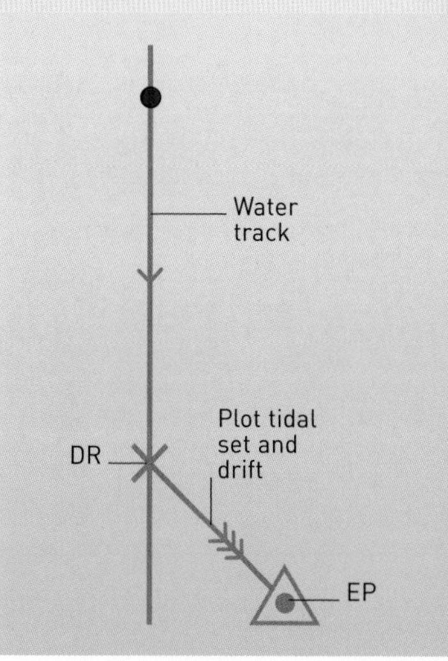

- **Plot the water track** from a known point (A), using the course steered as recorded in the logbook, and mark it with one arrowhead.

- **Mark the DR position (B)** by using dividers (see p.173) to measure off the distance sailed in the last hour according to the log. Use the standard plotting symbols (see p.183) to mark the water track and the DR position.

- **Plot the EP**, by finding the tide's set (direction) and drift (speed) for the last hour using the tidal atlas, the chart, almanac, or electronic source (see pp.178–79).

- **Plot the set of the tide** from the DR position by drawing a line on the correct bearing, and mark it with three arrowheads.

- **Measure the amount** of tidal drift along the line using dividers and the latitude scale on the chart. Draw a triangle with a dot in the middle to mark the EP.

HOW TO TAKE A FIX BY COMPASS

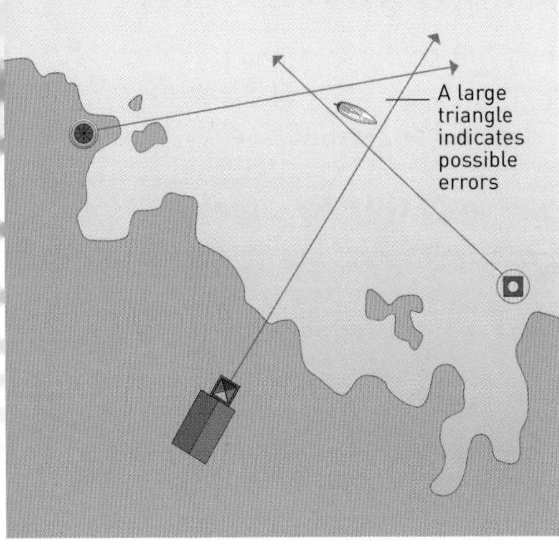

- **Use a hand-bearing compass** to measure the bearings of three landmarks or charted objects (such as buoys), each about 60° from the next. This is known as a three-point fix.
- **Plot their bearings** on the chart. The intersection of these bearings will form a triangle, or "cocked hat", that indicates your position.

USING RADAR

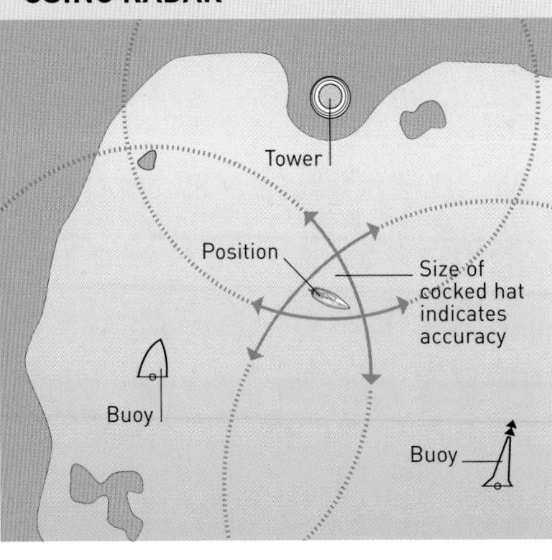

- **Note the ranges** of three or more identifiable radar targets in quick succession, to fix your position in the "cocked hat" where the three range arcs cross.
- **Radar bearings** are not as accurate as radar ranges so use radar ranges whenever possible.

ALLOWING FOR ERROR

- **Never assume** You may not be at the exact position marked on the chart. Errors in measuring distance sailed, course achieved, or tidal set and drift can easily introduce considerable errors.
- **Estimate possible errors** Draw a circle of uncertainty around your EP. When shaping a course from the EP, always assume you are at the closest point to any dangers.

Shaping a course

Setting a course to steer you safely from your departure point to your destination is known as shaping a course. A vital skill for accurate and safe navigation offshore, this process requires a chart of the area, plotting tools (see pp.172–73), information about tidal streams (see pp.178–79), and a compass (see p.174).

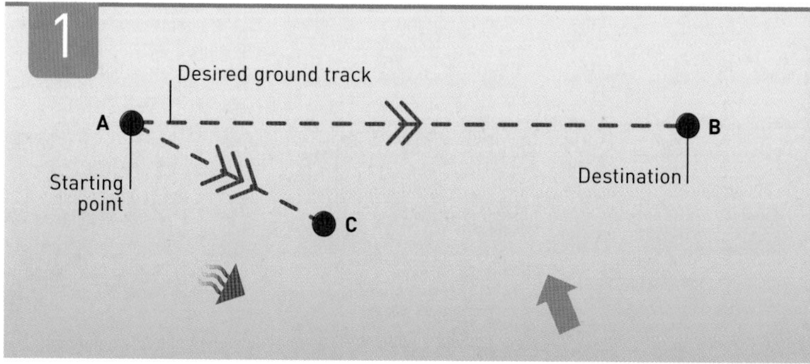

- **Mark your desired ground track** (course relative to the seabed) on the chart from A to B. Measure its length with the dividers and find the distance using the chart scale.
- **Plot the tide direction** from (A). Use dividers to mark the amount of drift in 1 hour (C). Mark the line with three arrowheads.

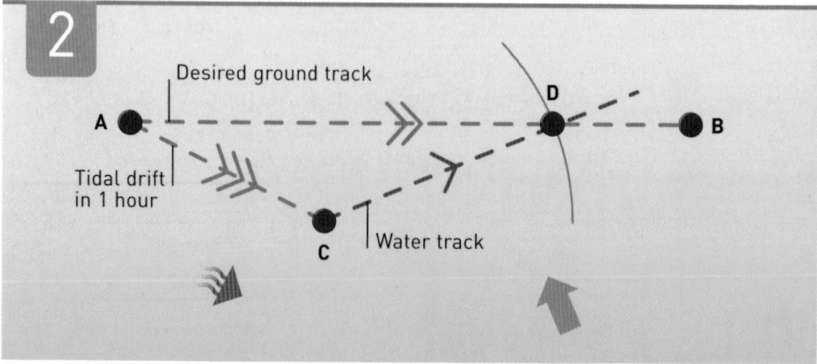

- **Open the dividers** to the distance you expect to sail in the next hour, using the scale on the side of the chart.
- **Place one point of the dividers** on C and mark where the other point meets the ground track (D). Join C and D to mark the water track – the course to follow.

Using symbols

Navigators plot courses and positions using symbols to save space and avoid confusion. Standard symbols are shown here. Time is written using 24-hour-clock notation and should include the time zone (for example, 1415 GMT).

Waypoint	Water track	Fix
Dead reckoning position	Ground track	Position line
Estimated position	Tidal stream or current	Transferred position line

3

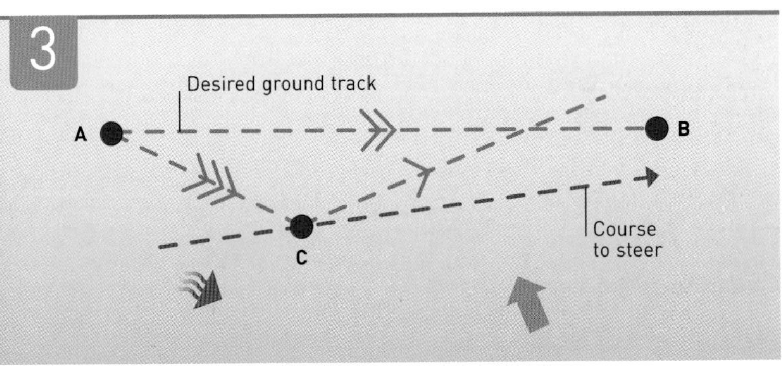

• **Once under sail**, use a hand-bearing compass to take a bearing on the wake. The difference between this and the back bearing on the main compass is the leeway.

• **Adjust the water track** to windward to allow for leeway in order to calculate the correct course to steer.

4

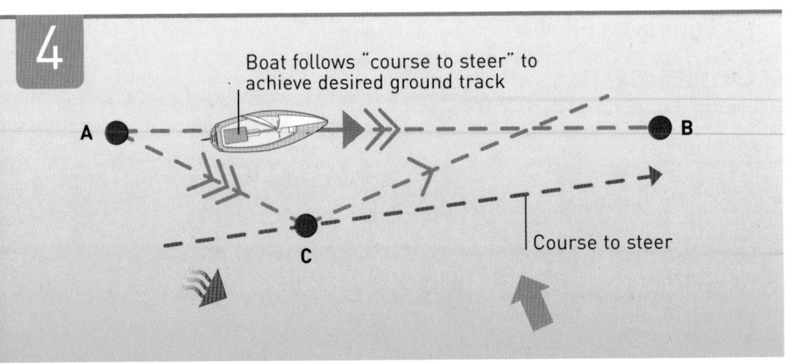

• **Steer the course** determined by the navigator, and the boat follows the desired ground track from A to B to reach its destination.

• **Monitor tide, wind, and leeway** every hour during a long trip. The tidal atlas gives hourly figures for the changing tide. Adjust your course as necessary.

HOW TO SHAPE A COURSE ON A LONG PASSAGE

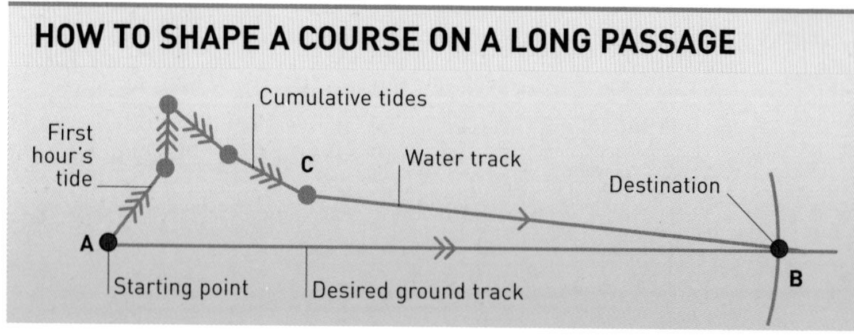

- **Use a simple plotting process** if there are no hazards near your intended track.
- **Estimate how long** the passage will take. From the departure point (A), plot the first hour of tide. On a long passage, you will need to deal with tidal streams that change hourly.
- **Plot the next hour** of tide from the end of the first tide line, and continue to mark the cumulative tidal effect for as many hours as the expected passage duration.
- **Open the dividers** to the distance you expect to sail in the number of hours of tide plotted, then put one point on C and cut the track A–B.
- **The line C–B** is the water track for the whole passage. It can be adjusted for leeway as normal.
- **When using this method**, it is important to know that the boat will not follow the track A–B.

STAYING CLOSE TO THE GROUND TRACK

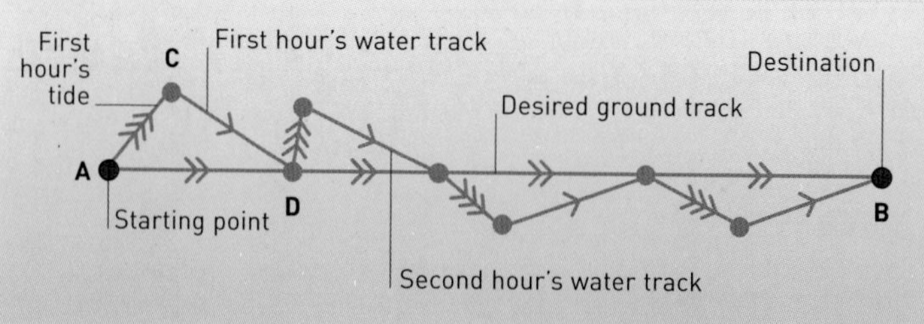

- **Keep the boat close** to the ground track at all times if there are hazards close to your track.
- **Mark the first hour's tide** and plot the course to steer for the first hour (C–D).
- **From point D**, lay off the second hour's tide and plot the course to steer for the second hour.
- **Continue this process** for the length of the passage. Each hour will require a different course to steer, but the boat will proceed along the desired ground track to point B.

USING WAYPOINTS TO NAVIGATE

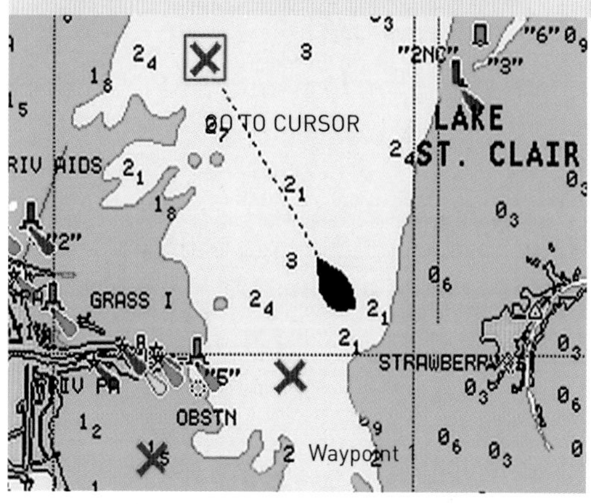

- **Waypoints** The positions stored into a GPS's memory are called waypoints.
- **Information** By entering waypoints along your route, the GPS can calculate the distance, bearing, and estimated time of arrival (ETA) from your position.

AVOIDING CROSS-TRACK ERRORS

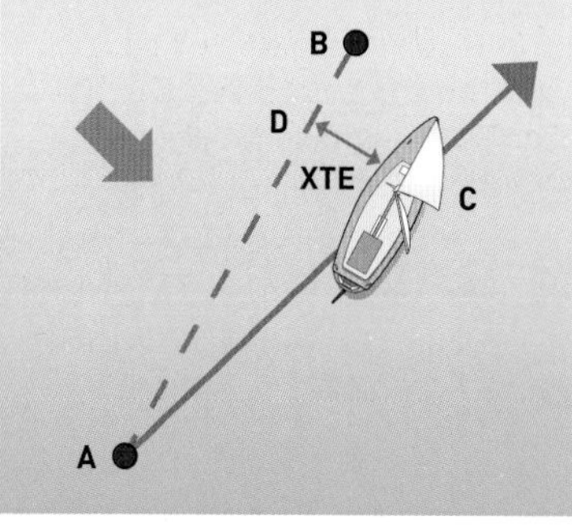

- **Cross-track error (XTE)** A GPS can monitor the XTE (the amount that the yacht has strayed from its planned course) from A to B.
- **Leeway** Here, the XTE DC is caused by greater leeway than anticipated. By monitoring the XTE, the navigator can correct the heading to compensate.

USING VMG

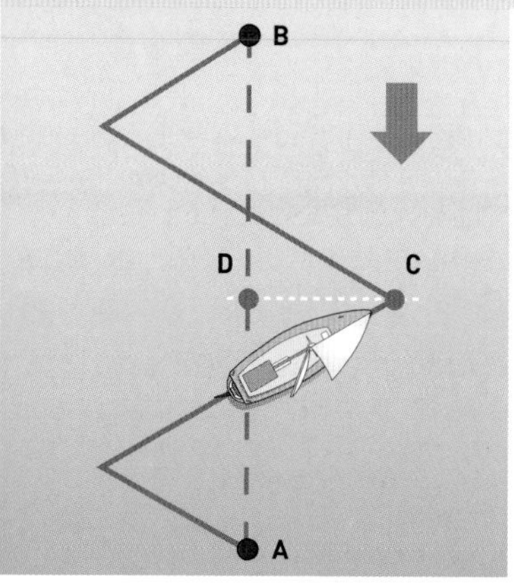

- **Velocity made good (VMG)** This is the speed at which you are closing on your objective.
- **Sailing to windward** It is useful to know your VMG when you are sailing upwind and are unable to point at your destination.
- **Calculation** A GPS calculates the VMG and ETA at your destination (B) by dividing the distance achieved from A–D by the time taken to reach C.

Avoiding collisions

The International Regulations for the Prevention of Collisions at Sea (Col Regs) specify the responsibilities of all types of craft. They apply to all vessels, and it is essential that you learn the most common rules. The skipper of a small boat has exactly the same responsibility for avoiding collisions as the skipper of a large liner or supertanker.

HOW SHOULD I PASS?

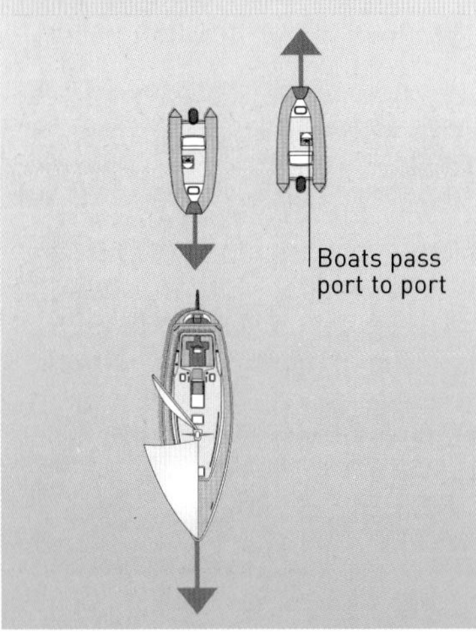

- **Keep to starboard** All vessels, whether under sail or power, must stay close to the starboard side of a channel, so that they pass port to port.

- **Give boats a wide berth** If crossing a busy shipping channel, pass behind large vessels and give them as wide a berth as possible.

HOW SHOULD I OVERTAKE?

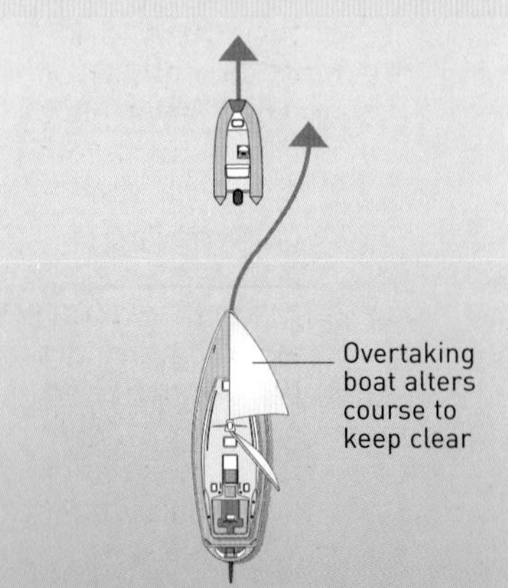

- **Keep clear when overtaking** An overtaking vessel must keep clear of the one being passed, even if it is a sailing boat that is overtaking a power boat. The onus to keep clear continues throughout the passing manoeuvre.

DO I HAVE RIGHT OF WAY?

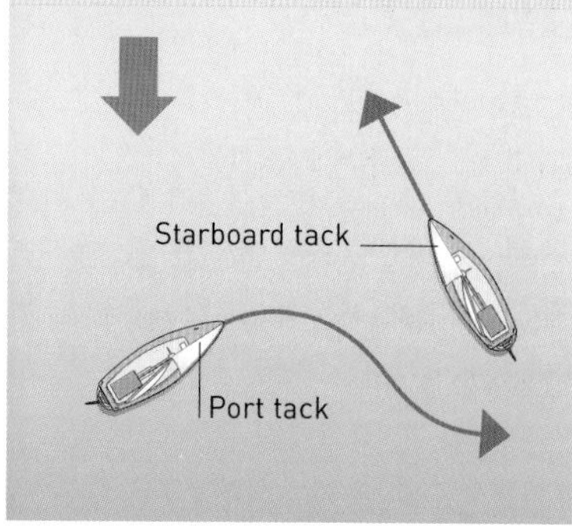

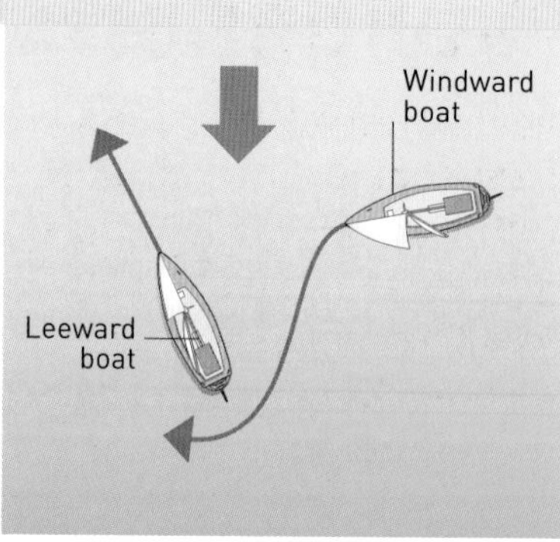

- **Opposite tacks** When sailing boats are on opposite tacks, the one on port tack must keep clear by tacking or, as above, by altering course to pass behind the boat on a starboard tack.

- **At night** Under sail at night it can be hard to identify the vessel that should give way, especially when one boat is sailing on a run and the other is close-hauled on port tack. The port tack boat must assume she has to give way.

- **On the same tack** When sailing boats are on the same tack, the windward boat must keep clear and steer to pass behind the leeward boat.

- **Early action** Keep a good look out and if you are the give-way vessel, make sure to take early and clear action, which is obvious to the vessel that has the right of way (stand-on vessel).

WHEN SHOULD I GIVE WAY?

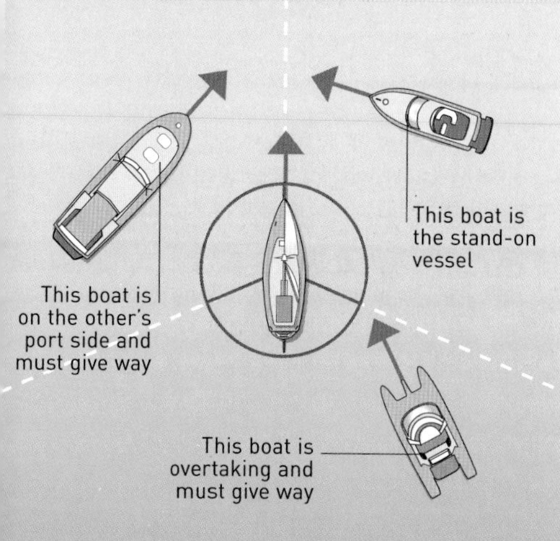

- **Stand on or give way?** The concept of there being (at least) one give-way and one stand-on vessel in any potential collision situation is fundamental.

- **Identify** In daylight, imagine the sectors of the navigation lights (see p.188) to assess the situation as you approach other boats on a potential collision course.

Navigation lights

The International Regulations for Preventing Collisions at Sea (the Col Regs) specify the type, size, layout, arc, and distance of visibility of lights to be used by all types of vessels. Various combinations indicate, among other possibilities, whether a boat is anchored or under way, under sail or power, or fishing or trawling.

WHAT LIGHTS SHOULD BE SHOWN AT NIGHT?

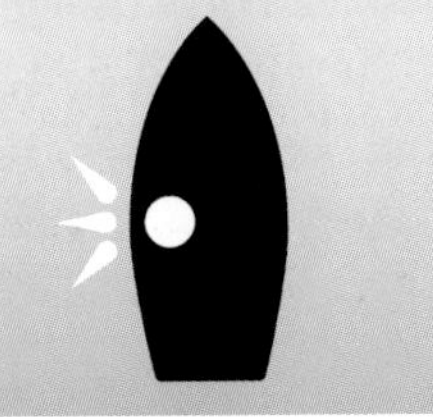

- **Dinghy under 7m (23ft)** Under sails or oars, this type of boat must carry a torch to show a white light when required.

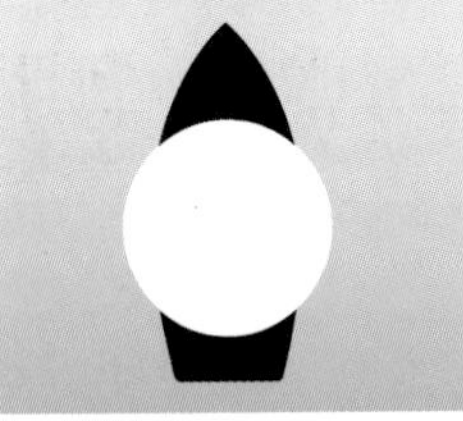

- **Boat up to 7m (23ft)** Under power but capable of less than 7 knots, this type of boat must have a fixed all-round white light.

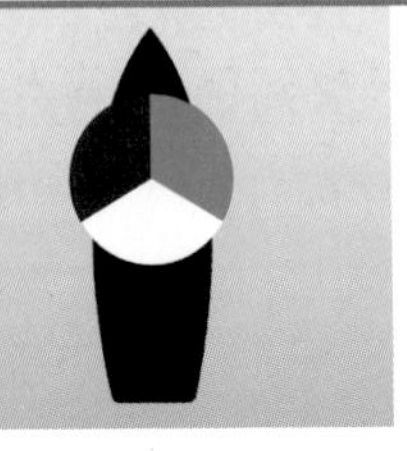

- **Boat under sail (under 20m/66ft)** Boats in this category may use sidelights and stern lights combined in a masthead tricolour light. A separate stern light and sidelights must still be fitted for use under power, with a steaming light, as for a powerboat of a similar size (opposite).

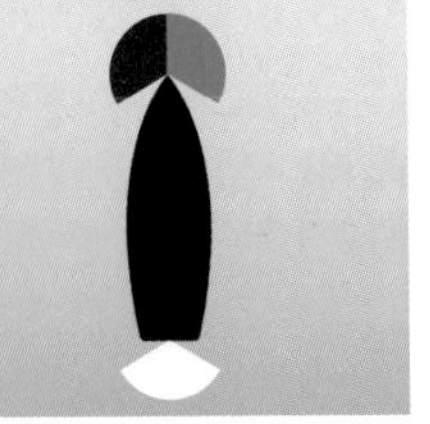

- **Boat under sail (over 7m/23ft)** These must show red and green sidelights, each covering an arc of 112.5°. The stern light must be visible over an arc of 135°. Under 20m (66ft), the sidelights can be combined in one lantern, or a tricolour light may be used (see above).

WHAT ARE THE NAVIGATION LIGHT SECTORS?

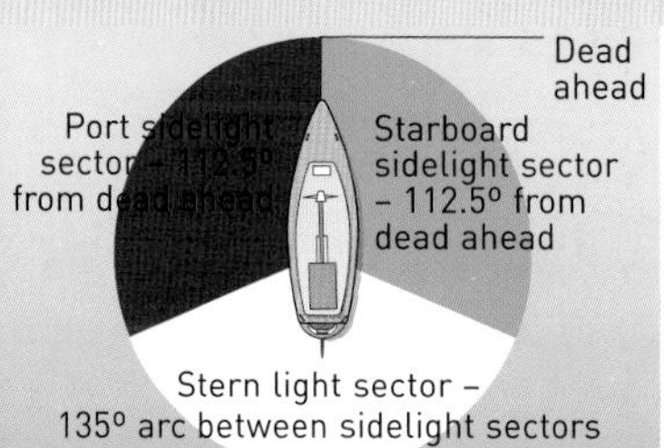

- **Under power at night** Use the other powerboat's light sectors to decide when you must give way. If you are in the white or red sectors, give way; if you are in the green sector, stand on (maintain your course and speed).

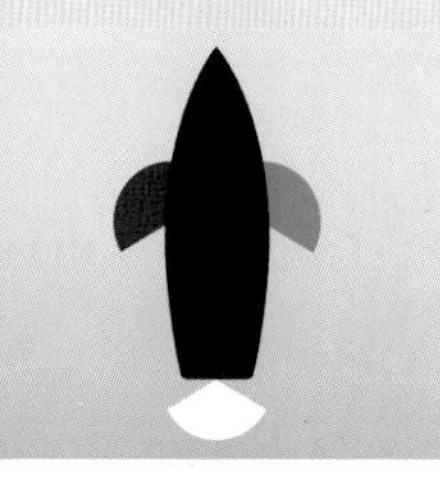

- **Boat under sail (over 20m/66ft)** Boats of this size must use two separate sidelights and a stern light. They may not use a tricolour masthead light, but they can choose to show the optional sailing lights that are often used on large sailing vessels.

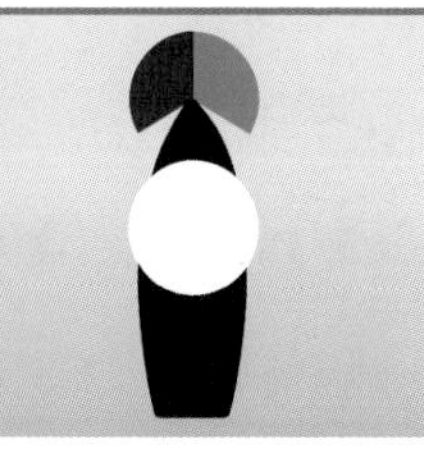

- **Boat under power (under 20m/66ft)** These can combine their stern and masthead lights. Sidelights may be combined in a single bow-mounted light.

- **Boat under power (under 50m/165ft)** Boats of this type must show a masthead steaming light, visible over a 225º arc, positioned above the sidelights.

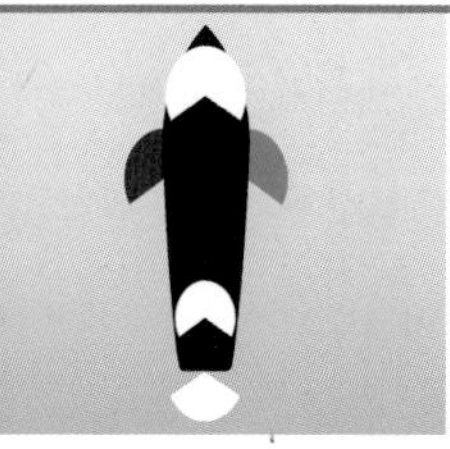

- **Boat under power (over 50m/165ft)** Large power-driven vessels are required to show two masthead steaming lights. The forward light should be positioned lower than the aft light.

Sailing at night

To enjoy the experience of night sailing fully, you and your crew must make preparations before darkness falls. For your first night-time passage, try to have at least one crew member who has had experience of night sailing. At night, all vessels must display navigation lights according to their size and type (see p.188).

WHAT SAFETY MEASURES ARE NEEDED?

- **Lights** Before sailing, check all navigation lights, torches, and electronic navigation aids. Replace any broken bulbs and flat batteries.

- **Reference** Make sure that you have a comprehensive reference book aboard, as it can be difficult to remember all possible light combinations (see p.188).

- **Nightfall** As dusk falls, dress warmly and wear a safety harness, which should be clipped on at all times when on deck.

USING A TRADITIONAL WATCH SYSTEM

Day 1 | Day 2

0000 HRS
0400
0800
1200
1600
1800
2000
2400

KEY

Team A on watch
Team B resting

Team B on watch
Team A resting

Mealtimes

- **Watch system** When setting out on a passage of more than a few hours, operate a defined watch system that allows all crew members to have time off watch for rest and sleep.

- **Tasks** Use a watch system that divides the crew into two or more watches, one of which is responsible for the sailing of the yacht, while the other rests or prepares meals.

- **Traditional system** Arrange watch systems to run from midnight to midnight, splitting the 24 hours into periods of on-watch duty and off-watch rest (see left).

- **Four-hour watches** Four-hour watches at night may be too long when sailing conditions are difficult. Adjust to suit your needs.

- **Personalized system** If you are an experienced skipper, you can devise your own system to suit the needs and size of your crew and the length of the passage.

- **Keeping time** Make sure everyone understands the importance of being on time for their watch. Be early, not late.

- **Lookout** The on-watch crew must keep a regular lookout as it is very easy to be taken unawares by a ship appearing over the horizon, especially from astern.

Sailing in fog

Fog is possibly the greatest of all dangers a sailing craft can face – even greater than rough weather to a small boat, as visibility can be reduced to near zero. This makes you vulnerable to collision with another craft or the shore. Do not put to sea unless you are certain that the fog is land-bound and that conditions at sea are clear.

WHAT DO I NEED TO DO WHEN FOG SETS IN?

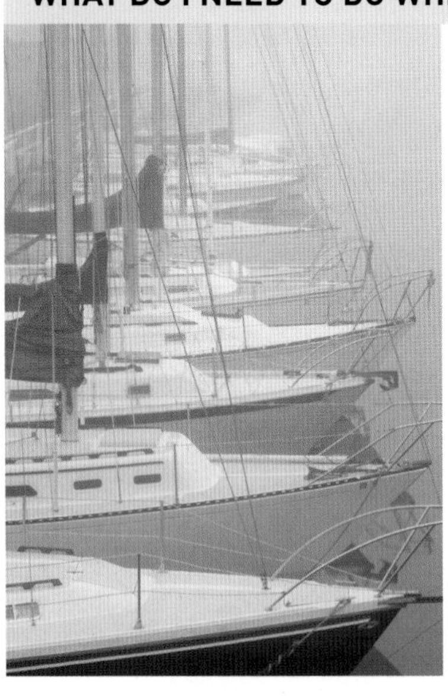

- **Before sailing** Check the weather forecast and note the visibility in your area.
- **If you are already at sea** Plot your position immediately and at frequent intervals thereafter.
- **Be visible** Turn on your navigation lights.
- **Avoid other boats** Head for shallow water away from shipping channels. Use the depth sounder to aid navigation.
- **Be prepared** Put on lifejackets but do not use safety harnesses in case of collision.

WHAT EQUIPMENT DO I NEED?

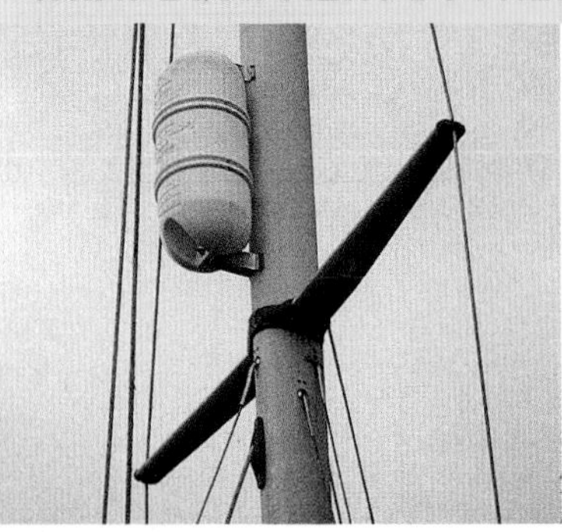

- **Radar reflector** If your boat does not have a permanently mounted radar reflector, hoist a removable one on a halyard.
- **Foghorn** Use a mouth-operated or aerosol foghorn to make the appropriate sound signals, as shown on the right, for your type of vessel.

What sound signals should I make?

When at sea in fog, be sure to make regular sound signals to indicate your presence and activity. The signals below are the most relevant ones but carry a reference book on board.

KEY ▬▬ Long blast ▬ Short blast ▲ Bell ▲▼▲▼▲ Rapid bell ○ Gong

Under sail	▬▬ ▬ ▬	One long blast and two short blasts with the foghorn, sounded every two minutes.
Making way under power	▬▬	One long blast with the foghorn, sounded every two minutes.
Under way but not making way	▬▬ ▬▬	Two long blasts with the foghorn at two-minute intervals.
Aground – under 100m (328ft)	▲▲▲ ▲▼▲▼▲ ▲▲▲	Three bells, rapid ringing, three bells, at one-minute intervals.
Aground – over 100m (328ft)	▲▲▲ ▲▼▲▼▲▼ ▲▲▲ ○	Three bells, rapid ringing, three bells, a gong sounded aft, every minute.
At anchor – under 100m (328ft)	▲▼▲▼▲▼▲▼	Rapid ringing of the bell forward in the boat, at one-minute intervals.
At anchor – over 100m (328ft)	▲▼▲▼▲▼▲▼ ○	Rapid bell ringing forward, gong sounded aft, every minute.
Pilot boat on duty	▬ ▬ ▬ ▬	Four short blasts with the foghorn (under way or making way) every two minutes.

Sailing in strong winds

The definition of rough weather depends less on the wind strength than it does on the experience of the crew, the type of boat, the state of the sea, and the course you are sailing. Every skipper must know the strengths and weaknesses of the boat, its gear, and its crew, and must have tactics for dealing with heavy weather.

PREPARING FOR ROUGH WEATHER

- **Hatches** Make sure all hatches are closed and secured. Check with the skipper before opening a hatch in rough weather.

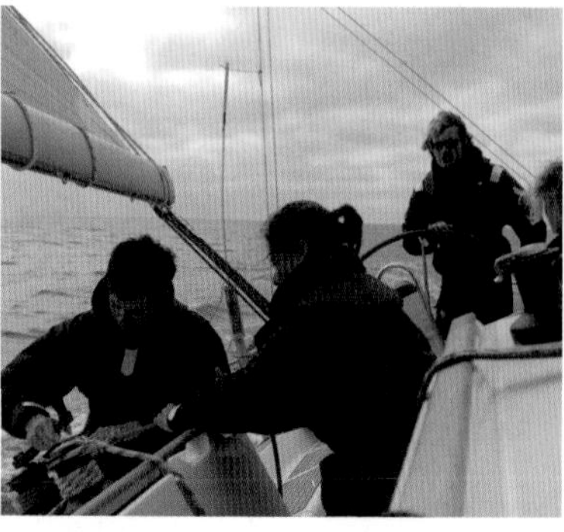

- **Lifejackets** In rough weather, always wear lifejackets on deck and in the cockpit.

- **Harness** Use safety harnesses and tethers in rough weather to ensure the safety of the crew on deck and in the cockpit.
- **Comfort** Adjust lifejacket and harness straps so that they are snug but comfortable (see p.16).
- **Secure** Clip the tether only to strong fittings or to the dedicated jackstays (see p.20).

MANAGING SAILS AND COPING WITH ROUGH SEAS

- **Reefing** Reef early (see pp.94–95), when you first think it might be necessary.
- **Balance** Reef the mainsail and jib in proportion to keep the boat balanced without excessive weather or lee helm.
- **Rough seas** In heavy weather, rough seas are usually more of a problem than the wind strength.
- **Shelter** Head for shelter before bad weather hits but beware trying to enter a harbour on a lee shore, where seas will build up.

USING STORM SAILS

- **Storm sails** Practise using storm sails such as a storm jib and trysail (instead of a mainsail).
- **Change early** If you think that you need to use storm sails, change to them before conditions get too dangerous to work on deck.

WHAT STORM TACTICS SHOULD I USE?

- **Preparation** If you know bad weather will arrive soon, prepare in advance. Cook and eat a meal before the weather gets rough and dress warmly ready for the bad weather.

- **Tactics** Your choice of tactics will depend on the design of the boat, the severity of the weather, and your closeness to shore.

- **Heave-to** The normal procedure is heaving-to (see pp.82–83) under a deeply reefed mainsail and storm jib.

- **Motor-sail** Some modern cruisers can motor-sail to windward with just a deeply reefed mainsail.

- **Sail under bare poles** Running with all sails lowered can be a good tactic if the boat is easy to steer and you have sea room.

- **Tow a drogue** Streaming a drogue (an object towed over the stern) or trailing a warp (opposite) slows the boat and helps hold the stern into the waves.

- **Lie a-hull** Remove all sails and lash the tiller to leeward, or wheel to windward.

- **Use a sea anchor** This is a parachute-like arrangement made of nylon and connected to the boat by a stretchy nylon rope (see opposite). It may be more comfortable than heaving-to or lying a-hull. This can hold the yacht's bow into the waves and reduces downwind drift.

HOW TO SLOW THE BOAT

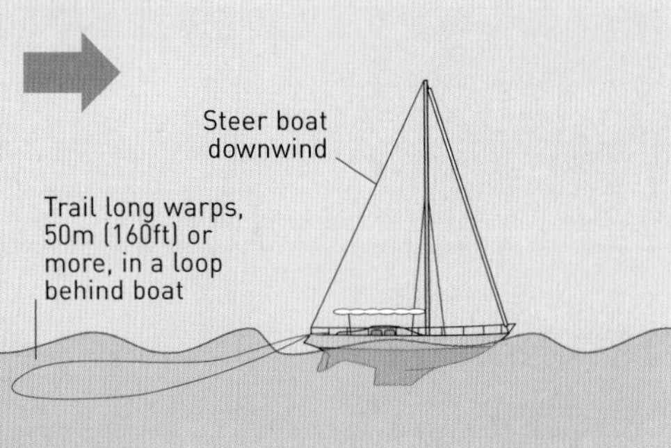

- **Trail warps** If there is plenty of sea room to leeward and if it is too rough to heave-to, steer downwind and slow the boat by trailing a warp or towing a drogue. Tying a heavy object in the middle of the warp will keep it submerged.
- **Rig a sea anchor** Attach the warp of a sea anchor to the end of the anchor chain. Let out at least 10–15 times the boat's overall length.

MANAGE YOUR SAIL AREA

- **Reef early** Reduce sail early (see p.94) so that you do not have to do it when conditions worsen and working on deck becomes much harder.
- **Race boats** Racers often sail over-canvassed, but do not do this when you are cruising.

Understanding weather

Weather is critical to sailors, who depend on wind for propulsion but for whom the "wrong" strength or direction of wind can make sailing slow or even dangerous. Fortunately, there is much weather information available today to help the sailor.

Weather information

Today, weather information based on advanced computer models and satellite information is available from a range of providers, giving mariners a level of detail that would previously have been thought impossible. Use as many sources of information as possible to build a good picture of the weather you can expect.

WHERE DO I FIND FORECASTS BEFORE I SAIL?

- **Printed weather forecasts** These are often posted daily on marina, harbour office, and sailing club notice boards.
- **Public radio** Most countries with a coastline broadcast marine or shipping forecasts, usually with forecasts split into sea areas.
- **Coastguard** Weather forecasts are available from the coastguard via VHF radio.

UNDERSTANDING FORECASTS

- **Content** Forecasts usually include gale warnings, general synopses, and any expected changes over the next 24 hours.

- **Changes** Make it a habit to check all available sources before you sail, and look for any changes in barometric pressure.

- **Advice** Harbour and marina staff can often provide good weather advice for their area and on any local weather effects.

- **Discuss** Improve your weather knowledge by discussing the forecast information with other sailors and your own crew.

VIEWING ONLINE WEATHER FORECASTS

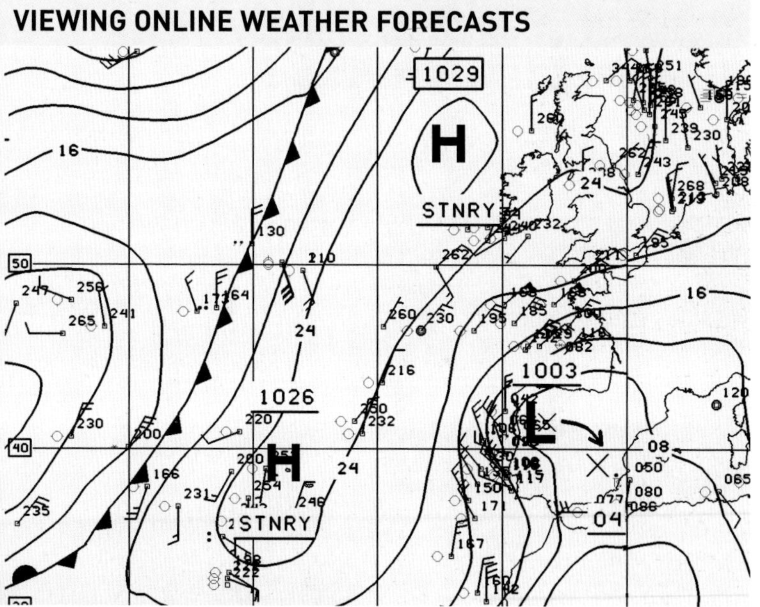

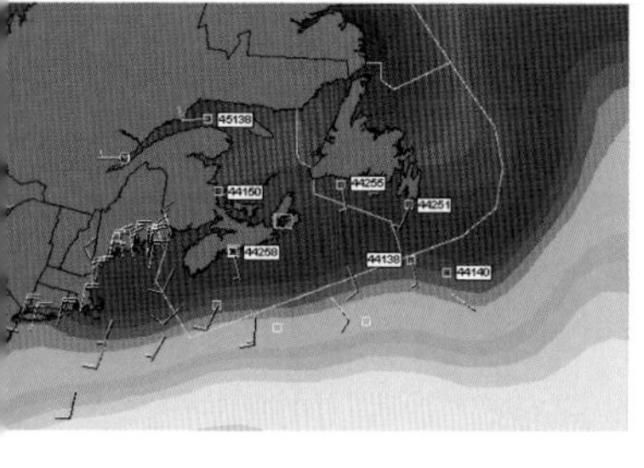

- **Water conditions** A variety of forecast information is available including water temperatures, as shown above, or wave heights.

- **Synoptic chart** Detailed synoptic charts, as shown above, showing movement of fronts, pressure systems, and wind strengths and directions, can be downloaded from the internet.

- **Weather fronts** Indicated by a line of triangles or semicircles, these are perhaps the most important features to look for and are explained in more detail on p.206.

USING NAVTEX

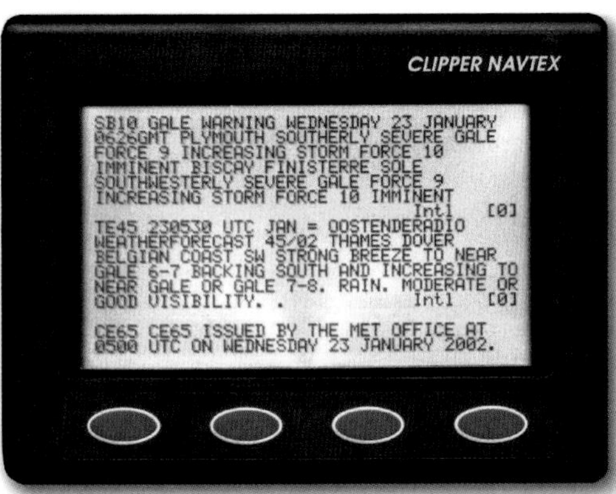

● **Navtex receiver** Weather, navigational, and safety information can be displayed on a Navtex system for a selected area. Some receivers have built-in printers and others, as shown on the left, use only an LCD screen to display information.

WHAT DOES WEATHERFAX DO?

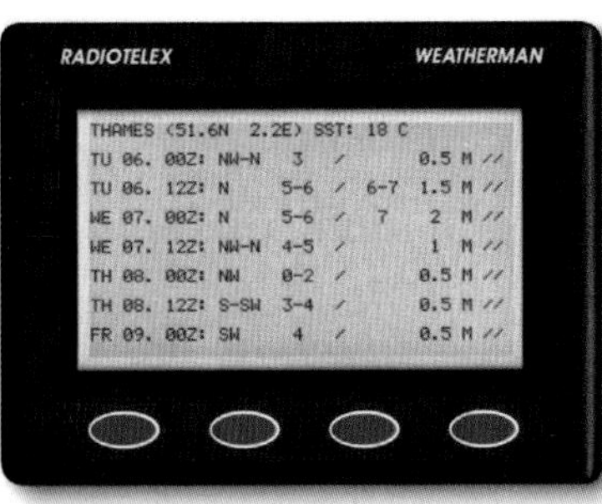

● **Weatherfax system** This provides access to a range of weather information, including ocean frontal positions and gale warnings up to 96 hours from the time of issue, and charts of similar quality to those on the internet.

● **Receiver** Weatherfax transmissions can be received on a dedicated receiver. Weatherfax software may also be installed on a computer that is linked to a radio receiver.

ELECTRIC BAROMETER – HOW CAN IT HELP?

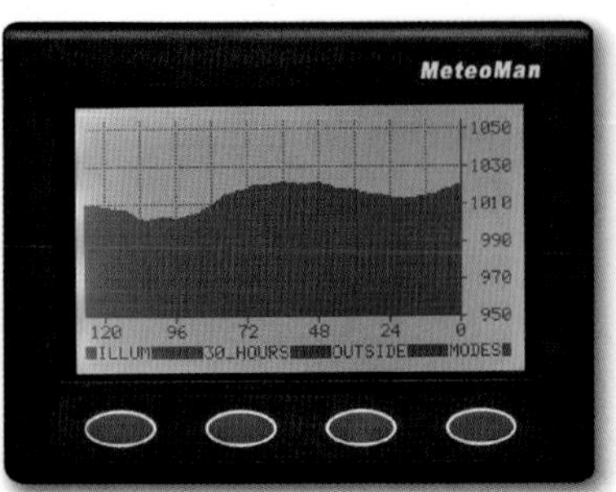

● **Electric barometer** This instrument displays pressure and changes over time on a graphical display that can also show temperature, humidity, time, and other information.

WHAT ARE GRIB FILES?

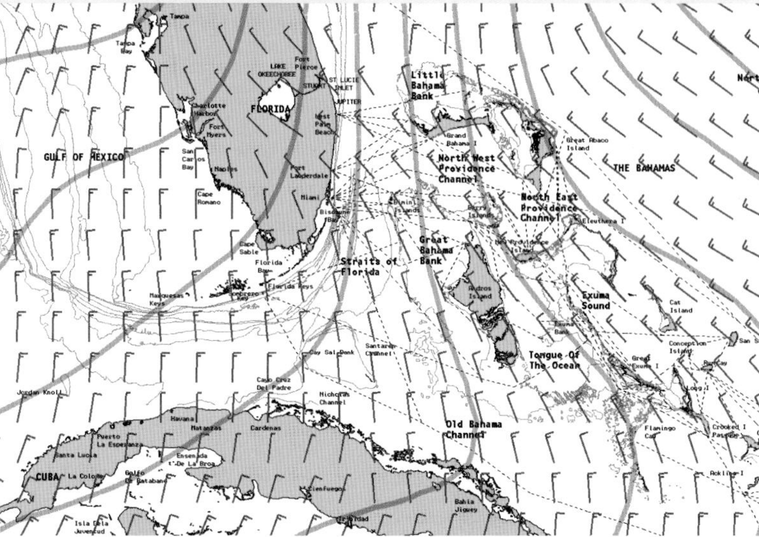

- **Gridded Binary (GRIB) files** These are small output files generated by computer weather forecasting models, at least daily.
- **Useful data** GRIB files display data such as wind speed and direction, ocean currents, seastate, and temperature.

DO I NEED HAND-HELD EQUIPMENT?

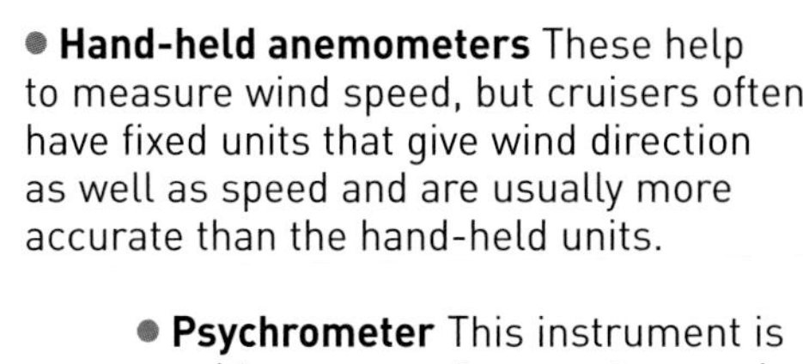

- **Hand-held anemometers** These help to measure wind speed, but cruisers often have fixed units that give wind direction as well as speed and are usually more accurate than the hand-held units.
- **Psychrometer** This instrument is used to measure temperature and humidity. It provides information on dew point (the temperature at which excess water vapour in warm air condenses into droplets) and is also useful for predicting fog.

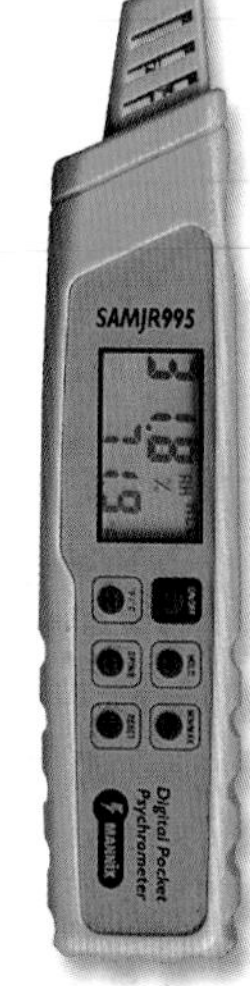

Hand-held anemometer

Psychrometer

Interpreting forecasts

Despite the sophistication of modern weather forecasting, there is still no substitute for direct observation and recording at sea to enable the sailor to determine the most likely short-term weather and to evaluate the accuracy of the forecast. In order to interpret forecasts, it is useful to understand basic weather concepts.

WHAT ARE DEPRESSIONS AND ANTICYCLONES?

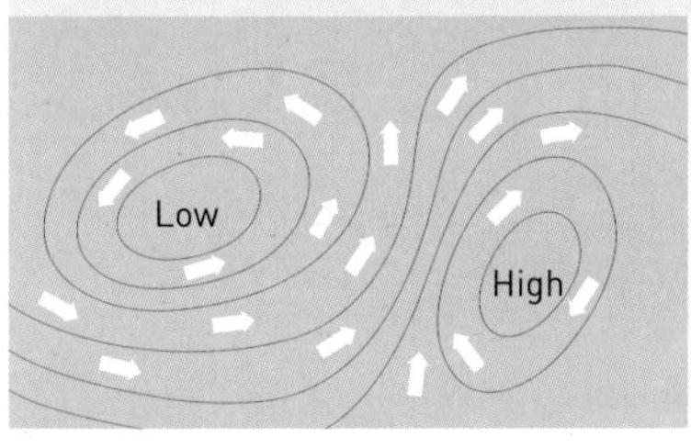

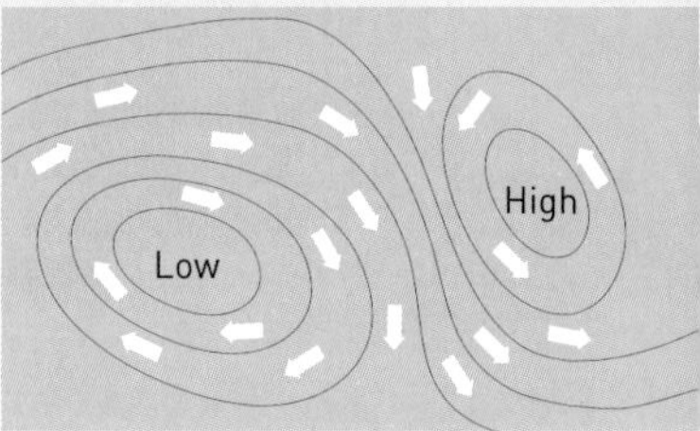

- **Northern hemisphere** Wind blows clockwise around high-pressure weather systems and anticlockwise around low-pressure systems north of the Equator.

- **Southern hemisphere** Wind blows anticlockwise around high-pressure weather systems and clockwise around low-pressure systems south of the Equator.

Northern hemisphere

Southern hemisphere

- **Lows** Areas of low pressure with warm air rising are called depressions. They often bring strong winds and heavy rain.

Northern hemisphere

Southern hemisphere

- **Highs** Areas of high pressure with cold air sinking are called anticyclones. They generally bring good weather.

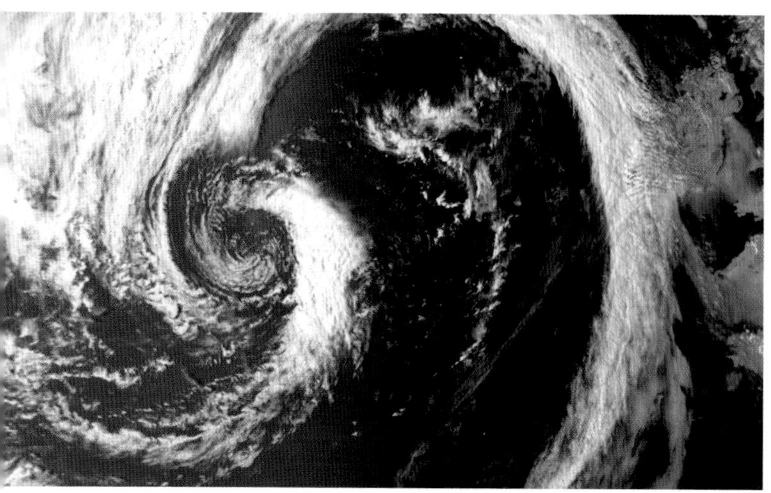

Satellite images Weather systems show up well on satellite images, which can be downloaded from the internet.

Fronts The position of weather fronts can be deduced from cloud cover, as in this depression seen approaching the British Isles.

Weather forecast terms

TERM	MEANING
Gale warnings	Imminent (within 6 hours); Soon (within 6–12 hours); Later (more than 12 hours after forecast)
Strong winds	Average wind above Force 6 to 7 expected
Fair	No precipitation expected
Backing	Wind direction expected to change in anticlockwise direction
Veering	Wind direction expected to change in clockwise direction
Visibility good	Greater than 9km (5nm)
Visibility moderate	Between 4–9km (2–5nm)
Visibility poor	Less than 4km (2nm)
Sea moderate	Wave height 1.25–2.5m (4–8ft)
Sea rough	Wave height 2.5–4m (8–13ft)
Sea very rough	Wave height 4–6m (13–20ft)

Weather fronts

Understanding the passage of a frontal depression and the associated changes in conditions is important for the cruising sailor. Depressions are often forecast in advance, but their speed and direction of movement can be unpredictable. It is an advantage if you can make your own judgments, based on observation.

WHAT IS A DEPRESSION?

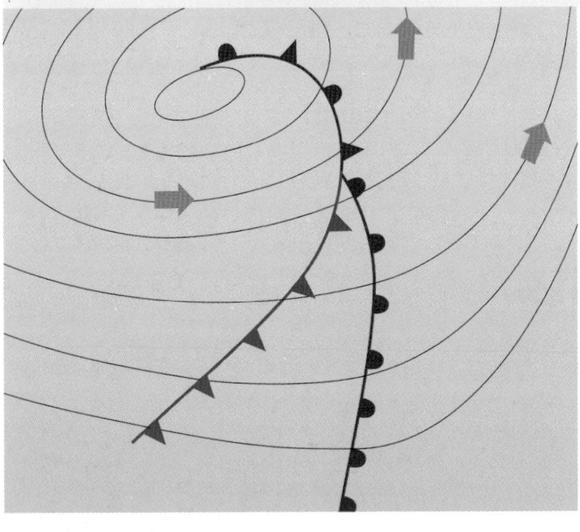

- **Direction** Mid-latitude depressions tend to travel from east to west in both hemispheres.
- **Fronts** Depressions are associated with fronts, which are the forward edges of an advancing air mass.

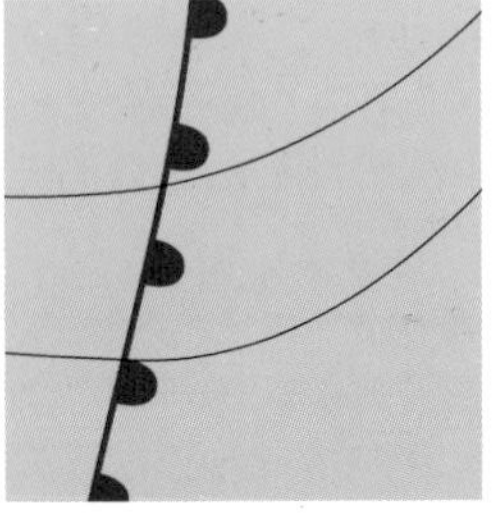

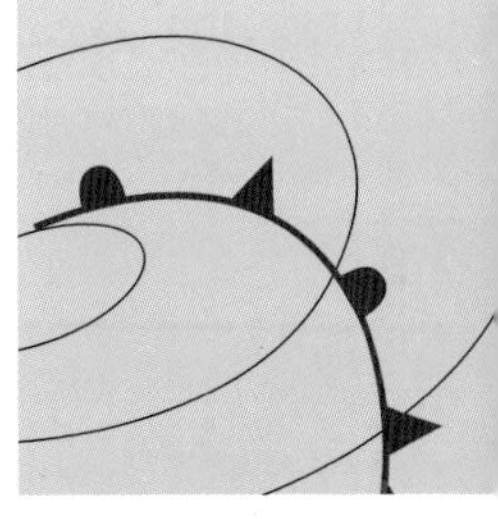

- **Warm front** The leading edge of a mass of warm air (the warm sector) pushing over cooler air is a warm front. It may create heavy rain and poor visibility.
- **Cold front** The leading edge of a mass of cold air pushing under warmer air is a cold front. Showers and thunderstorms may follow it.
- **Occluded front** A fast-moving cold front catches up the warm front ahead in an occluded front. Its effect depends on the temperature of the air ahead.

HOW DO I SPOT A DEPRESSION?

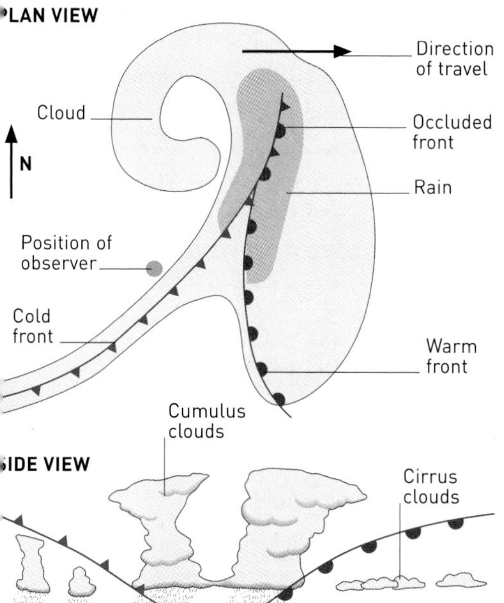

● **Passing depression** This example of a northern hemisphere depression is shown from the point of view of an observer looking north.

● **Succession of fronts** In turn, a warm front, a warm sector, and a cold front pass in front of the observer's position.

● **Clouds** Changes in the cloud cover provide good clues to the passage of the depression.

WHAT ARE THE KEY INDICATORS?

● **Cirrus clouds** These thin, high clouds, which are composed of ice crystals, indicate an approaching depression 12–24 hours away.

● **Speed** The speed and extent of the cirrus clouds are guides to the depth of the depression, also indicated by a fall in air pressure.

● **Cumulus or cumulonimbus clouds** These huge, heaped clouds often mark a cold front.

● **Squalls** There may be heavy rain, fierce gusts and squalls, and sometimes thunderstorms. At the cold front, the wind usually veers sharply north-west.

Wind speed

The Beaufort Scale was created by Admiral Sir Francis Beaufort in 1805 to help sailors estimate wind speed by observing conditions on sea or land. To get an accurate measurement of wind speed, use an anemometer. A fixed rather than hand-held anemometer will provide direction information as well as speed.

Beaufort Scale

FORCE	MEAN SPEED	DESCRIPTION	ASHORE
0	Less than 1 knot	Calm	Smoke rises vertically and flags hang limp.
1	1–3 knots	Light air	Smoke drifts slightly, indicating wind direction.
2	4–6 knots	Light breeze	Light flags and wind vanes move slightly.
3	7–10 knots	Gentle breeze	Light flags extend outwards.
4	11–16 knots	Moderate breeze	Paper lifted off the ground. Small branches move.
5	17–21 knots	Fresh breeze	Small trees sway visibly and tops of trees move.
6	22–27 knots	Strong breeze	Large trees sway and wind whistles in telephone lines.
7	28–33 knots	Near gale	Whole trees are in motion. It is difficult to walk against the wind.
8	34–40 knots	Gale	Twigs are broken off trees. Progress on foot very much impeded.
9	41–47 knots	Severe gale	Chimney pots and slates blown off roofs. Fences blown down.
10–12	48+ knots	Storm to hurricane	Trees uprooted and considerable structural damage likely. Extremely rare inland.

• **Windex** Fixed to the masthead (far left), a Windex indicates the wind direction.

• **Anemometer** This instrument (near right) sends wind direction and speed data to a display unit in the cockpit or at the chart table.

CRUISER SAILING	WAVE HEIGHT	SEA STATE IN OPEN WATER
Becalmed. Use engine.	0m (0ft)	Mirror-like water.
Very slow sailing upwind. Downwind spinnaker hard to keep filled.	Less than 0.1m (¼ft)	Ripples form on the water.
Slow sailing upwind with little heel. Spinnaker fills downwind.	Up to 0.3m (1ft)	Small wavelets with smooth crests.
Pleasant sailing. Spinnaker fills and sets well downwind.	Up to 0.9m (3ft)	Large wavelets with crests starting to break.
Hull speed achieved by most yachts. Some small cruisers start to reef.	Up to 1.5m (5ft)	Small waves and frequent white horses.
Medium-sized cruisers start to reef. Crew wear and clip on safety harnesses.	Up to 2.5m (8ft)	Moderate waves and many white horses.
Most cruisers reefed. Wear and clip on harness. Seek shelter if inexperienced.	Up to 4m (12ft)	Large waves, white foamy crests. Spray likely.
Seek shelter or sail away from land to ride out any forecast storms. Family crews may have problems coping. Most cruisers deep-reefed.	Up to 6m (20ft)	The sea heaps up and waves break. Much spray.
Use a deep-reefed mainsail and small headsail. Close and secure hatches and companionways against water. Only essential crew should be on deck.	Up to 8m (25ft)	Moderately high waves of greater length that frequently break.
Danger of knockdown. Some crews may continue to sail; others heave-to or run before. Depending on the sea state, a trysail could be set.	Up to 10m (30ft)	High waves with breaking crests and flying spray.
Stay well away from coastlines. Survival conditions. Danger of 90° knockdowns and full capsizes.	10–16m (30–52ft)	Very high waves. Sea becoming heaped up and white. Visibility affected.

Daily changes

If you are sailing near the coast in settled conditions, the weather you experience will change throughout the day. Thi effect is known as the diurnal weather variation. It is caused by the sun heating the land, and to a far lesser extent, the sea. Understanding diurnal effects enables you to predict wind speed and direction changes during the day.

READING CLOUDS AND SKY

- **Cumulus** Early convection currents produce small cumulus clouds and variable winds. Deep clouds indicate that the good weather may not continue through the day.

- **Enlarging cumulus** Cumulus may increase in size. Large clouds with high tops may produce rain showers Stronger gusts with wind shifts are found near the clouds.

Mixed cumulus Larger cumulonimbus may develop among smaller cumulus. These areas are very active and can produce heavy showers and even hailstones.

Thunderstorms A rising air mass under a large cumulus or cumulonimbus cloud may produce a thunderstorm. Heavy gusts and big wind shifts occur at the base of the storm.

Clear skies As the land cools, convection currents die and the clouds disappear. With nightfall, the land cools quickly as there are no clouds to trap the heat. An inversion (a condition in which warm air lays on top of cold air) may form.

Dawn mist At dawn, winds will be very light or calm and fog may develop. Near to land, the fog is likely to evaporate as the sun rises and warms the ground.

Land effects

When sailing close to shore, the effects of land may have a major influence on the weather you experience, unlike when sailing offshore where the prevailing weather system determines the conditions. From simple effects such as wind shadows to more complex ones such as sea and land breezes, the land has an impact on the sailing conditions.

UNDERSTANDING SEA AND LAND BREEZES

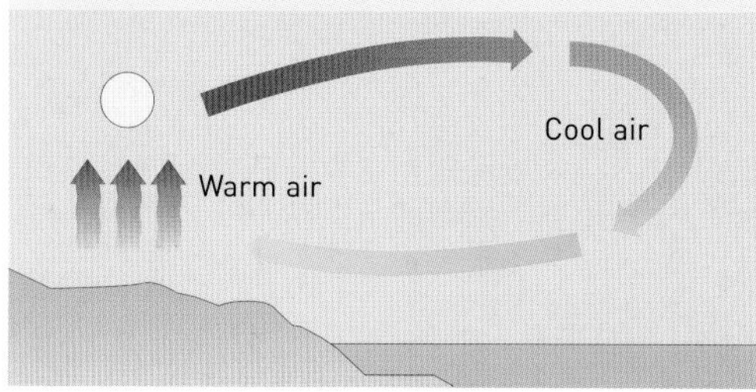

● **Sea breeze** As the land heats up, warm air begins to rise, forming a low-pressure area which draws in cold air from over the sea, creating an onshore breeze.

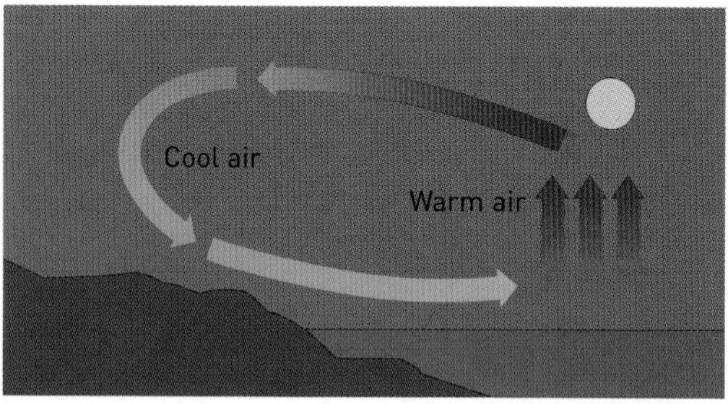

● **Land breeze** The sea breeze fades as the land cools and air above it starts to sink. Warm air above the sea now starts to rise, creating an offshore breeze that may blow through the night.

WHAT HAPPENS IN THE LEE OF HIGH LAND?

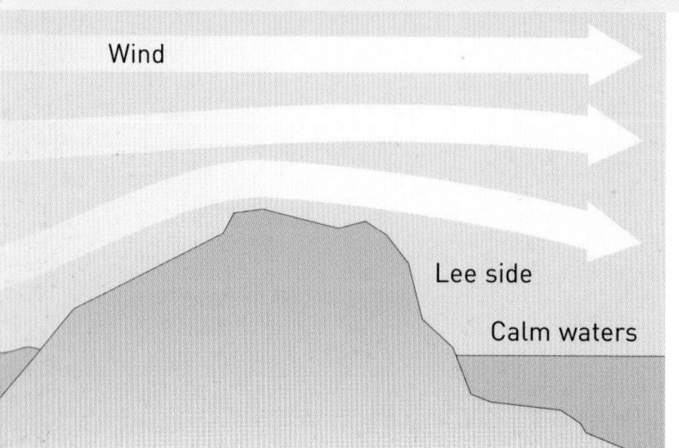

● **Wind shadow** High land creates a wind shadow in its lee as the wind lifts over the land and blows for some distance before sinking back to sea level.

KNOW THE IMPACT OF HEADLANDS AND BAYS

- **Acceleration** The wind often gathers speed around headlands, creating gusty conditions, especially when it is blowing nearly parallel to a coastline.

- **Steep valleys** Wind can be channelled along a steep-sided valley creating strong gusts that travel some way offshore in line with the valley.

- **Corners** When rounding a headland from the leeward side, be prepared for a large increase in wind strength on the windward side of the headland.

- **Tidal streams** These streams often accelerate off a headland. If the stream is running against the wind, it can cause a rough sea. If tide and wind are together, the apparent wind speed increases.

- **In the lee** Sailing in the lee of a headland or steep shoreline the wind may be light if it is blowing offshore, but be prepared for a significant increase in wind strength as you move farther away from the land.

- **Off-lying dangers** Beware of rocks and shoals close to the headlands that may pose a hazard and can cause rough seas.

- **Waves** Watch for waves being bent around a headland and rolling into a bay. This effect can turn an attractive anchorage into an uncomfortable one.

- **At anchor** When anchored in a bay, check the forecast for any change in wind direction that could turn the bay into a dangerous lee shore.

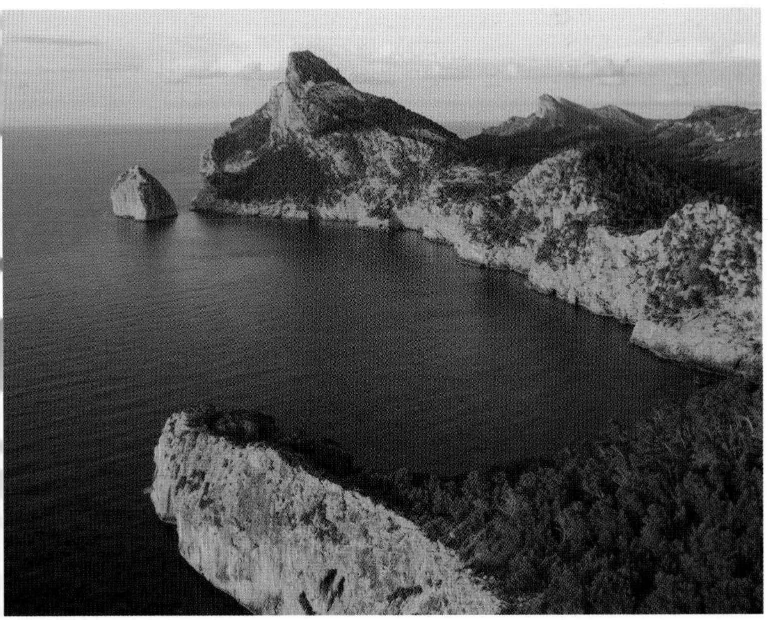

Wind, tide, and depth

While the weather you experience when coastal sailing will be affected by proximity to the land, the wind direction relative to the land, strength of a tidal stream and its direction relative to the wind, and depth of water will also have an impact – sometimes a major one. Variations in any of these factors can cause a major change in sailing conditions.

WHAT EFFECT CAN WIND AND TIDE HAVE?

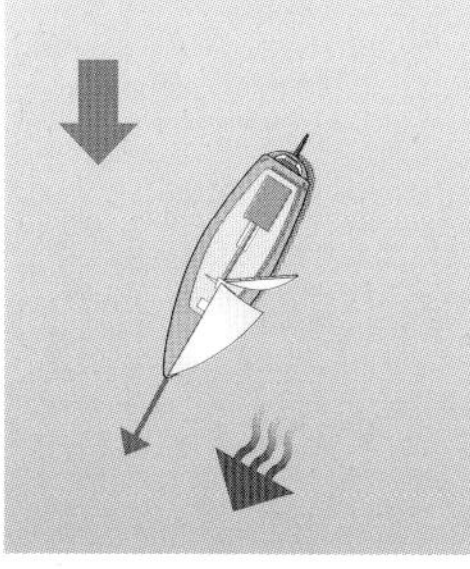

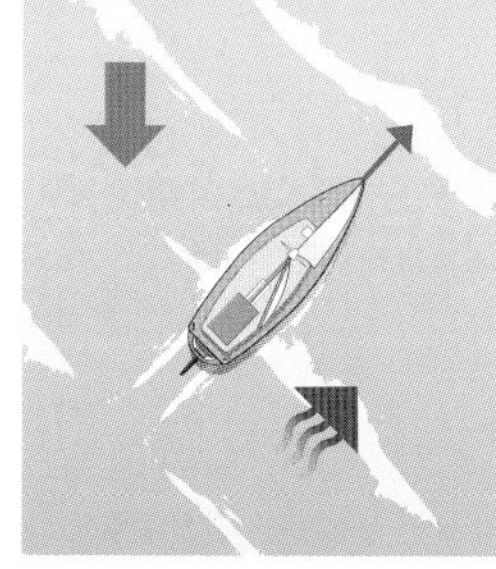

- **Wind and tide together** These conditions provide for a fast passage, when sailing downwind with flat seas, and comfortable sailing.
- **Wind and tide opposed** Sailing to windward with the tide is likely to be uncomfortable as the wind against tide creates steep waves.
- **Running with wind against tide** Running downwind in rough, wind-against-tide conditions, the boat may roll, which makes steering difficult.

DEEP AND SHALLOW WATER – WHAT ARE THE EFFECTS?

- **Depth of water** This influences the type of waves created when the wind blows.
- **Shallow water** In shallower water waves will be lower, closer together, and steeper than in deep water, and will break earlier.
- **Short, sharp seas** Sailing in steep waves in shallow water can be very uncomfortable.
- **Deep water** Waves may be higher in deep water, especially if a strong wind has been blowing from one direction for a while, but they will be further apart, and will be less steep, at least until they start to break. They are also usually easier to sail in.
- **Slowing the boat** If sailing upwind in steep waves becomes uncomfortable, slow the boat down by reducing sail (see p.94).

AVOIDING OVERFALLS AND TURBULENT SEAS

Rough conditions Overfalls are turbulent waters caused by a sudden change in depth, an uneven bottom, or where two tidal streams meet.

Avoiding hazards Look for chart symbols (see pp.170–71) that indicate overfalls and avoid them in strong winds, as conditions in these areas can be very rough.

KEEPING CLEAR OF PROBLEMS

Plan ahead When planning a passage (see pp.156–57) along a coastline, consider different scenarios according to whether the wind is offshore or onshore.

Lee shore Be careful to avoid being caught on a lee shore in deteriorating weather conditions. Strong onshore winds can be very dangerous.

Repairs and maintenance

Modern sailing yachts have many systems that must be regularly maintained, and repaired when necessary. All boat owners need to understand what is needed and even occasional sailors should become familiar with essential boat maintenance skills.

8
CH
ROP
FO
ANADIUM

Engine care

As well as being used for propulsion when needed, the engine also charges the batteries. Carry out regular checks and maintenance to ensure the engine functions reliably. Clean fuel and dependable cooling are important for engine reliability. Always check the oil level and cooling water before starting the engine.

MAINTAINING FUEL LEVELS

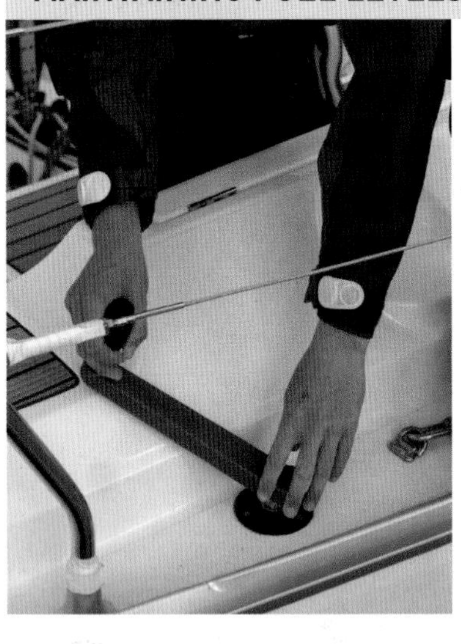

- **Avoid spillage** Take care when refuelling not to mix up the water and fuel fillers and make sure not to spill any diesel into the water or get water into the fuel filler. Some boats have a fuel cap that needs to be opened with a winch handle.

- **Carry sufficient fuel** Make sure you have enough fuel for the entire journey, even if you are intending to sail, as running out of fuel is one of the main causes of engine failure. On long passages carry spare fuel in plastic fuel cans and also carry a funnel.

HOW TO ACCESS THE ENGINE

- **Engine access** Most yacht engines are situated under the companionway steps, which are removable for engine access and maintenance.

TOPPING UP THE OIL

- **Oil levels** Check the engine and gearbox before you start the engine. Ensure the level on the dipstick is between maximum and minimum.
- **Oil change** Check your engine manual for the recommended oil change intervals and carry spare oil and oil filters on board.
- **Gearbox oil** Your gearbox may require special oil. Make sure you have spare gearbox oil on board.

CHECKING THE COOLING SYSTEM

- **Heat exchanger** Check the level of fresh water in the heat exchanger before you start. Top up if necessary.
- **Cooling water** When you start the engine, make a visual check of the exhaust to make sure that cooling water is being pumped.
- **Raw water filter** Shut off the cooling-water seacock, then remove any seaweed or other debris that may be sucked into the engine from the filter.

Simple repairs

Every cruising yacht should have sufficient tools and spare parts on board to enable basic repairs to be carried out at sea, so that the boat can get back to harbour. The selection of spare parts that you need to carry depends on the type of boat that you own and the distances you sail.

HOW CAN I BE WELL-PREPARED?

- **Don't wait** Deal with small problems immediately before they escalate into a major situation.

- **Crew** Know the skills of the crew so that you can use their expertise to help with repairs.

- **Maintenance logbook** It is useful to have a logbook in which you note the maintenance schedules of all the equipment on board.

- **Notebook** Have a repairs and maintenance notebook so that you can keep track of jobs to be done.

- **Tool kit** Have a basic tool kit, which contains the most commonly used tools, in an accessible spot, so that it can be easily grabbed when a job needs doing.

- **Spares** Stow spare parts and less commonly needed tools in a dry locker. Keep a list of the spares you carry aboard and update it when items are used for reference when restocking.

- **Imagine** A good way to spend a night watch is to imagine problem scenarios and their solutions.

KNOW YOUR ENGINE

- **Get familiar** Make sure you know the key parts of the engine and what to look for in case of a breakdown.

- **Skills** If you are unsure how to do essential repairs, ask an expert to show you, then practise the skills you have learned.

Basic tool kit

Choose tools of the best possible quality for use aboard your boat. Cheaper tools will quickly deteriorate in the damp conditions prevalent at sea. Keep your tools lightly oiled and stored securely. The following list is an example of the contents of a tool kit that would be useful for making basic repairs.

- Screwdrivers – all head types and sizes, including electrical screwdrivers
- Spanners – an assortment, including an adjustable spanner
- Socket set
- Mole wrench
- Electrical wire terminal crimper
- Wire cutter
- Hacksaw and spare blades
- Wood saw
- Power drill (12 volts), drill bits, and screwdriver bits
- Hand drill and bits
- Brace and bits
- Pliers and electrical pliers
- Hammers and a mallet
- Set of chisels
- Files
- Torch
- Mirror (to see into confined spaces)
- Bolt cutters

Useful spares

Some of the vital and most useful spares and kits are listed below. Consider carrying replacement units for essential items that are not repairable.

ENGINE SPARES

- Spark plugs and coil (petrol engine)
- Injectors (diesel engine)
- Repair kits for fuel and water pumps with seals and impellers
- Set of hoses
- Oil filters
- Fuel filters
- Sets of gaskets, seals, and O-rings
- Fuel
- Oil and grease
- Fuel antibacterial additives (diesel)
- Spare ignition key

ELECTRICAL SPARES

- Fuses – all types used on board
- Bulbs – including navigation lights
- Terminal fittings
- Connecting blocks
- Soldering iron and solder
- Wire – assorted sizes
- Tape – insulating and self-amalgamating
- Batteries (for torches etc.)
- Distilled water (to top up batteries)
- Hydrometer (for checking batteries)

ASSORTED SPARES

- Sail repair kit (p.227)
- Sticky backed sail repair tape
- Piston hanks
- Whipping twine
- Mainsail slider
- Rope – spare lengths of various sizes
- Shackles – assorted
- Bottlescrew
- Clevis pins
- Split pins and rings
- Bulldog clamps and rigging wire – a length equal to longest on board
- Marine sealant
- Underwater epoxy
- Waterproof grease
- Petroleum jelly
- Paint and varnish (minor repairs)
- Epoxy glue and fillers
- Glass-fibre tape and cloth
- Nails, screws, and bolts – assorted
- Wood – assorted pieces

Steering maintenance

A failure in the steering system will disable the boat and could put it in imminent danger if close to the shore or another vessel. In strong winds, it is likely to result in a knockdown. Check the system before sailing and maintain all the parts regularly. It is sensible to have an alternative steering method and to practise using it.

MAINTAINING TILLER STEERING

- **Greater reliability** One of the big advantages of tiller steering is its simplicity and reliability.
- **Potential weak points** The only areas where it can fail is a problem with the rudder or its fittings or, more commonly, a tiller breakage.
- **Transom-hung rudders** It is easy to inspect these rudders and to check the fittings which attach them to the transom.
- **Spade- or skeg-hung rudders** In these designs, the rudder shaft passes up through the hull and deck. Check that there is no slack in the bearings. If you find there is slack, have them replaced.
- **Rudder loss** If the shaft fails on a spade rudder, it could fall out through the bottom leaving a large hole. Carry a suitably-sized softwood bung to seal the hole.
- **Spares** Carry a spare tiller.

MAINTAINING WHEEL STEERING

- **Less reliability** Wheel steering has more components to fail than tiller steering, and these may be in an area that is hard to access.
- **Cable drive** This is the most common system on medium-sized cruisers. Check for stranded cables and pulleys that are out of alignment. Replace or repair any damage immediately.
- **Hydraulic system** Check for leaks, which often warn of failure. Carry spare seals and hoses.
- **All systems** Check for tightness or stiffness in the system by turning the wheel from lock to lock, and check the shaft bearings for wear. If problems are found, have them checked by an expert and repaired immediately.
- **Spares** Carry a spare drive cable and fluid for hydraulic systems. Remember to carry an emergency tiller even when wheel steering.

HOW TO USE EMERGENCY STEERING

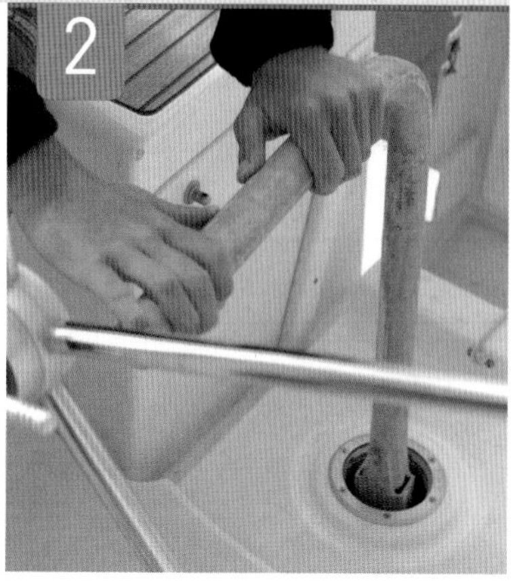

- **Some wheel-steered boats** have a removable cover in the cockpit, which gives access to the top of the rudder stock and allows an emergency tiller to be fitted.
- **Check that the emergency tiller** fits properly into the rudder head and practise fitting and using it with your crew.
- **The emergency tiller** is likely to be very short and you may have to rig lines from it to winches on either side to control it.
- **If your autopilot** connects directly to the rudder at the rudder quadrant, use it for emergency steering if a wheel-steering system fails.

COPING WITH RUDDER FAILURE

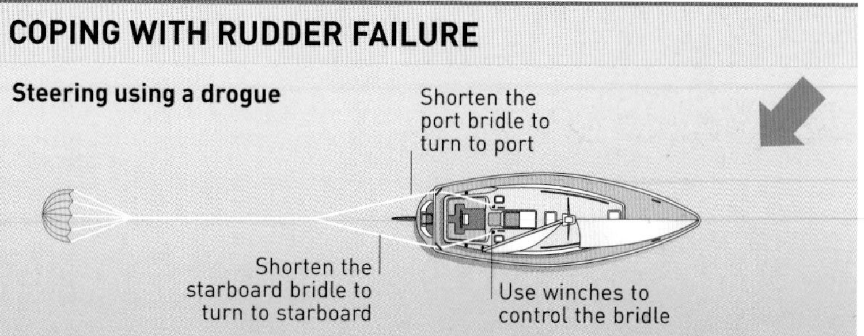

- **Preparation** If you are the skipper, be prepared for a total rudder failure and have a system worked out for your boat. This is difficult to achieve in most boats and you will need to practise it. Do not be surprised if it takes several attempts to find a system that is suitable for your boat.
- **Drogue** You can tow a drogue behind the boat with a bridle to each quarter to allow for steering.
- **Jury-rig steering** Another approach is to make a steering oar with a plywood blade lashed to the spinnaker pole along with some chain to weight it.

Rig checks and repairs

Whatever the size of your craft, the condition of its rig and related fittings is critical for handling efficiency and safety. Most equipment should require little maintenance, but you must check it regularly for wear and the appearance of small cracks that indicate stress damage.

THE RIG – WHAT TO CHECK

- **Check the rig** This will involve at least an annual trip to the masthead unless you unstep the mast when laying up the boat for the winter.
- **Go aloft** Have at least one helper to hoist you aloft and use a spare halyard as a safety line.

- **Terminals** Check rigging wires where they enter terminals and look for any signs of corrosion and frayed strands.
- **Wire** Replace the stainless-steel wire at least every 10 years or immediately if you find broken strands or corrosion at terminals.

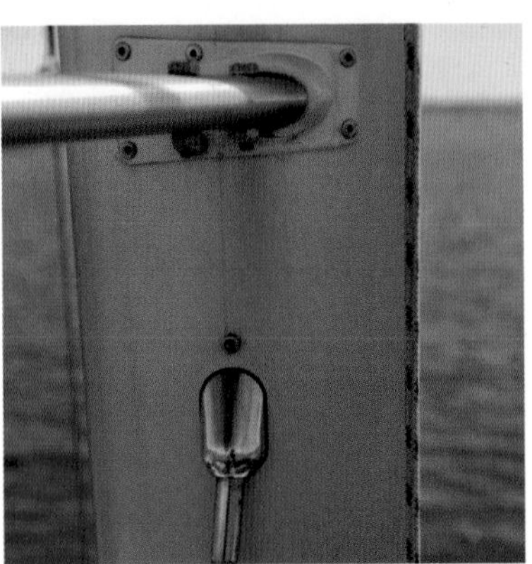

- **Fittings** Look for corrosion where stainless-steel fittings are attached to aluminium spars.
- **Stress cracks** You can identify potential failure by small stress cracks radiating from fittings and their fasteners.
- **Loose fittings** Look for fittings that are working loose. Remove, re-bed, and re-fasten them.

CHECKING THE GUARDRAILS

- **Inspect** Guardrails take a lot of abuse – for example, from chafing caused by attaching fenders to them. They are vital to safety so check them regularly and replace if you find any signs of damage.

MAINTAINING THE BOOM AND MAST

- **Aluminium spars** Most modern yachts use aluminium spars that require little maintenance. Simply wash off the dirt and salt and finish with a wax polish.

- **Check** Inspect all fittings and the mast step area for damage and corrosion.

SERVICING A WINCH

- **Dismantle and inspect** Service winches at least once a season. Use a large cloth to prevent the small parts from being lost overboard.

- **Grease** Clean all parts thoroughly in paraffin. Lightly grease these before reassembly.

Sail maintenance

The sails are the driving force of a sailing boat and expensive to replace. However, all too often they are not inspected and maintained regularly. The old clichés – "a stitch in time saves nine", and "prevention is better than cure" – are nowhere more applicable than in sail care. Make it a habit to scan your sails every time you hoist them.

HOW TO PROTECT SAILS

- **Prevent flogging** Sails are damaged much more by flogging than when full of wind, so limit the amount of time that the sails flog.
- **Avoid chafing** Apply sacrificial patches to areas that rub against the spreaders.
- **UV light** Sunlight damages sails, so always put on the sail cover when the mainsail is lowered.
- **Protect from light** Protect furling headsails from UV light with a heavier layer of cloth along the leech. Replace it when damaged.

WHERE TO LOOK FOR DAMAGE

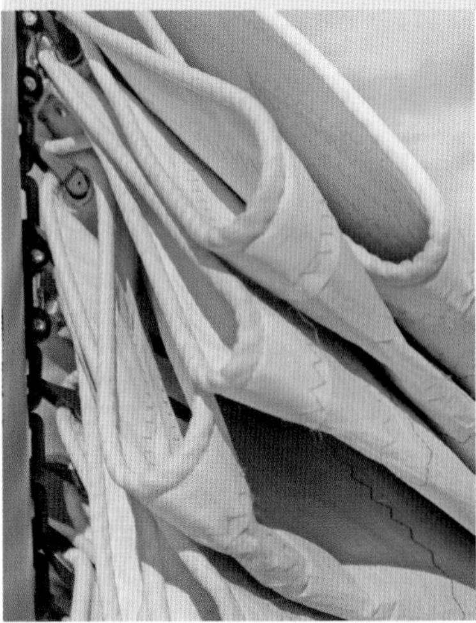

- **Stitching** This is where most damage occurs, so check along seams and batten pockets, edges, and around high-load areas such as corners.

- **High-load areas** Check the corners where the loads are high and seams come together. Look also for chafe in areas where the sail rubs against the rigging.

WHAT TOOLS DO I NEED?

Sailmaker's needle

- **Sewing kit** Have a small set of tools, sail repair tape, adhesive, and various sizes of needles and thread so that you can make early repairs when you spot sail damage.

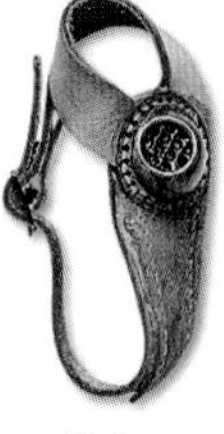

Palm

- **Specialist tools** Always use proper sailmaker's needles and a sailmaker's palm, which makes it much easier to push a needle through heavy sailcloth.

HOW TO PATCH A SAIL

- **Stitching a sail** This method of repairing a torn sail only applies in the case of cloth sails that can be stitched.

- **Laminate sails** Hi-tech laminate sails made of low-stretch fibres cannot be stitched – make repairs by glueing patches to the sail.

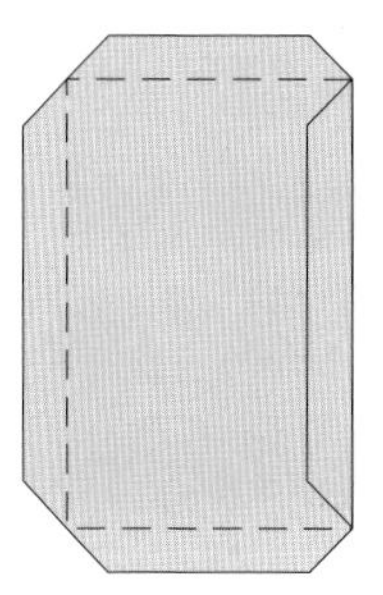

1 **Cut a patch** to cover the tear. Trim the corners, and turn the edges under.

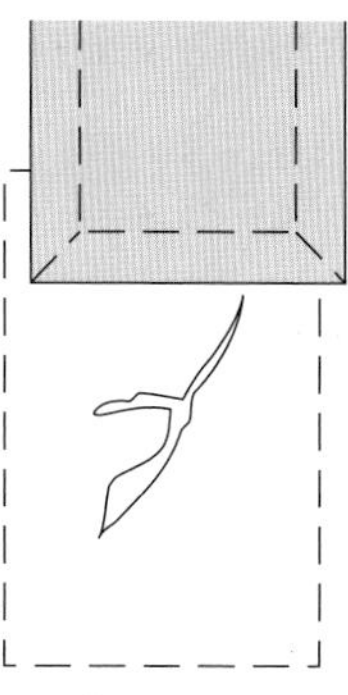

2 **Place the patch** centrally and glue it so that it covers the tear on all sides.

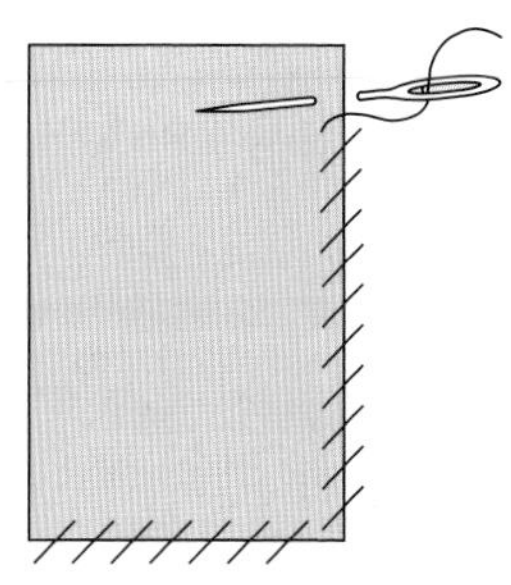

3 **Oversew neatly** around the turned-under edges of the patch.

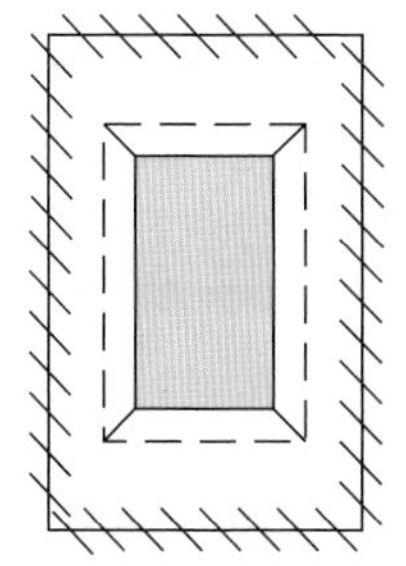

4 **Turn the sail over,** and then trim the torn area to make a neat rectangle.

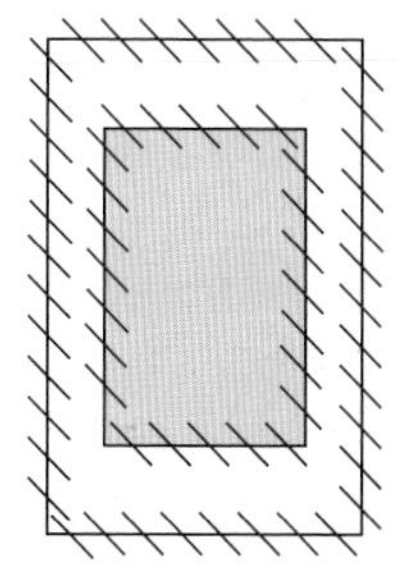

5 **Oversew** around the edges of the rectangle to finish the repair.

Hull maintenance

The amount and type of maintenance that a hull requires depends on the material used in its construction. Glass-reinforced plastic (GRP) combines strength with relatively low maintenance. It is used for almost all production-built boats. Maintain the hull in good condition by keeping it clean and polished, and repairing small scratches quickly.

HOW TO PREVENT DAMAGE

- **Gelcoat** A GRP hull has a relatively soft outer layer of gelcoat, which provides the smooth finish and colour.
- **Protect** Keep the gelcoat clean and use a polish to help it shed dirt and grime.
- **Repair** Fix any gelcoat damage quickly to prevent water getting into the underlying laminate and weakening it.
- **Let it dry** Lift the boat out of the water for the winter and store ashore to allow the laminate to dry out. The boat can slowly absorb water into the laminate when left in the water for long periods.

DAMAGE TO FITTINGS – WHAT TO LOOK FOR

- **Loose fittings and cracks** Many yacht fittings take a lot of load when sailing or even when moored or anchored. Over time, fittings bolted to the deck will loosen, and the bedding sealant on which they are bolted down will crack. Look for cracks in the gelcoat around fittings.

- **Deck leaks** Often caused around loosened fittings, deck leaks allow water to find its way through the bolt holes. Remove and re-bed fittings if they become loose.

- **Hatch seals** These harden over time. Replace any hatch seals that start to leak.

CHECKING RUDDER, PROPELLER, AND BEARINGS

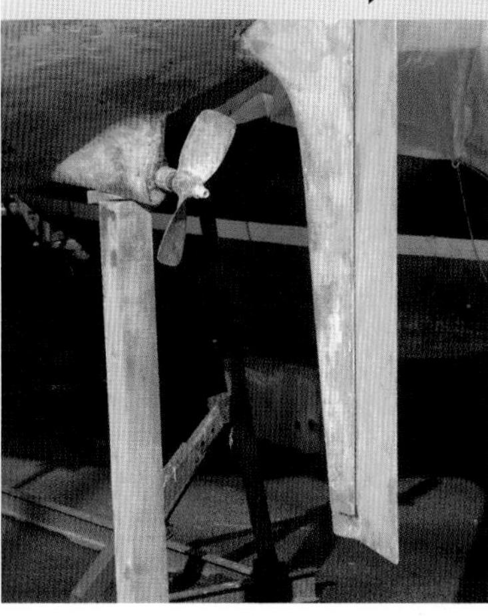

- **Rudder** A yacht's rudder can be vulnerable to impact, especially if it is a spade rudder rather than one that is hung on a skeg, as here, or the back of a long keel.

- **Bearings** Regularly check the rudder bearings for movement by vigorously pulling the rudder at the bottom. If there is movement, have it checked by an expert.

- **Propeller** Check the propeller shaft and its bearings in the same way as the rudder.

PREVENTING GALVANIC CORROSION

Strap for bolting anode to the hull

Pear-shaped anode for fitting to hull with minimum resistance to water flow

- **Galvanic corrosion** This type of damage occurs when different metals in close proximity and immersed in sea water form an electric cell. A current flows, and one of the two metals is eaten away.

- **Sacrificial anodes** Made of zinc, these fittings come in various shapes and sizes. They are fastened underwater near hull fittings, the rudder, and the propeller shaft to protect these important fittings from corrosion. The zinc corrodes before other metals and so protects them. Always replace anodes when more than half their bulk has been corroded away.

Dealing with damage

Production-built glassfibre reinforced plastic (GRP) hulls are strong and fairly long-lasting, but they can be damaged by impact, abrasion, and by water absorption over a long period. Have your boat taken out of the water each winter to allow the GRP to dry out and to reduce winter damage.

ASSESSING THE PROBLEM

1

- **Check for blisters** on the underwater surfaces, which may be a sign of osmosis – water ingress into the laminate or confined to the antifouling layer.

2

- **Expose the gelcoat** by scraping off a patch of antifouling. This enables you to check if the blisters are in the laminate or merely in the antifouling paint.

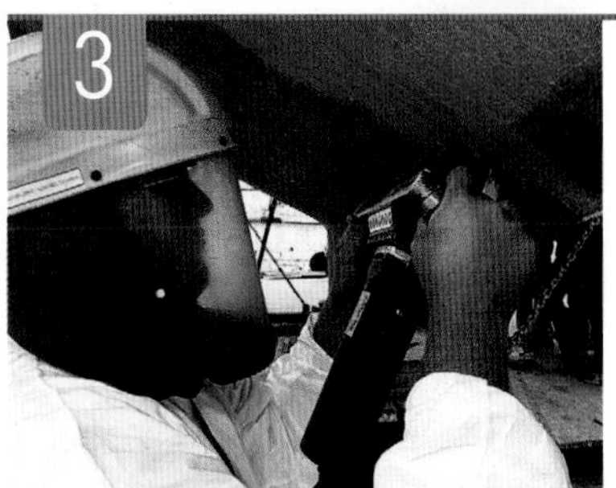

3

- **If osmosis is diagnosed**, have a professional remove the gelcoat using a hand-held peeling machine, before drying out the laminate and coating with epoxy resin.

REPAIRING MINOR GELCOAT DAMAGE

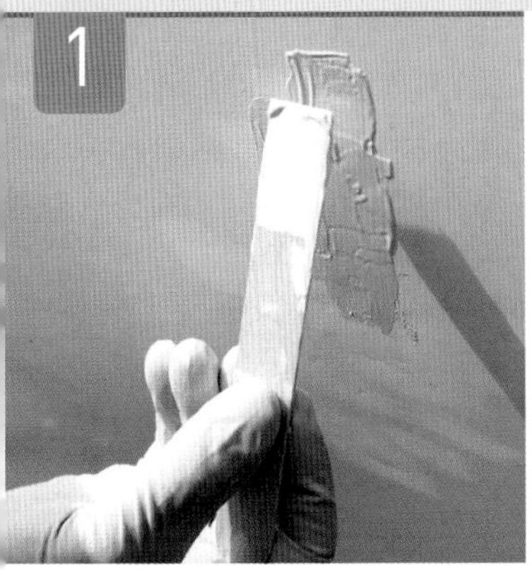

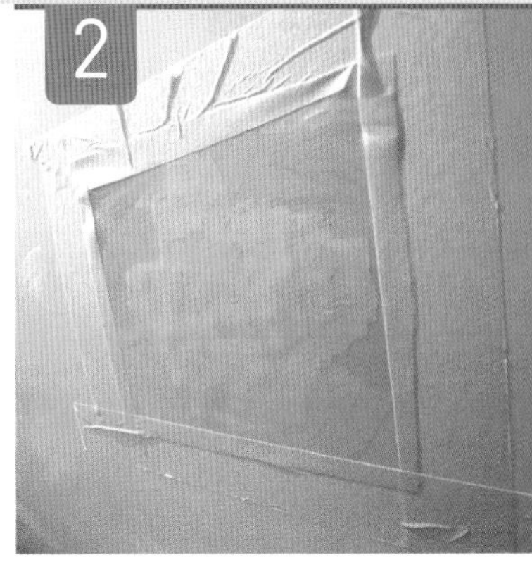

- **Use polyester gelcoat** of the appropriate colour to repair minor chips and grazes in the gelcoat of a GRP boat. Mix gelcoat and hardener and apply to the damaged area using a wooden spatula.

- **Use a piece of acetate film** to keep air off the gelcoat while it cures. Cut the film oversize, smooth over the repair to eliminate air, and fix with masking tape.

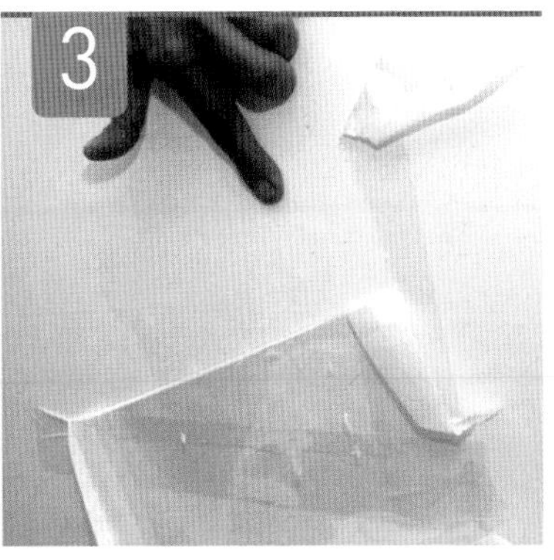

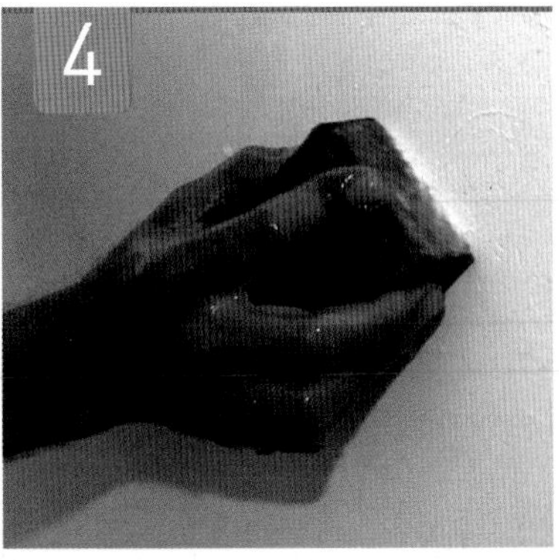

- **Peel back the acetate** to test the hardness of the new gelcoat with a finger nail. Re-cover with the acetate, if it is not yet cured, and leave until it has hardened.

- **When the repair has cured**, remove the film, and wet sand the repair with fine wet-and-dry paper wrapped around a cork or wood block. Finish off with a rubbing paste to polish the surface.

Knots and rope skills

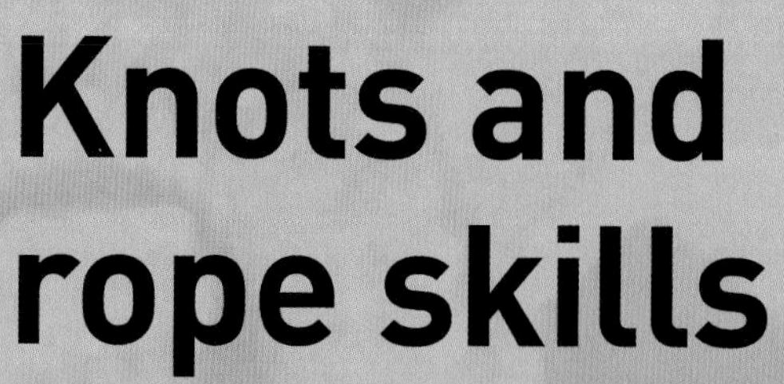

Ropes and knots play quite a large part in sailing, but the knowledge needed to use and maintain ropes and to tie knots is simple and fun to learn. If you are interested in ropework, there is a wealth of practical and decorative knots to explore.

Types of rope

Modern sailing ropes, from the thin ropes used for halyards and control lines to the thick ropes used for mooring, are made from synthetic materials, which are lighter and much stronger than natural fibres. Learning a little about the different properties of the various types of rope will enable you to select the most suitable rope for any particular task.

CHOICE OF ROPE

- **Materials and construction** Rope can be made from many different fibres and in a number of ways. These factors determine how the finished rope behaves in terms of stretch, strength, durability, and flexibility.

- **Synthetic materials** Modern ropes are lighter and much stronger than natural fibres and are immune to rot caused by dampness. They are available in a wide range of colours.

ROPE CONSTRUCTION

- **Three-strand (laid) rope** Yarns are twisted together in one direction to create the three strands. Strands are then twisted together in the opposite direction to create the rope.

- **Braided rope** A core of braided or lightly twisted strands is covered by a braided sheath, which, depending on type, can provide the strength for the rope, or may just protect the inner core.

ROPE MATERIALS

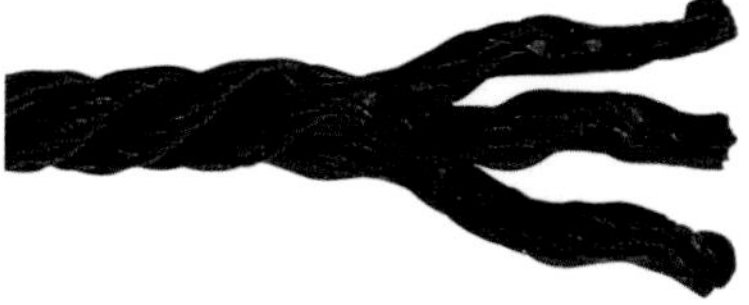

• **Polypropylene** A low-cost material, polypropylene, is used to make general-purpose, three-strand ropes that are light and will float. They are used mainly for cheap mooring lines. Watch them for UV degradation.

• **Polyester** This type of rope can be of braided or three-strand construction. It is strong, with low stretch, and does not float. It is often used for halyards and sheets on cruisers.

• **Nylon** Strong and elastic, this rope does not float and loses strength when wet. It is used mainly for mooring lines and anchor cables where its strength and stretchiness are an advantage.

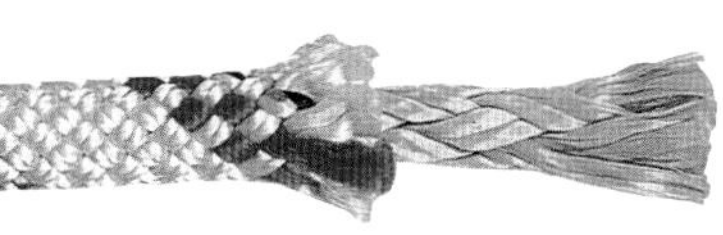

• **Aramid and HMP (high-modulus polyethylene)** These ropes are strong and light and have low stretch. They are used on racing boats for low stretch sheets and control lines.

HOW TO CARE FOR ROPES

• **Coil and stow** When not in use, keep ropes, ideally, out of the sun and weather in a place where they can dry.

• **Remove salt** Wash ropes occasionally in soapy fresh water to remove salt and dirt, which can damage fibres by abrasion.

• **Seal ends** Avoid frayed rope ends by whipping the ends (see p.254) or heat sealing them.

• **Deal with damage** Do not use a frayed rope. If the damage is near the middle, consider cutting the rope and creating two shorter lengths. Otherwise, discard it.

Coiling a rope

Loose rope not in use should be coiled so it does not become tangled. It can then be stowed neatly so that it is accessible and ready when needed. Rope tends to twist when it is coiled. To avoid kinks, coil three-strand rope clockwise, in the same direction as the strands are twisted. You may need to coil braided rope in figure-of-eight loops.

1

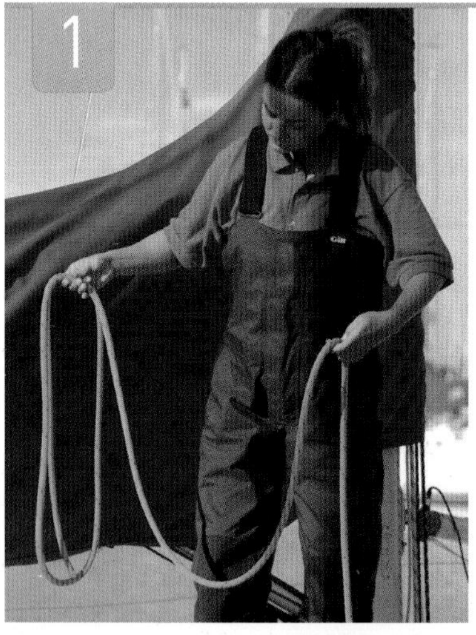

- **Make loops** with one hand and gather the coils in the other one.
- **Twist the rope** between the thumb and forefinger each time you make a loop.

2

- **Keep the coils** of rope evenly sized by paying out an arm-span length for each loop you make.
- **Leave plenty of rope** to secure the coils. Take a horizontal turn round the top of the coils.

- **Continue wrapping** the rope tightly around the coils.
- **Take at least** two more tight turns around the coils to keep them secured.

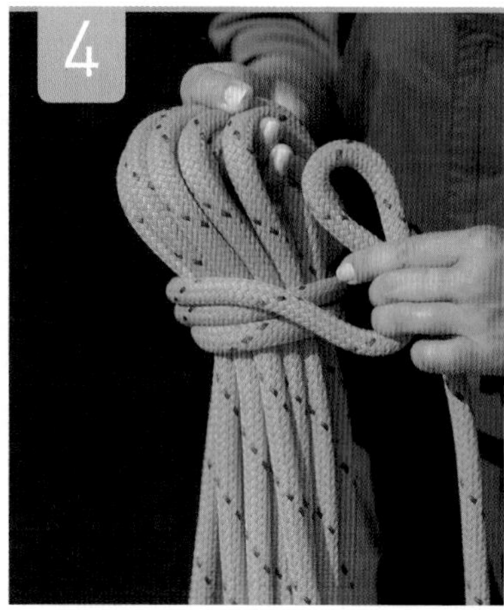

- **Make a small loop** in the rope close to the last turn.
- **Push the loop** through the centre of the coils, above the horizontal turns.

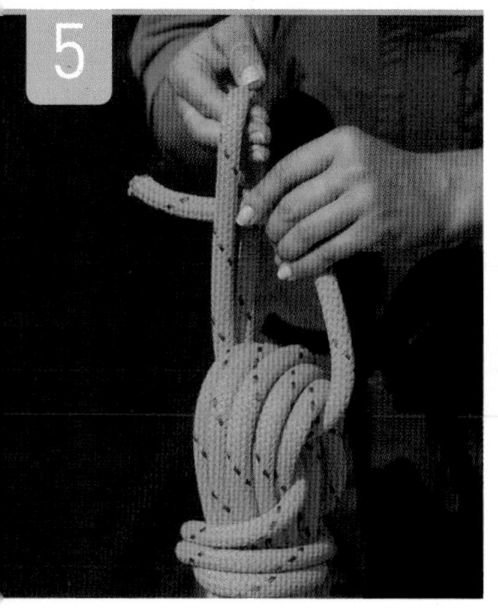

- **Hold the loop** firmly in place to secure the coils.
- **Pull the free end** of the rope up and over the coils.
- **Insert it through** the centre of the loop.

- **Pull the free end** tight to secure the coil.
- **When you need** to use the rope, pull the free end out of the loop and unwind.

Stowing ropes

When ropes are not in use, they should be coiled and secured so that they are out of the way but easy to retrieve and use when necessary. If they are left loose, they will tangle quickly and be difficult to unravel when they are needed. Dirty ropes should be washed in soapy water and hung up to dry.

WHERE TO STOW ROPES

● **Cockpit locker** Warps are often stowed in a cockpit locker. Avoid dumping them in a heap as they will tangle and be hard to retrieve and prepare for use when needed.

● **Hang on hooks** If possible, have a row of hooks at the back of the locker on which coiled ropes can be hung. This keeps them neater and less prone to tangling, makes them easier to retrieve, and allows them to drain.

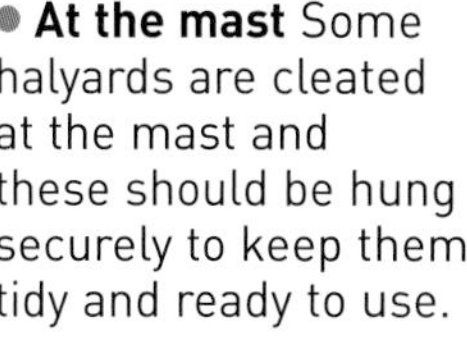

● **At the mast** Some halyards are cleated at the mast and these should be hung securely to keep them tidy and ready to use.

● **Decorative stowage** It is important to stow ropes so you do not trip over them on the dock. However, the ends should be made fast to the dock cleat and the rest of the warp kept aboard. Decorative "cheeses", as shown above, collect dirt and are hard to use in a hurry.

STOWING THE HALYARD

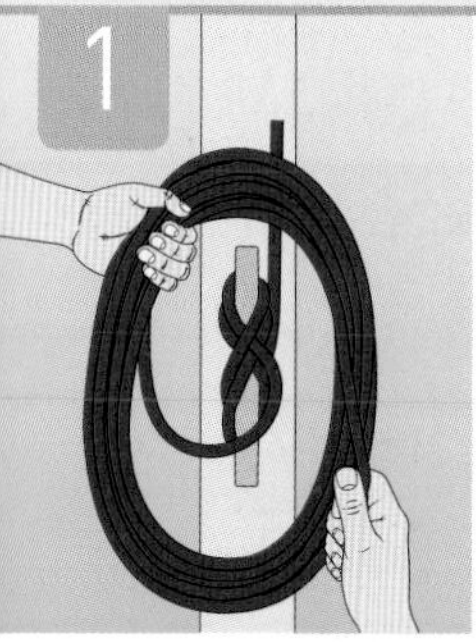

● **Cleat the halyard** and coil up the tail, starting from the cleat to avoid putting twists into the halyard, which may jam and be hard to remove.

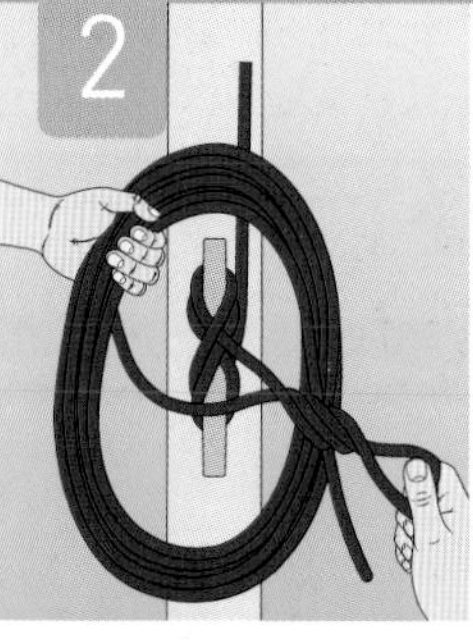

● **Grasp the part** of the halyard that leads to the cleat and bring it through the coil centre, twisting it once or twice.

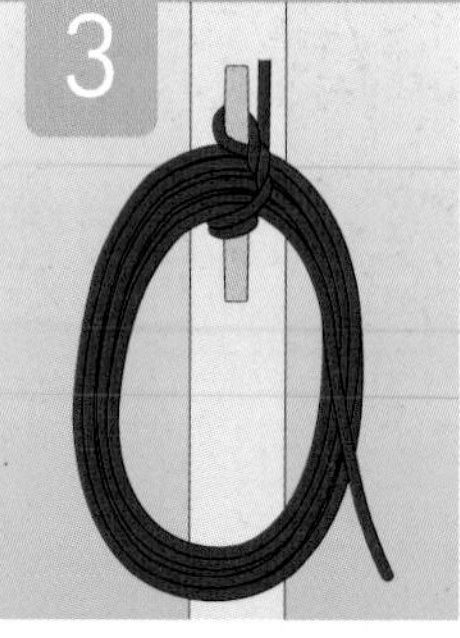

● **Pull the twisted** loop over the coils and drop the loop over the top horn of the cleat to hold the coils securely.

Figure-of-eight

A stopper knot is used in sailing to ensure that the end of a rope cannot run out through a block or fairlead. The basic stopper knot is the figure-of-eight. Simple and effective, it does not jam and is easily undone. It is most often used for retaining the end of a sheet.

• **Make a small loop** by crossing the working end over the standing part of the rope.

• **Hold the loop** in one hand and use your other hand to twist the working end under the standing part of the rope.

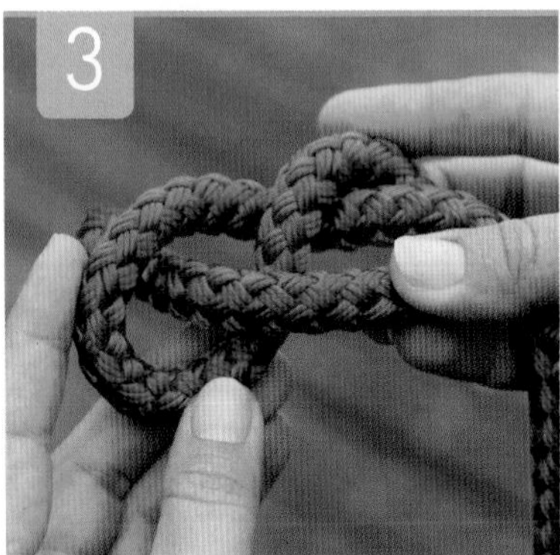

• **Feed the working end** of the rope down through the loop so that it makes a figure of eight.

• **Pull the end tight** to ensure the figure of eight is secure. The knot should take only a few seconds to tie.

Double overhand knot

The double overhand knot is an alternative stopper knot. Less versatile than the figure-of-eight knot, it can be difficult to untie. Its main advantage is that it can be made bulkier by adding extra turns – for example, if you need to stop a thin piece of rope from running through a large hole.

- **Make a loop** by crossing the working end under the standing part of the rope.

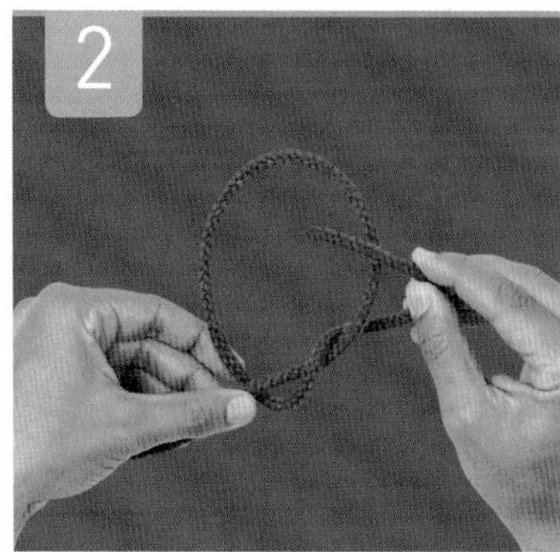

- **Pass the working end** through and over the loop twice.

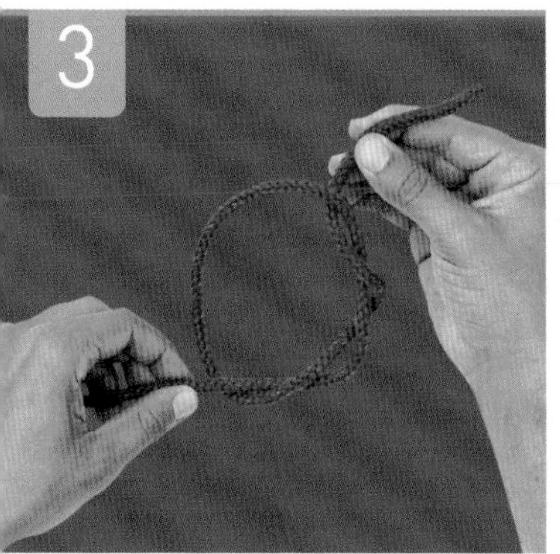

- **Pull the working end** through the loop.

- **Pull both ends tight** to create a secure knot.

Bowline

The bowline is a key knot for sailing. It forms a loop in the end of a rope and is secure under tension but quick and easy to untie. However, it cannot be untied under load. The bowline (pronounced bow-lynn) is particularly useful when mooring or tying a sheet to the clew of a sail. It is a useful skill to be able to tie it one-handed.

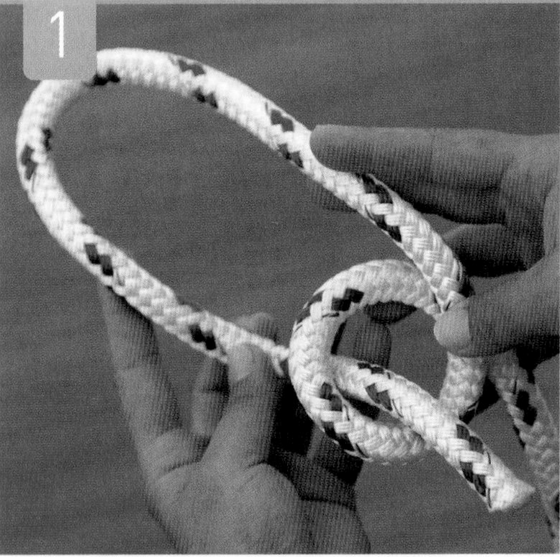

- **Make a loop** with the working end on top, hold it in place, and pass the end through the centre of the loop.

- **Holding the crossing turn** in place, take the working end under and over the standing part of the rope.

- **Still holding the crossing turn** in place, feed the working end of the rope back through the loop.

- **Pull the bowline tight** with both hands, ensuring there is not an excess of rope at the working end.

WHEN SHOULD I USE A BOWLINE?

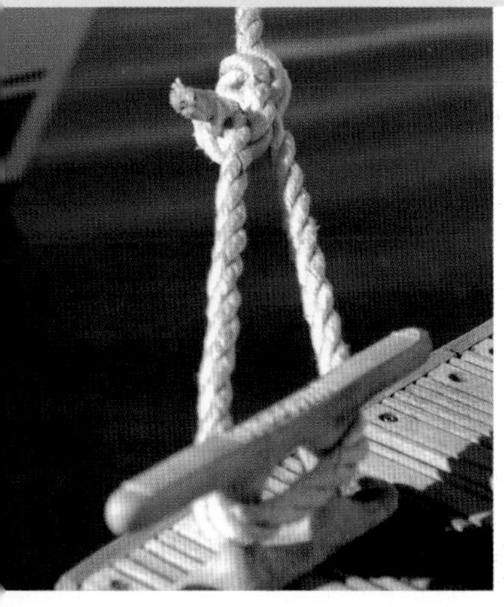

- **Mooring** Tied in the end of a mooring warp, a bowline can be dropped over a cleat on the pontoon.
- **Assisting man overboard recovery** Tie a large bowline in the end of a line to pass under the shoulders to secure the person to the boat or to lift him or her from the water.
- **Fastening** Attach jib sheets to the sail's clew with a bowline.

Round turn and two half-hitches

The round turn and two half-hitches is useful for tying fender lines to a rail, where it is much more secure than a clove hitch. It is also useful for tying a warp to a mooring ring. The principal advantage over the bowline is that it can be untied easily when the rope is under heavy load.

1

- **Make a round turn** by looping the working end of the rope twice round the mooring ring, post, or rail.

2

- **Pass the working end** over the standing part of the rope. Ensure the working end is long enough for this knot.

3

- **Take the working end** back under the standing part and over itself to form the first half-hitch.

Pull the first half-hitch tight, then repeat to tie the second half-hitch, which must loop round in the same direction as the first.

Pull the working end of the rope tight to close up the second half-hitch and lock the knot.

Always leave plenty of length for the working end when you tie this knot and slide the two half-hitches tight against each other.

Clove hitch

The clove hitch provides a quick and easy way to secure a rope to a rail, ring, or bollard. It is usually used for a short-term requirement, such as mooring a small tender or tying fenders to a rail. Be cautious about how you use it as it can easily come undone if there is repeated tugging on the rope.

- **Make a turn** with the working end of the rope, then pass it over the standing part of the rope.

- **Make a second turn** with the working end in the same direction as the first turn.

- **Feed the working end** of the rope under itself.

- **Tighten** the clove hitch by pulling on both the standing part and the working end.
- **Leave a long tail** on the working end to make it more secure.

- **To undo** the clove hitch, just push the working end and the standing part together to release the tension.

QUICK-RELEASE ALTERNATIVE

- **Tie the clove hitch** as normal up until Step 3. Then make a loop in the working end. Feed the loop under the last turn.
- **Tighten** by pulling the top of the loop and the standing part.
- **Undo** quickly and simply by pulling on the working end.

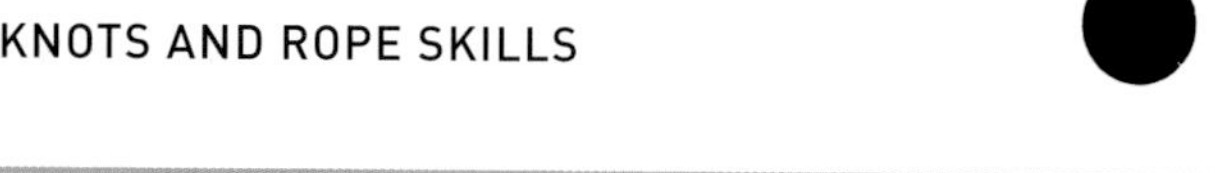

Reef knot

The original purpose of the reef knot was to tie the mainsail reefing lines securely together. Modern reefing systems mean a majority of modern yachts do not use reefing lines, but the reef knot is still useful when you need to tie the ends of two lines of equal diameter together – for example, when using sail ties to secure a sail.

- **Cross the two working** ends of the rope, with the left end (red) over the right end (blue).

- **Take the left working end** (red) and, with the forefinger and thumb, bring it under the right working end (blue).

• **Cross the left working end** (red) over the right working end (blue) and bring it up to create a loop.

• **Pass the left working end** (red) down through the loop and back towards you to form a reef knot, as shown.

• **Pull both ends taut** to close the knot. If in doubt, remember to tie the reef knot "left over right, then right over left".

Sheet bend

The sheet bend is a simple way of tying two separate pieces of rope together when you need to temporarily extend one – for example, when you need to row a mooring warp ashore using the tender and the warp is too short. Use the sheet bend for equal diameter ropes but tie a double sheet bend (see p.252) when the two ropes are of different diameters.

- **Make a loop** in the end of one rope (red). Pass the working end of the other rope (blue) up through the loop.

- **Continue** to feed the working end (blue) around the back of the initial loop (red).

• **Bring the working end** (blue) up under itself while crossing over the loop of the other rope (red).

• **Pull both pieces** of rope – the working end and the initial loop – tight in order to close the sheet bend.

• **Despite its simple appearance**, the sheet bend is a secure knot when kept under tension.

Double sheet bend

This knot is a useful variant on the sheet bend (see p.250) that is particularly recommended for joining ropes of different diameters, as shown here. It involves making an additional turn around the loop, which provides extra security when tying two ropes together.

- **Follow steps 1, 2, and 3** for the sheet bend (see pp.250–51), using the thicker rope (green) to form the loop.

- **Take a second turn** around the initial loop (green) with the thinner rope (white).

- **Cross the working end** of the thinner rope (white) over the loop of the thicker rope (green) and tuck it under itself.

- **Pull the ends** of both the thin and the thick rope tight in order to close the double sheet bend.

Fisherman's bend

This knot is similar to the round turn and two half-hitches (see p.244), but is more secure. It can be used for tying an anchor warp to the anchor, or for attaching a mooring warp to a ring on a pontoon or quay.

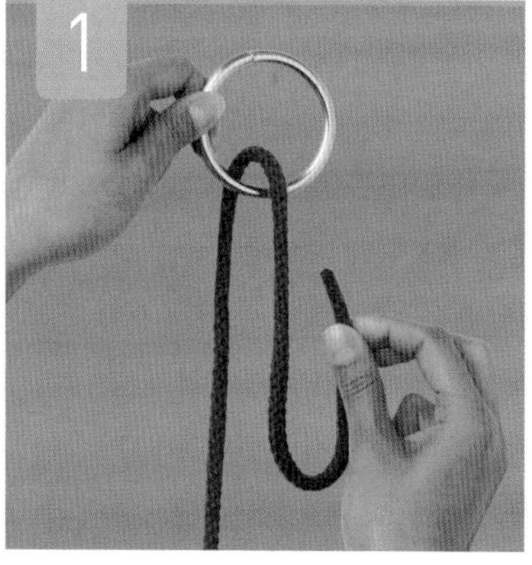

- **Bring the working end** of the rope forwards through the ring.

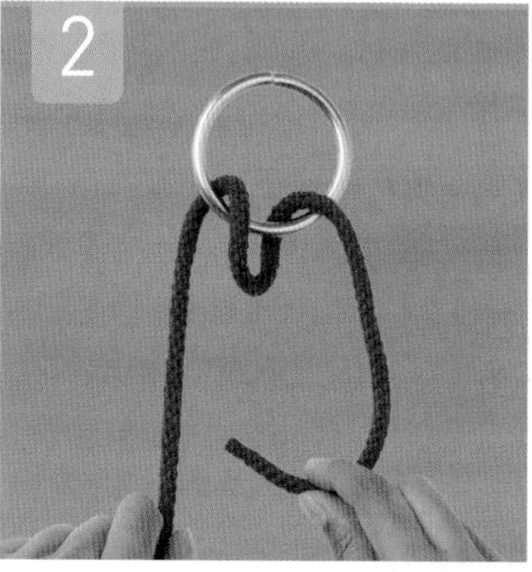

- **Take a turn** around the ring and bring the working end behind the standing part.

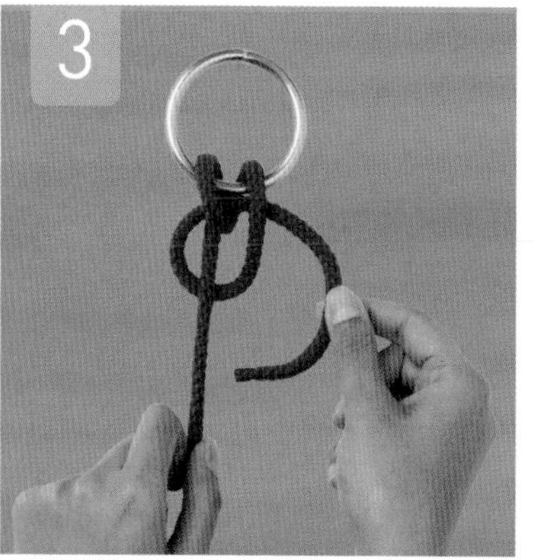

- **Pass the working end** through the loops around the ring and bring it behind the standing part.

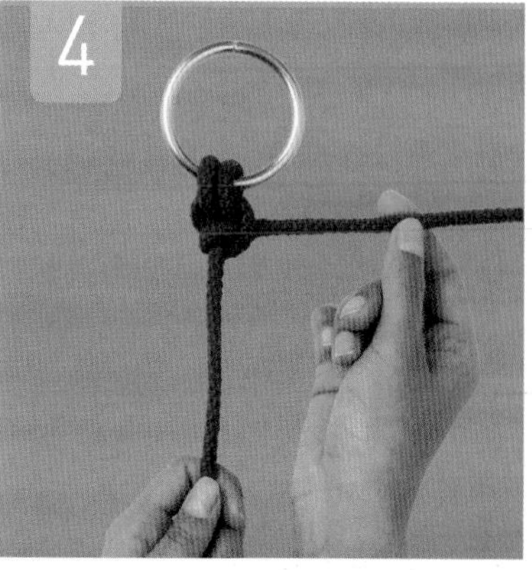

- **Take the working end** over the standing part and under itself. Pull both ends tight to complete the knot.

Sealing rope ends

If a rope end is left unfinished, it will quickly fray and will jam in blocks and fairleads. If not dealt with promptly, the rope will continue to fray or unravel and may become useless. The best and most permanent way to seal a rope end is with whipping twine, but a quick seal can be made with adhesive tape, shrink tubing, and proprietary sealants.

WHAT ARE THE TEMPORARY SOLUTIONS?

- **Liquid whipping** Proprietary liquids are available that will seal a rope end. Simply dip the end in the liquid and leave to dry.

- **Plastic tubing** Slide a suitably sized length of heat shrink tubing (available from chandlers) over the rope end, and apply heat until the tubing shrinks tightly around the rope end.

- **Glue** Dip thin ropes into a latex-based or polyvinyl acetate adhesive and leave to dry.

- **Plastic adhesive tape** Form a temporary seal by wrapping adhesive tape tightly around the rope end.

HOW TO TIE A COMMON WHIPPING

1

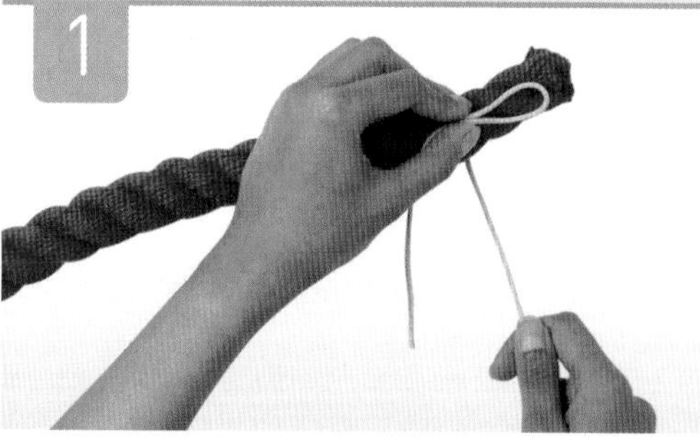

• **Form a loop** in the end of the whipping twine and lay it along the rope with the loop towards the end of the rope.

2

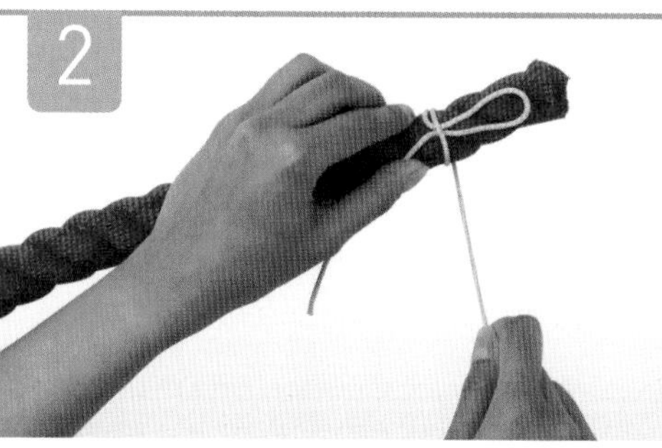

• **Wrap the long end** of the twine repeatedly around the rope, moving towards the rope end. Pull each turn tight.

3

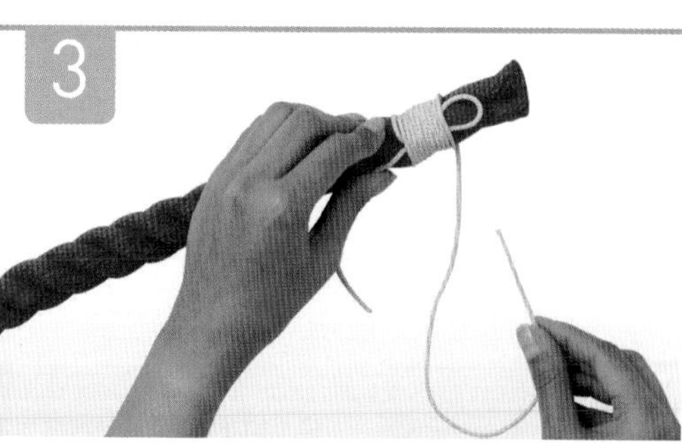

• **Pass the end** of the twine through the loop when the turns approach the end of the rope.

4

• **Pull hard** on the short tail of the loop to bury it under the turns. Trim both twine ends close to the whipping.

Sailmaker's whipping

This type of whipping is a secure method of binding the end of three-strand rope without the need for you to use a sailmaker's needle to sew twine. For a long-lasting result, make the length of the whipping about one and a half times the diameter of the rope.

1

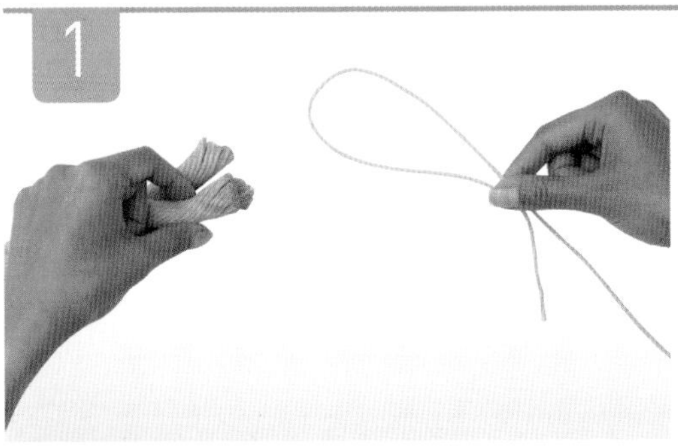

- **Unlay the end** of the rope and pass a loop of whipping twine over one of the strands.

2

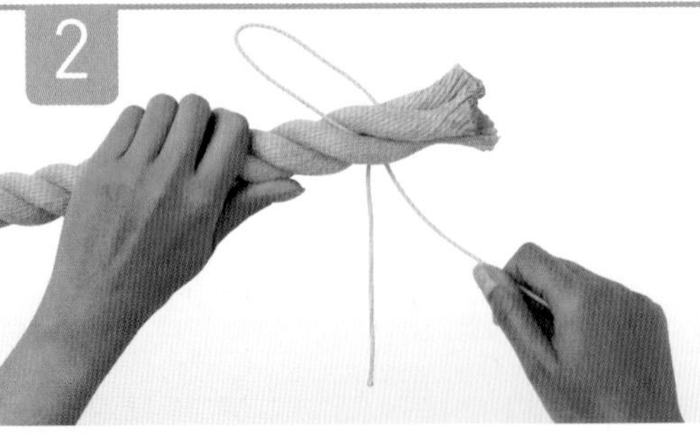

- **Relay the strands** of the rope with the loop protruding from the rope. Leave a short tail on the loop.

3

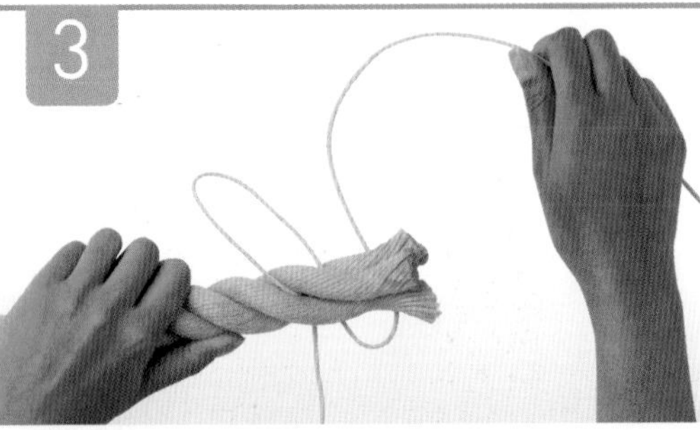

- **Start to wind** the long (working) end of the twine around the end of the rope.

4

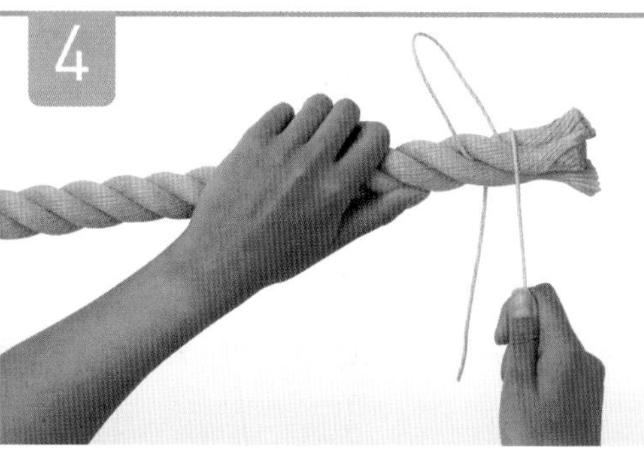

- **Continue to wrap** the twine tightly around the rope.

5

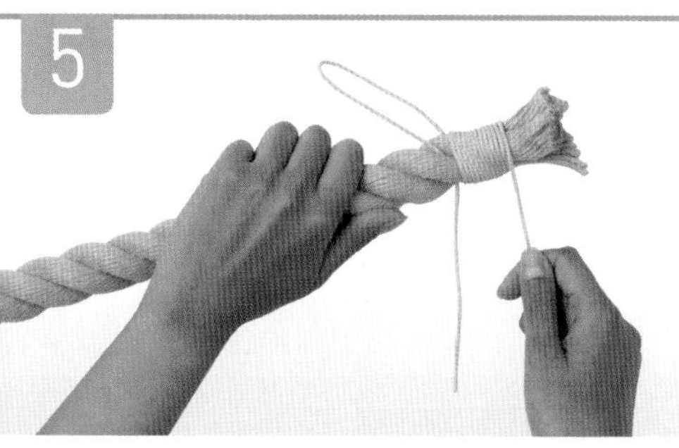

- **Work towards** the end, leaving the loop and tail free.

6

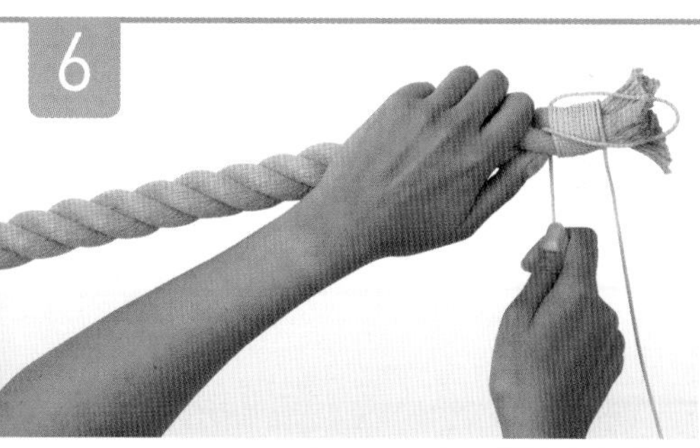

- **Pass the loop** over the end of the rope strand over which the loop was placed in step 1.

- **Pull the short tail** of twine until the loop tightens.

7

- **Take the tail** of the twine along the groove from which it emerges to the end of the whipping.

- **Tie a reef knot**, with the tail and the working end, in the centre of the strand ends. Trim the strand ends.

Seizing

Often used to create a loop in the end of braided rope, this technique binds two parts of a rope alongside each other. The friction that results from seizing two parts of the rope enables the loop to hold very heavy loads. You will need to use whipping twine.

1

- **Form an eye** in the end of the rope.
- **Tie a clove hitch** (see p.246) with a length of whipping twine around the two parts of the rope to be seized to each other.

2

- **Pass the twine** around the two parts of the rope in a series of turns, working away from the loop end.
- **Pull each turn tightly** as it is formed.

3

- **Continue making turns** until the length of the seizing is three times the diameter of the rope.
- **Take the twine** back to the start of the seizing, and bring the twine up between the two parts of the rope.

4

Pass the twine over the seizing and down through the eye in the end of the rope.

5

Pull the twine tight, then repeat steps 3 and 4.

6

Pass the twine between the two parts of the rope, and thread it under one of the turns.

7

Create a knot as shown by taking the twine through the turns you have just made. Pull the end tight so the knot disappears between the two ropes. Trim the end of the twine, leaving a short end.

Splicing

Use this method if you want to form a fixed eye in the end of a rope, as shown below, to join two ropes (or to join a rope tail to a length of wire), or to bind the end of a rope. Once completed, a splice is stronger than a knot and is permanent. An eye splice is used to form a fixed eye in the end of a three-strand rope such as a mooring warp.

WHAT TOOLS DO I NEED?

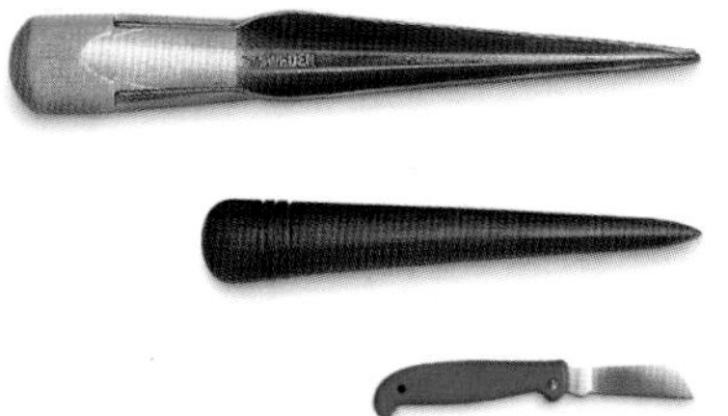

- **Swedish fid** This hollow-bladed tool is used for threading and separating strands when splicing.
- **Fid** This tool has a pointed end used to separate rope strands.
- **Sailor's knife** The straight blade of this knife gives neat cuts.

MAKING AN EYE SPLICE

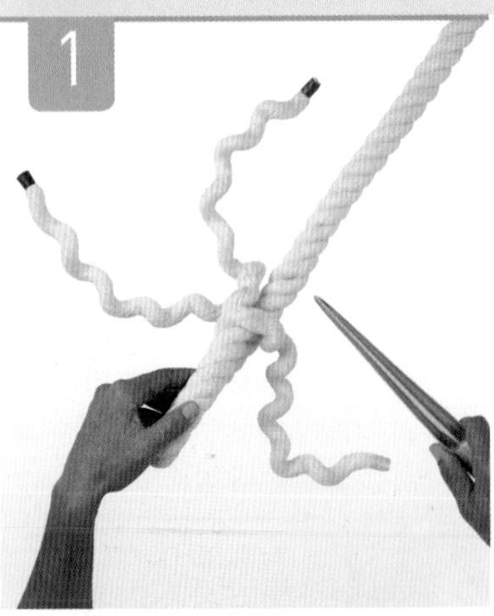

- **Separate the rope strands** some way back from the end and form an anticlockwise loop of the size required for the eye.

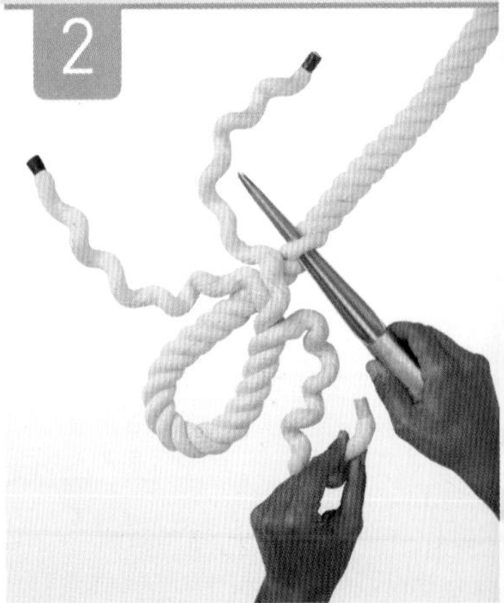

- **Take the end** of the top strand and tuck it under a strand on the rope at the place where you want the eye to start.

3

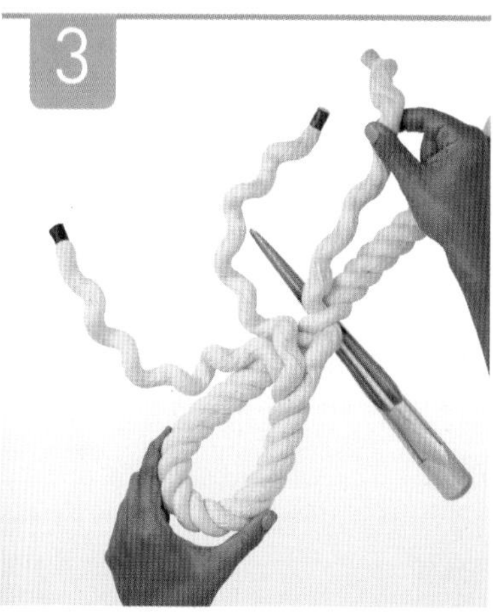

• **Turn the splice over** and tuck the end of the second strand under the next strand in the rope.

4

• **Turn the splice again** and tuck the third end under the third strand on the rope.

5

• **Turn and tuck**, repeating steps 2 to 4, up to three more times for maximum strength. Trim the ends.

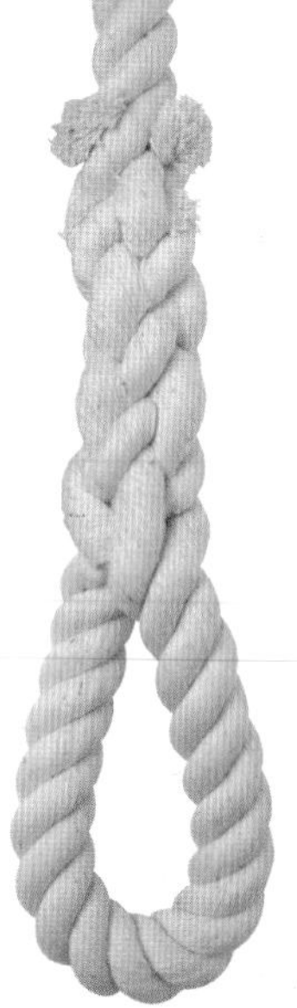

• **The finished eye** creates a fixed loop in the end of the rope.

Emergency procedures

Sailing is an active sport that has a good safety record. However, emergencies can occur, and you should make sure that you have learned the correct safety procedures and know how to use vital safety equipment.

OCEAN SAFETY

First-aid basics

The crew's welfare is the skipper's responsibility. If you are the skipper, be aware of any existing medical conditions among your crew, and whether medicines or treatment are required. Ask crew members to inform you of any condition that may affect their performance and ability to contribute to the sailing of the yacht.

FIRST-AID KIT – ACCESS AND CONTENTS

- **Easy accessibility** Keep the first-aid kit readily accessible and ensure that all crew members know where to find it.
- **Stowage** Keep it in a dry space close to the galley and the chart table area so it can be reached quickly.

Typical contents

A first-aid box should include:
- Sterile dressings
- Gauze pads
- Adhesive dressings
- A selection of bandages (with clips, tape, and safety pins)
- Scissors
- Tweezers
- Sterile wipes
- Disposable gloves
- Painkillers
- Thermometer
- A first-aid manual

Replace any items as soon as they are used and before they expire.

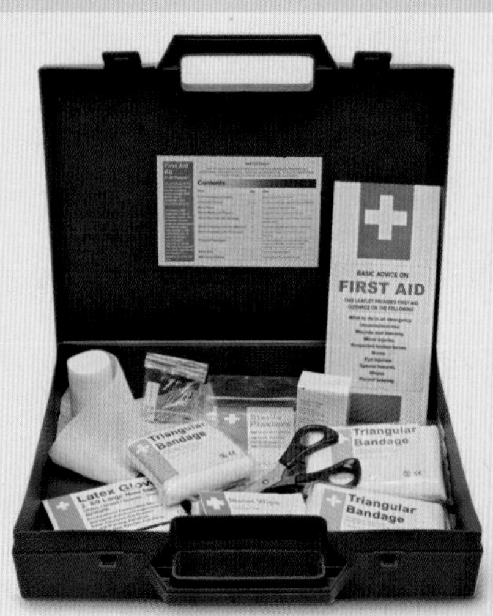

HOW AND WHEN TO USE THE RECOVERY POSITION

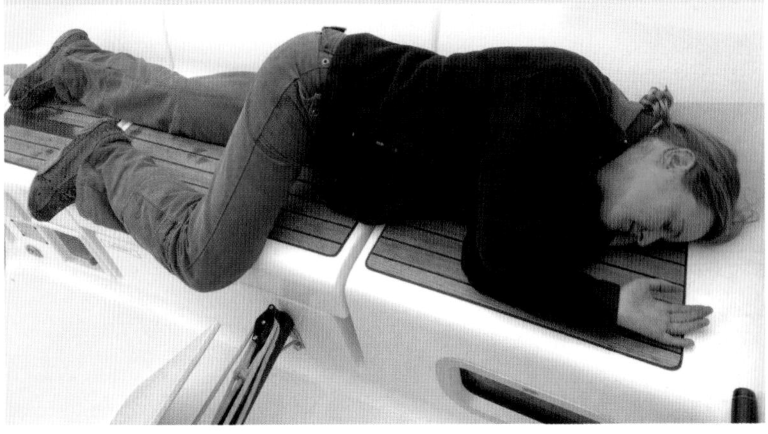

- **Put a casualty who is unconscious** but breathing in the standard recovery position. Use a cockpit seat, as shown here, a saloon berth, or the cabin floor.

- **Put the casualty** on his or her back and open the airway (see p.271). Position one arm at right angles to the body.

- **Place the back of the other hand** against the cheek. Bend the leg on the same side.

- **Roll the casualty** towards you by pulling on the bent leg. Bend the upper leg at right angles to support the casualty.

- **Monitor the casualty** for any changes while waiting for help.

TREATING CUTS AND GRAZES

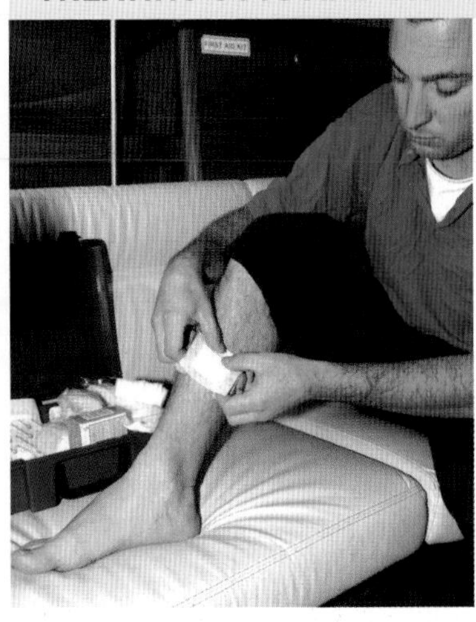

- **Treat cuts and grazes** to stop any bleeding and prevent infection.

- **Raise the injured part** and rinse the wound with fresh water to remove salt and dirt.

- **Use sterile gauze swabs** to clean around the wound, then gently pat the wound dry.

- **Use an adhesive dressing** to cover a small wound, and a dressing and bandage for a larger wound.

TREATING BURNS

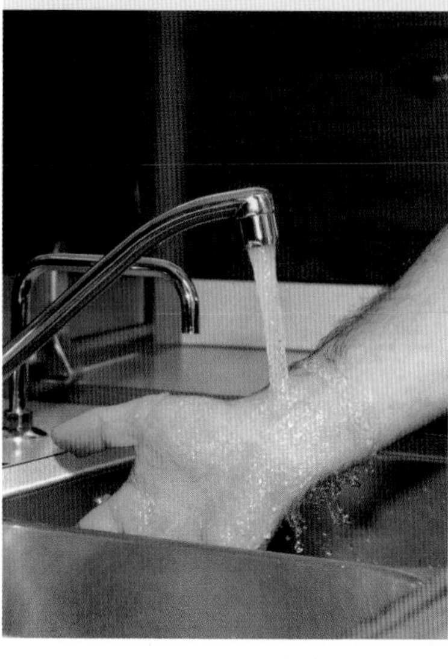

- **Hazardous** Burns are a hazard on a boat, especially in the galley and around the engine.

- **Degree of burn** A burn may be superficial or affect deeper layers of the skin. Burns can be very painful and there is a risk of shock (see p.270) developing through fluid loss.

- **Treatment** For all but small superficial burns consult a doctor as soon as possible. Immediately cool the area using cold water for 10 minutes or until pain ceases, and cover it with plastic kitchen film or a loose sterile dressing.

WHAT TO DO FOR SPRAINS AND STRAINS

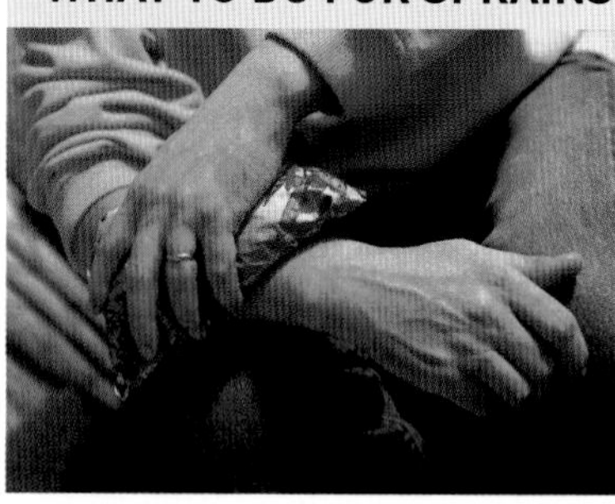

- **Sprain** This type of injury occurs when the ligaments that support a joint are damaged.

- **Strain** Damage to the muscles or their tendons can occur if they are stretched or torn. This can be very painful and the injury may be mistaken for a broken bone.

- **Swelling** The area around a sprain or strain swells and any movement will make the pain worse. Later, bruising develops.

- **Rest** For both sprains and strains, rest and raise the injured limb.

- **Cool** Place a cold compress (a packet of frozen peas wrapped in a cloth is ideal) over the area to cool it and minimize bruising.

- **Compression** Wrap the injured area in padding and apply a crepe or conforming bandage that extends from the joint below the injury to the joint above.

- **Dislocation** This is caused by a twisting strain that displaces the bones of a joint. There may be a sickening pain and the joint may be immobile. The area will look deformed and will swell. Immobilize the limb in the most comfortable position for the casualty; use a sling if necessary.

HOW TO DEAL WITH FRACTURES

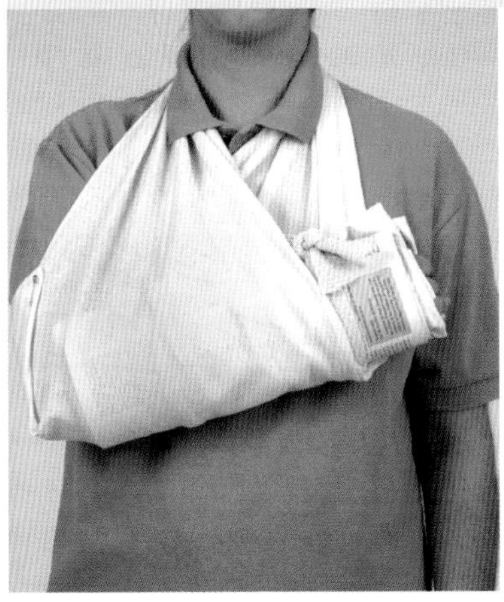

- **Broken bone** If you suspect a fracture, avoid unnecessary movement, immobilize the limb (a rolled-up newspaper can make an improvised splint), and seek medical aid.

- **Support** Splint an arm or leg to an uninjured part of the body. Support an arm injury with a sling. If there is an open wound, first cover the area with a sterile dressing.

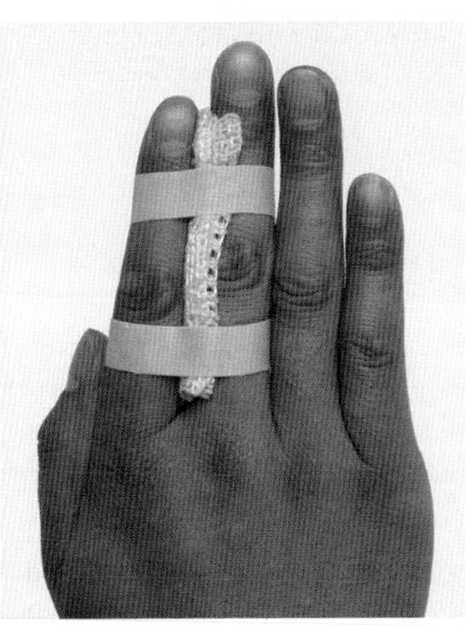

- **Broken finger** Immobilize a broken finger by strapping it to adjacent fingers with plasters or a bandage.

- **Leg injury** Bring the uninjured leg to the injured leg. Place padding between the legs and rolled towels on either side. For extra support, secure folded triangular bandages at the knees and ankles.

CARING FOR A HEAD INJURY

- **Medical assistance** An impact with a boom is a common cause of head injuries on boats. A scalp wound, fracture, concussion, or brain tissue damage can result. A head injury is potentially serious. If the casualty has lost consciousness, always call for medical help.

- **Watch out** Stay alert for signs of deterioration, such as drowsiness, nausea, vomiting, and dilated or uneven pupils, which may not develop for hours.

- **Keep awake** Avoid letting the casualty sleep until certain he or she has completely recovered.

HOW TO DEAL WITH HYPOTHERMIA

● **What is hypothermia?** This is a dangerous condition that occurs when the body's temperature drops below 35°C (95°F).

● **Symptoms** Intense shivering and difficulty with speech are signs of hypothermia. Further heat loss leads to physical and mental incapacity, eventual loss of consciousness, and possible death.

● **Immediate action** Aim to prevent further heat loss and warm the casualty gradually. Move him or her into a sheltered area. Replace wet clothes with dry ones. Wrap him or her in a space blanket or sleeping bag, and keep the head warm. Do not use a hot water bottle to give warmth. Get medical assistance.

● **Warm drinks** If the casualty is fully conscious, give warm drinks and high-energy food.

HANDLING HEATSTROKE AND HEAT EXHAUSTION

● **What is heatstroke?** This life-threatening condition occurs when the body's temperature control system fails – after prolonged exposure to heat and humidity.

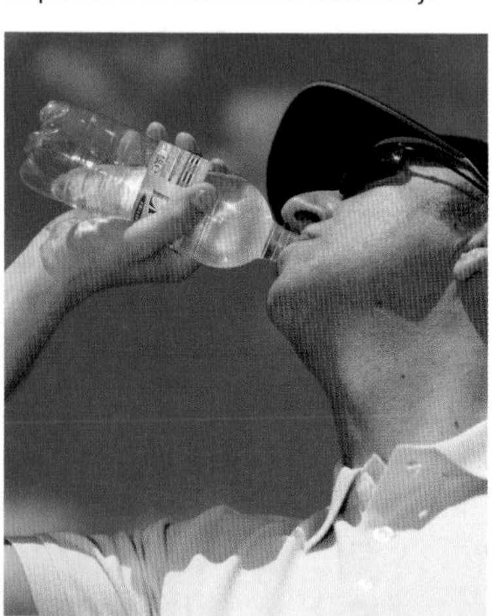

Symptoms include raised body temperature, flushed and hot skin, headache, dizziness, and fast, shallow breathing. Urgent medical help is required.

● **What is heat exhaustion?** This is a milder condition caused by overheating. It may cause profuse sweating, faintness, nausea, and headache. Look out for additional symptoms of heatstroke.

● **Action** For both conditions, try to lower the temperature quickly. Lay the person in a cool place with raised legs. In cases of suspected heatstroke, remove the person's clothes and cover with a cold, wet sheet and fan him or her. Encourage the person to drink plenty of water.

PREVENTING AND TREATING SUNBURN

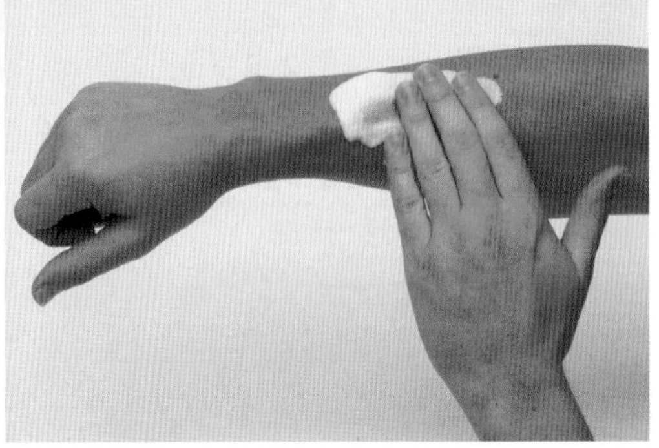

- **Prevention** Always use sunblock and wear a hat and long-sleeved shirt to avoid sunburn.

- **Treatment** If you get sunburnt, cool the area with fresh water, cover the skin with light clothing, and move into the shade.

SEASICKNESS – WHAT TO DO

- **Cause** Seasickness is caused by disturbance to the body's balance mechanism.

- **Anti-seasickness medication** Always carry anti-seasickness medication aboard, and take a preventive remedy before sailing or the onset of rough weather. These medications take time to work and will not be effective once sickness has begun. Some products may cause drowsiness.

- **Alcohol and food** Avoid over-indulgence in rich food or alcohol before you start sailing.

- **Fresh air** If you start to feel sick, sit where there is a good supply of fresh air and keep your eyes on the horizon – this helps the sense of balance.

- **Distraction** Take your mind off your feelings of sickness by getting involved in tasks on deck.

- **Stay warm** Avoid becoming cold or damp. Go below if you start to feel cold and lie down and keep warm until you feel better.

- **Snacks** Nibble dry food to reduce feelings of nausea.

- **Activities to avoid** Try not to work at the galley or at the chart table if you are feeling sick.

- **Extreme cases** If a member of the crew is suffering from severe seasickness, he or she can become weak and immobilized. In this case, if you are the skipper, you should return to harbour as speedily as possible.

HOW TO DEAL WITH SHOCK

- **Shock** This serious medical condition is caused by a dramatic fall in blood pressure. This can follow any serious injury, severe blood loss, dehydration, or, more rarely, a serious allergic reaction.

- **Symptoms** Key symptoms of shock include a rapid pulse, grey-blue lips, and a cold and clammy skin. Further symptoms may include weakness, giddiness, nausea, thirst, and shallow and rapid breathing.

- **Treatment** The recommended treatment is to keep the casualty warm and maximize blood supply to the heart and brain by raising their legs above the level of the heart and loosening tight clothing.

- **Keep watch** Do not leave the casualty alone or allow them any food or liquid – just moisten their lips with a little water if required. Unless their condition improves rapidly, get medical help as soon as possible.

NEAR DROWNING – WHAT TO DO

- **A risk of sailing** Drowning – death as a result of immersion in water – is among the most serious risks you face when sailing. It is most likely to occur if someone falls overboard without a lifejacket.

- **Reduce the risk** The longer a person is in the water the greater the risk of drowning. This underlines the importance of practising man overboard manoeuvres (see pp.274–77).

- **Treatment** If you recover a person who is unconscious from the water, immediately open the airway and check breathing.

- **Resuscitation** If the casualty is not breathing, start CPR (right) without delay. Continue until breathing has restarted or until help arrives.

- **Recovery** Once breathing has restarted, place the casualty in the recovery position (see p.265) and treat for hypothermia (see p.268).

HOW TO PERFORM CPR

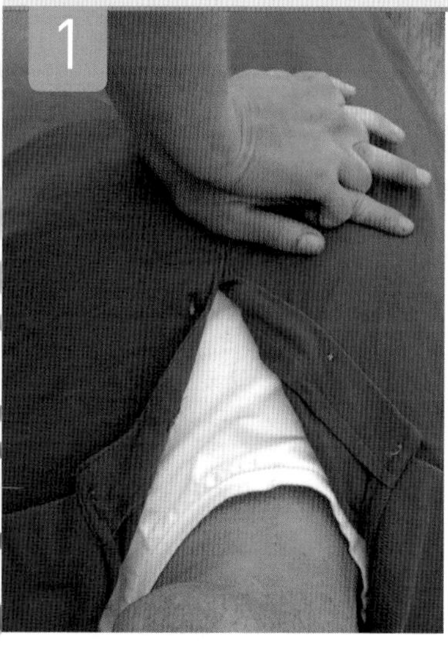

- **Give cardiopulmonary resuscitation** (CPR) to an unconscious casualty whose breathing has stopped – whatever the suspected cause – while someone else calls for immediate medical help.

- **Kneel beside the casualty** and place the heel of one hand on the centre of the person's chest, then place the heel of your other hand on top of the first and interlock your fingers.

- **Depress the chest** by about 5–6cm (2–2½in) 15 times at the rate of 100 compressions a minute.

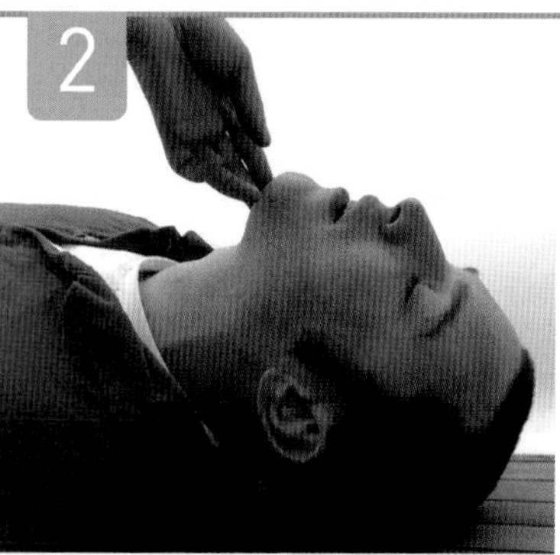

- **Open the airway** by tilting back the casualty's head by gently placing your hand on the forehead. Then lift the chin with your fingertips.

- **Pinch the nostrils**, take a deep breath, seal the casualty's lips with your lips, and blow in.

- **Repeat the cycle** of 15 chest compressions followed by two rescue breaths. Continue until help arrives, the casualty starts to breathe normally, or you are too exhausted to continue. If the person starts to breathe normally, place him or her in the recovery position (see p.265).

Onboard emergencies

You can help keep yourself, your crew, and your boat safe by careful planning and regular maintenance of the yacht's equipment and rigging. Calling out the rescue services should be the last resort. If an emergency does occur, you must be able to deal with the shock, stay calm, and instruct the crew in the immediate steps necessary.

WHAT ARE THE TYPES OF EMERGENCY?

- **Use judgment** A skipper must have a clear idea of what justifies a call for help. While this depends on experience, training also helps.
- **People emergencies** The most critical type involves injury or accident to the crew. These must be dealt with as soon as possible.
- **Get advice** Call the coastguard for help in any situation beyond the scope of simple first-aid skills and the onboard first-aid kit.
- **Boat emergencies** This is any incident that threatens the boat and crew. It may be a fire, collision, grounding, or equipment damage.

WHAT ARE THE FIRST STEPS?

- **Immediate action** Deal with the first shock of any accident. Put into action your pre-made plan.
- **Check crew** After any accident, you must check on the safety of your crew. Get them to focus on immediate steps. Your pre-sail safety briefing really pays off here.
- **Identify damage** Quickly identify the extent of damage and the threat resulting from it. Prioritize your actions accordingly.
- **Delegate work** If you are the skipper, give each crew member a job to do, depending on their experience and capabilities.

GETTING HELP

- **Choose your signal** If you require assistance, decide whether the situation demands an urgency signal or distress signal.
- **Urgency signal** This signal repeats the words PAN PAN three times before an urgent message concerning the safety of the boat or the crew (see p.160).
- **Distress signal** When you are in grave and imminent danger, use the distress signal. It repeats the word MAYDAY three times before the message (see p.160).

Do I need emergency help?

If an emergency arises on board, it is easier to deal with if you have thought through your reaction to a range of emergencies in advance and if you use a step-by-step process to confirm whether you need to call for help.

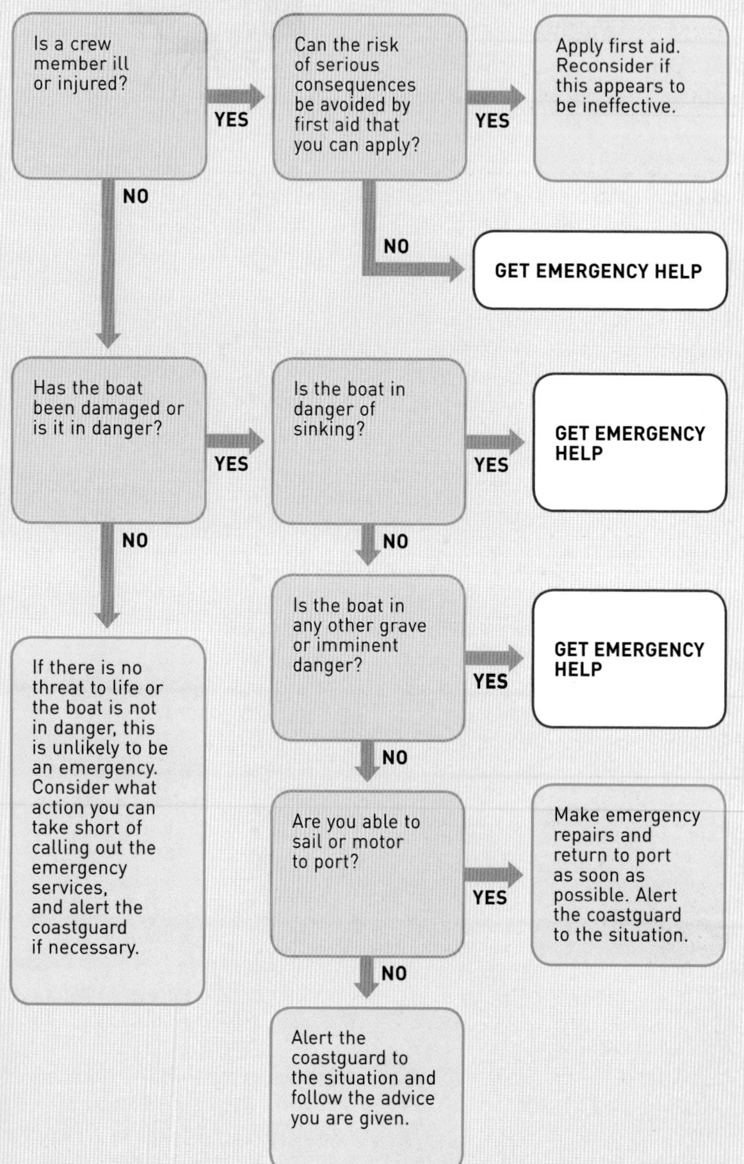

Man overboard

Having a man overboard (MOB) is one of the greatest fears of any skipper. If a person falls overboard, he or she is in grave danger, but prompt and efficient action can prevent a fatality. The skipper should brief the crew on what to do in this situation and practise both the "sail away and return" and the "crash stop" drills (see pp.275–77).

WHAT ARE THE IMMEDIATE ACTIONS TO TAKE?

- **Throw a heaving line** or, ideally, a lifebuoy and danbuoy (floating pole with flag), as shown here, if you can stop the boat close to the man overboard.
- **Keep the MOB** in sight. If you are the skipper, delegate one person to keep a constant watch and point at the MOB throughout the recovery manoeuvre.

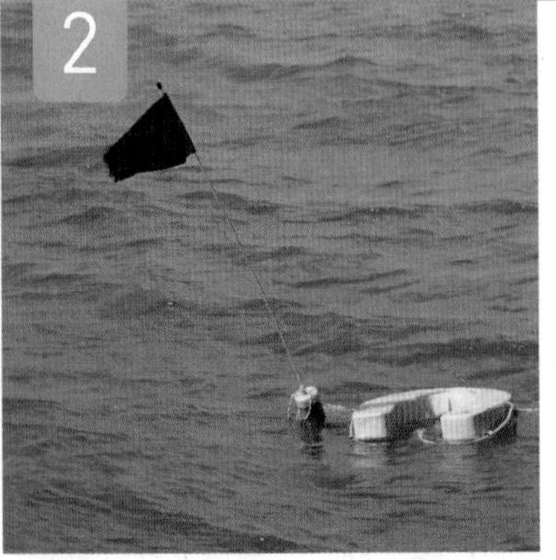

- **Pull the MOB back** to the boat if he or she is conscious and can reach the heaving line or lifebuoy. The danbuoy is easier to see than the lifebuoy from the water. It is also much easier to see from the boat than in the water.
- **Perform a recovery manoeuvre** if this is not possible for any reason. Use either the "sail away and return" or "crash stop" manoeuvres (see opposite).

HOW TO SAIL AWAY AND RETURN

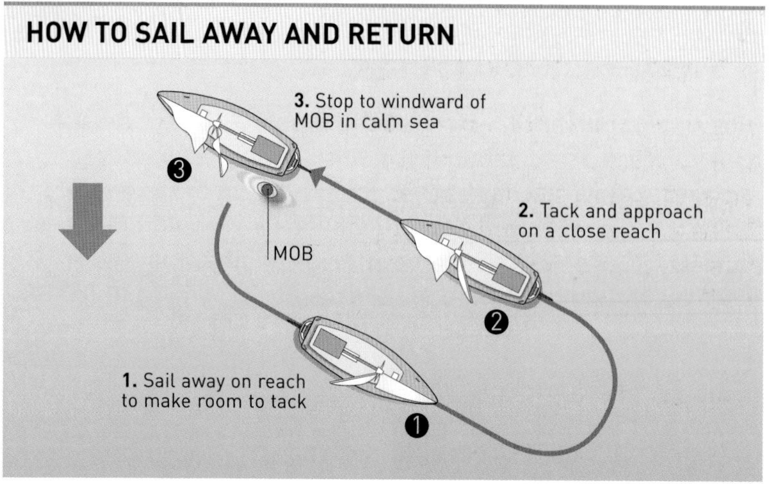

- **Sail away and return** When under sail, you can bear away to a broad reach, sail away to get space to tack, and return.
- **Approach** Head back to the MOB on a close reach and slow down by easing the sails. Stop to windward of the MOB if possible.

PERFORMING A CRASH STOP

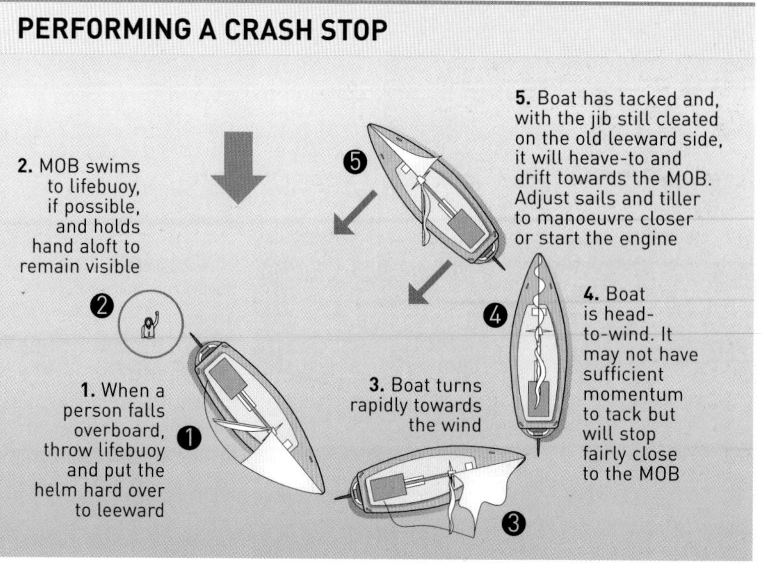

- **Crash stop** Use full helm to turn towards the wind. Depending on the course, the boat will tack or stop head-to-wind.
- **Use the engine** Check that there are no ropes in the water, then start the engine to help you manoeuvre. Consider dropping the mainsail and furling the jib.

Practising the drill

It is very important to practise the man overboard (MOB) drill as often as possible. It is useful to have a quick practice at the start of a passage to remind the crew of the preferred techniques on your boat and the location of the lifebuoys and danbuoy. Use a weighted fender as an MOB and avoid giving the crew notice of when a practice is about to take place.

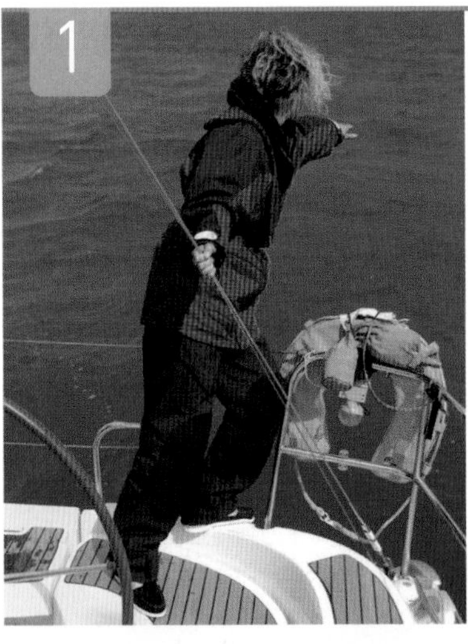

- **Make sure all crew** don lifejackets as they will be working in an exposed situation.
- **Call "Man overboard"** to alert the crew. If the MOB is not connected by a harness line, instruct a crew member to point continuously at the MOB to keep him or her in sight.
- **Deploy the lifebuoy and danbuoy** if the MOB is close enough to reach it.
- **Heave-to and stop the boat** at once if possible.

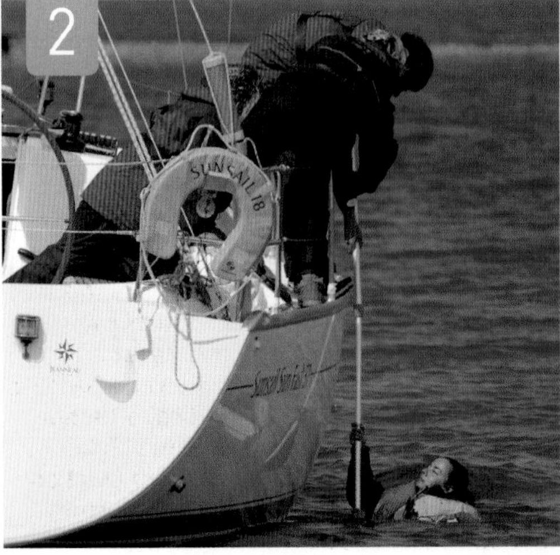

- **Complete your chosen manoeuvre** (see p.275) to bring the boat to windward of the MOB.
- **When you are close enough**, hold a boathook or an oar for the MOB to grasp. You can also use the boathook to hook the MOB's lifejacket or clothing to hold him or her alongside.

• **In calm water**, guide the MOB to the boarding ladder at the stern. In rough weather, this could be dangerous, with a risk that the MOB will be pushed under the stern.

• **Make sure** that the propeller is not turning when the MOB is near the stern. It is safest to stop the engine. In rough seas, recover the MOB from the side of the boat. It is usually easiest to do this from the leeward side, but it is not always possible. Use a halyard to hoist the MOB aboard.

• **Be ready** to help the MOB climb the ladder, which can be difficult in sodden waterproofs.

• **As soon as the MOB** is back on board, get him or her below and assess if medical attention is required. Take action to prevent and treat hypothermia (see p.268).

Fire on board

Fire is one of the worst emergencies that can happen afloat. If not dealt with very quickly and effectively, it can result in the boat burning to the waterline and sinking. As usual, prevention is better than cure, and you should understand the causes of fire and how to minimize the risks, as well as what to do if a fire does break out.

WHERE TO KEEP FIRE-FIGHTING EQUIPMENT

- **In the galley** Mount a foam or dry powder extinguisher in the galley and have a fire blanket mounted right by the stove for smothering pan fires.
- **In the engine compartment** Fit a fire extinguisher (this can be manual or automatic).

Which fire extinguisher?

The choice of the correct fire extinguisher for the type of fire is essential for effective fire-fighting. If you are the skipper, know how and when to use each type of extinguisher and brief the crew thoroughly in their use (see p.24).

TYPE OF FIRE	EXTINGUISHER AND USAGE
Combustible materials	Foam or dry powder extinguisher. Aim extinguisher at the base of the fire.
Engine fire	CO_2, foam, or dry powder extinguisher. Turn off fuel supply at tank.
Electrical fault	CO_2 or dry powder extinguisher. Turn off battery system at isolating switch.
Cooking fire	Foam or dry powder extinguisher, or fire blanket. Use the blanket to smother flames.

PREVENTING AND DEALING WITH A FIRE ON BOARD

- **Causes** Fire on board is most typically the result of a cooking accident, an electrical fault, or an explosion in the gas (see p.147) or fuel supply.

- **Prevention** Avoid bringing naked flames near gas fittings, and do not run the engine or other machinery when refuelling or when working on the engine. Keep all fire-fighting equipment well maintained.

- **Speed** Combat the fire as soon as it starts, to bring it under control with minimum damage.

- **Explosions** There is little to be done in the event of an explosion, as it is likely to destroy the boat. Prevent such an eventuality by fitting and maintaining the gas and fuel supply properly, and installing a gas detector with a loud warning bell.

- **Evacuation** If a fire starts, tackle the blaze immediately and have other crew retrieve additional extinguishers to fight the blaze. Other crew should move on deck away from any fumes.

DEALING WITH A FIRE IN A PORT

- **Fire services** Fires can occur as easily when moored as at sea. A fire in a marina will be attended by land-based fire services.

- **Moving boats** If a boat close by catches fire, immediately move your boat and any others away from the fire and keep the area clear for fire services.

Dismasting

The loss of a mast usually occurs when a piece of rigging or a terminal fitting gives way. This mostly happens in rough conditions, but can occur in calm weather if the fitting has been weakened earlier. The mast will fall roughly downwind as the sails pull it over the side. In this situation, it may be necessary to summon towing assistance.

WHAT SHOULD I DO?

- **Priority action** Check that the crew are safe and unhurt, then assess the situation.

- **Take care** Be careful when moving about on deck as the boat's motion will be jerky without the mast, so there is an increased risk of falling overboard.

- **Make safe** Get the broken pieces on board or cut away as fast as possible so that they cannot damage or pierce the hull.

- **Propeller alert** Do not start the engine until you are certain that there are no ropes, wires, or sails in the water. If your propeller is fouled, you will be disabled.

- **Slow the boat** Use the anchor to hold you in place if you are in danger of drifting onto the shore or a hazard.

- **Get help** Inform the coastguard as soon as you have assessed the situation and your requirements.

GETTING HELP FROM A RESCUE BOAT

- **Cautious approach** Whatever the type of accident, a rescue boat must look out for wires, ropes, and sails in the water near a damaged yacht. These could foul the rescue boat's propeller.

- **Give warning** Alert the rescue boat to any obstructions in the water and their location.

- **Extra help** A small rescue boat may be able to evacuate crew if necessary, and assist by calling for a larger towing boat.

PREPARING FOR A TOW

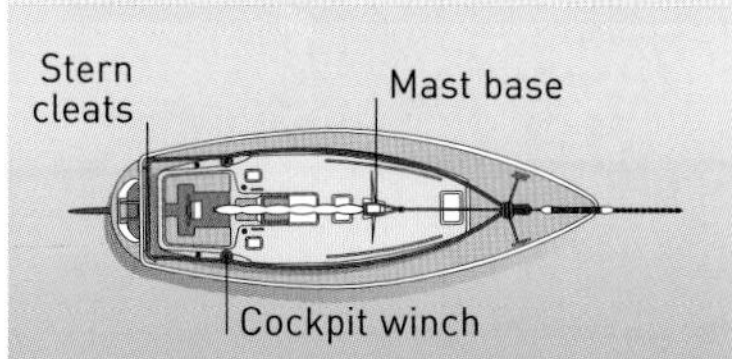

- **Spread the load** Attach the tow rope to all strong points including cleats, the mast base, and the sheet winches. Rig a bridle if it will be a long tow or if the water is rough.

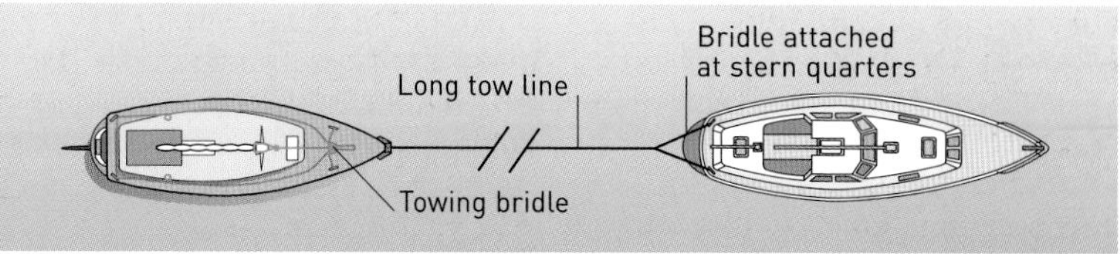

- **Sudden jerks** Use a long tow line to reduce sudden jerking that can break the rope or fittings. Nylon rope is a good choice because it is stretchy.

- **Steering** Rig a bridle at the stern of the towing vessel to allow it to steer without being hampered by the towed boat. Pad all areas where the rope and bridle may chafe.

Collisions at sea

A collision is most likely to occur in fog or poor visibility, but can also occur in clear conditions in busy waters, such as harbours, or when the crew are not attentive. When entering or leaving a harbour or marina, the crew on deck should be careful not to obscure the helmsman's view. If a collision does occur, it is vital to assess the situation quickly.

HOW CAN I AVOID COLLISIONS?

- **Pay attention** In crowded waters, boats and ships are often in close proximity, so keep an eye on other vessels and observe the Col Regs (see p.186).

- **Know the rules** Consider every situation and make sure you know whether you are the "give way" or "stand-on" vessel (see p.187).

- **Be ready to alter course** Have crew ready to ease or trim sheets to allow quick course changes.

- **Poor visibility** In fog or poor visibility, turn on navigation lights, make the right sound signal (see p.193), delegate crew to lookout duties, and hoist a radar reflector if you do not have a fixed one.

- **Stay out of channels** Where possible, stay out of shipping channels, especially in poor visibility. If you have to follow a channel, stay on the starboard side, as close to the edge as possible.

WHAT IF I EXPERIENCE A COLLISION?

● **Act immediately** If a collision occurs and your boat is holed, it is essential that you act speedily to stem an inflow of water. Use anything available that can fill the hole to slow down water ingress.

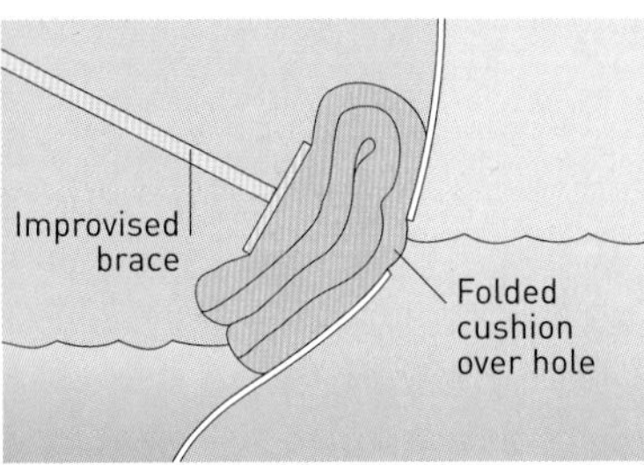

● **Small holes** Block these with soft wood or rubber plugs that you should be carrying aboard.

● **Padding** Fill a larger hole with soft materials such as cushions and mattresses, backed up with bracing to hold them in place. If the hole is below the waterline, there will be a lot of water pressure to overcome.

● **Bilge pumps** If the boat is holed, turn on the electric bilge pumps and delegate a crew member to work the manual bilge pump.

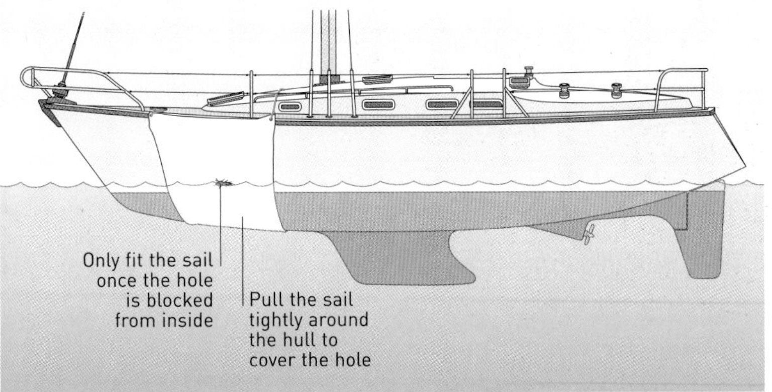

● **Bandage** Drag a sail over the hole on the outside of the hull; it will be sucked into the hole and will help to stem the flow. Secure it tightly in place.

● **Call for help** As soon as you have assessed the situation and taken immediate action to keep the boat afloat, call the coastguard and report your position and situation, or put out a general distress call, depending on the severity of the damage (see p.160).

● **Other damage** A collision may result in lesser damage, such as to the hull/deck joint, the rails, or the rig. First check for water ingress and crew safety, then decide whether you can make port under your own power or whether you need assistance. If you need help, call the coastguard using VHF radio (see pp.158–59).

Signalling for help

Distress signals are only ever used when a boat or crew member is in grave danger and immediate assistance is required (see pp.272–73). If you see or hear a distress signal, you must render assistance. Radio is the best way to summon help, but you may need to use flares (pp.286–87) or flags if this is not functioning, or if you are in a liferaft.

WHAT IS GMDSS?

- **GMDSS** The Global Maritime Distress and Safety System is a worldwide maritime communications system that uses Digital Selective Calling (DSC) via radio or satellite systems.

- **Complex relay** An alert sent via DSC connects to GMDSS and initiates a chain of actions from the emergency services.

- **Distress alerts** GMDSS is designed primarily to be a ship-to-shore and ship-to-ship distress alert system, but also delivers other routine maritime information.

- **EPIRB link-up** GMDSS also provides for locating signals to be sent using emergency position indicating beacons (EPIRBs, see p.161).

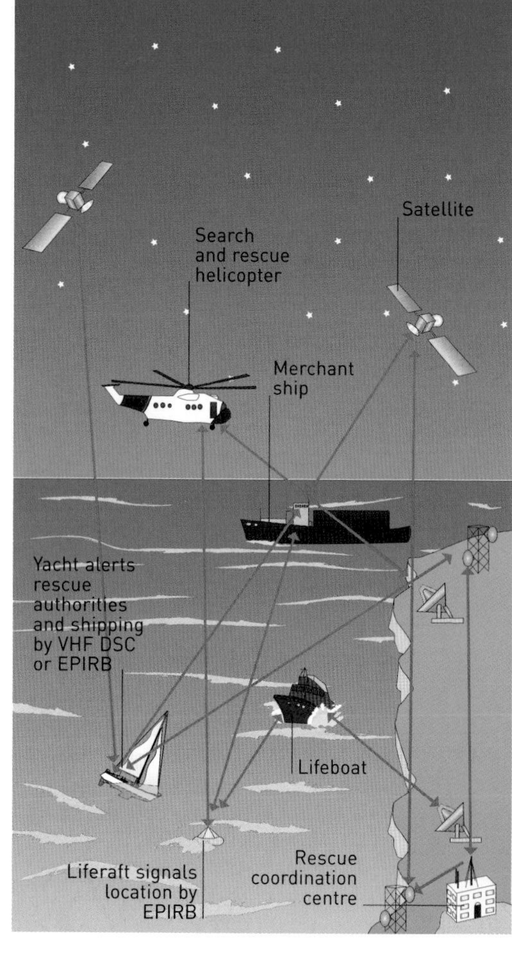

CALLING FOR HELP BY RADIO

- **Press the red DSC button** In an emergency, use the red DSC button on your radio to activate GMDSS. Operators will listen on the distress channel for a subsequent MAYDAY call. The DSC signal contains your yacht's MMSI number (see p.159) and GPS position.

- **Call for help** Summon help by alerting the coastguard, and other vessels, using emergency distress signals on Channel 16, including the MAYDAY signal (see p.160) for grave and imminent danger requiring immediate assistance.

- **Check regularly for new guidance** At present you can send distress alerts via Channel 16, but be aware that these procedures are being phased out, so make sure you and your crew are aware of any new developments.

USING FLAG SIGNALS

- **Flags and shapes** These methods of indicating the need for assistance are still used, but their importance has been reduced by the use of flares, radio, and, most recently, GMDSS.

- **Visibility** If you do carry flags, ensure that they are large enough to be seen from a distance. Flags are made of cloth, but painted boards can also be used.

- **Code flags N hoisted over C** This indicates "I am in distress and require assistance".

- **Code flag W** Hoisting this flag signals "I require medical assistance".

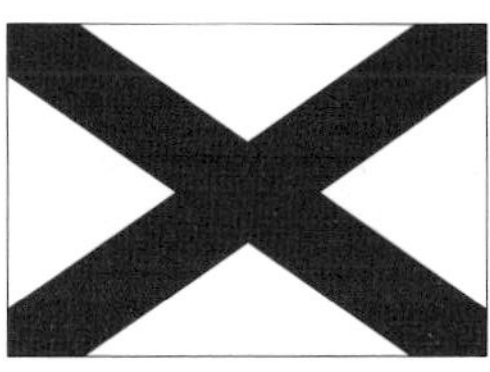

- **Code flag V** This code flag signals "I require assistance".

Black square over black ball These shapes indicate that "I require assistance".

TYPES OF FLARE

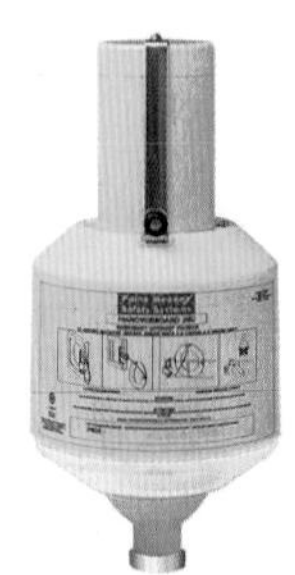

- **Red parachute flare** This fires a bright red flare up to 300m (1,000ft) that burns for about 40 seconds. Use it when you are far from help.

- **Buoyant smoke flare** This flare emits dense orange smoke for about three minutes. It is highly visible from the air and also shows wind direction.

- **Hand-held white flare** While not a distress signal, this flare warns other vessels of your presence. It burns for about 40 seconds. Stow one within reach of the helmsman.

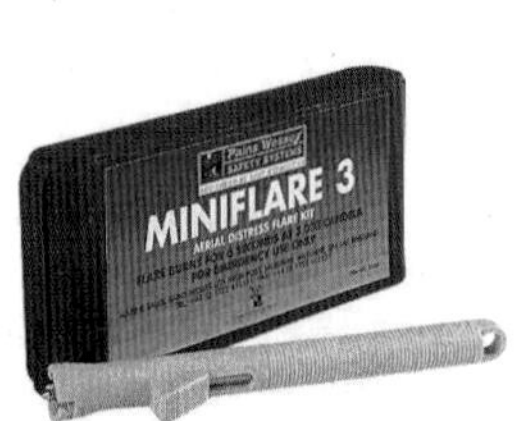

- **Mini-flare** For personal use and kept in the jacket pocket, it is ideal for use in tender. It fires eight red flare cartridges, for day or night – visible 8–16km (5–10 miles).

- **Hand-held red flare** This burns with a bright red light for about 60 seconds with a range of about 5km (3 miles). Use it to indicate your exact position to a nearby rescue boat.

- **Hand-held smoke** This flare emits bright, dense, orange smoke and is best used in daylight, good visibility, and light winds.

USING FLARES

- **Attract attention** Use flares to raise the alarm to a distress situation on your yacht or liferaft and to pinpoint your boat's position to rescue services.
- **Ready supply** Keep sufficient flares of various types (opposite) and ensure that they are within their expiry date.

HOW IS A FLARE FIRED?

- **Hand-held flares** These emit burning embers, so always hold them downwind, at arm's length and tilted away from your body. Avert your eyes to avoid being temporarily blinded by the light.
- **Parachute flare** When firing, turn your back to the wind and fire the flare downwind at an angle of about 15 degrees to the vertical. The flare will turn into the wind as it rises. However, if there is cloud, fire the flare at about 45 degrees to keep it under the cloud base where it can be seen. Never fire a parachute flare if there is a helicopter nearby.

MAKING AN SOS SIGNAL

- **SOS signal** This can be signalled by sound or light. The rapid sounding of a horn is also recognized as a distress signal.

Liferaft procedures

Speed is vital if you have to abandon a sinking yacht and a liferaft is the only option you have. First, prepare the raft for launching and ensure that the crew are in their warmest clothing, with waterproofs, harnesses, and lifejackets. If time allows, the crew should gather items that may be useful in the raft. Consider a sea survival course to learn best practice.

LAUNCHING AND BOARDING A LIFERAFT

1

- **Cut or untie** the lashings of the liferaft when you are ready to launch it.
- **Tie its painter** to a strong point on the vessel, as this is needed to inflate the raft.
- **Have two people** to launch the raft, if possible, as rafts are quite heavy and bulky. Some yachts have a raft locker built into the transom, which ensures that launching is straightforward.

2

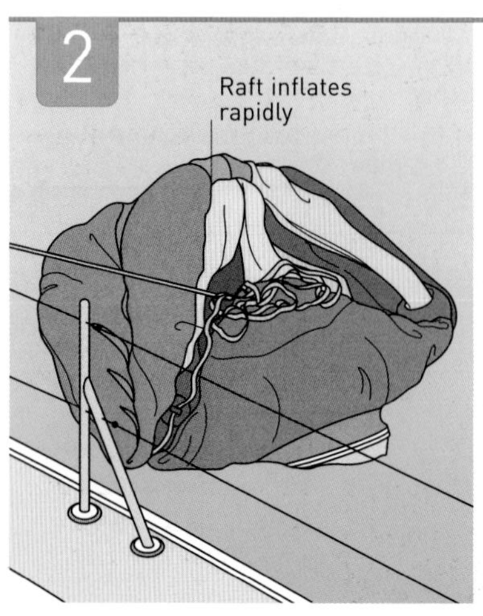

- **Throw the liferaft** over the side of the yacht. Tension on the painter should cause the raft, to inflate, but you may need to give a sharp pull on the line to ensure it will inflate.
- **If the raft inflates** upside down, you must correct its position before boarding.
- **Be ready to board** immediately. In a strong wind or a rough sea, an inflated raft cannot be towed or held alongside for long periods without damage.

3

- **Board the liferaft** directly from the deck of the yacht if possible. It is much harder to get into the raft from the water.
- **Heavier people** should transfer first to make the raft as stable as possible for the other crew.
- **The first person** to board the raft should move into the raft to balance it and clear the doorway for the next person.

4

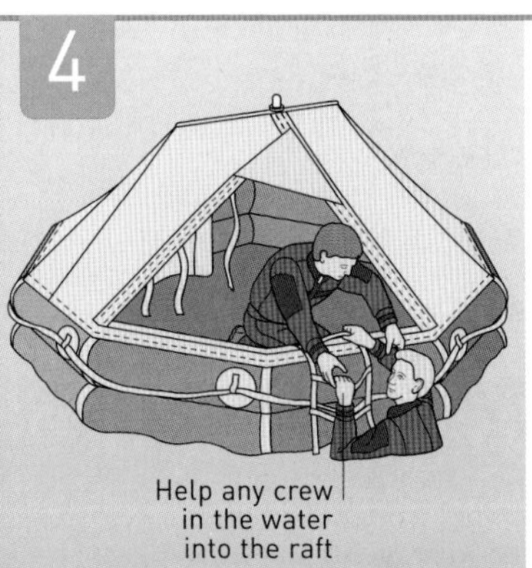

- **Help any crew** in the water to board the liferaft. Other crew in the raft should balance it as the person is helped in.
- **When all the crew** are in the raft with spare equipment and the grab bag (see p.25), cut the painter to release the raft from the yacht.

WHAT TO DO IF YOU NEED RESCUE FROM A RAFT

- **Attracting attention** Use a VHF radio, an EPIRB (see pp.158–61) if available, and flares to attract attention.
- **Means of rescue** Rescue from a liferaft is likely to come from a helicopter, lifeboat, ship, or another yacht.
- **Rescue procedures** Obey the instructions of your rescuer as speedily as possible.

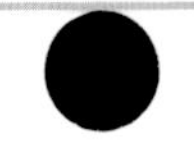

Rescue at sea

If you are involved in a rescue by marine services, such as a lifeboat or coastguard helicopter, remember that they are the experts – follow their instructions, and do exactly as they say. If your rescuer is another yacht, you will need to assess if the skipper's skill at manoeuvring close by and providing assistance is sufficient for the job.

RESCUE BY ANOTHER VESSEL – WHAT CAN I DO?

- **Hazard alert** Always advise an approaching boat of hazards such as ropes or sails in the water.
- **Towing warp** Prepare your own towing warp and attach it to several strong points, such as deck cleats, anchor windlass, mast base, and cockpit winches to spread the load. Use a long nylon warp to tow, as its stretch will help absorb shock loads without snapping.
- **Knots** When securing the tow line, avoid using knots or loops that cannot be released under load (see pp.240–53). Protect the tow rope from chafing against a fairlead or bow roller – for example, with plastic tubing.
- **Salvage fees** If you accept a tow from a commercial or private vessel, check whether a fee is expected, or you may be vulnerable to a claim for salvage.
- **Self-help** The more you can help yourself by supplying your own warp and controlling the rescue, the less vulnerable you will be to a salvage claim.
- **Use a drogue** If your rudder has failed, tow a drogue or long loop of heavy rope behind the boat to help to hold it on a straight course under tow.
- **Avoid side-by-side towing** Never use a side-by-side tow in anything but completely flat water and then only for a short distance.

HELICOPTER RESCUE – WHAT TO KEEP IN MIND

- **Helicopter rescue** Yachtsmen who get into serious difficulties may require search and rescue services provided by helicopter.

- **Speed** Helicopters provide a vital alternative to a lifeboat since they can get to a rescue location quickly, take off crew in hazardous sea conditions, and transport them quickly to medical facilities.

- **Flares** Use red or orange hand-held flares (see pp.284–85) as a signal to the helicopter, if you have summoned air rescue and this signal has been requested (orange smoke by day and red by night). Do not fire parachute or mini-flares, which can be dangerous to the helicopter.

- **Listen carefully** Make sure you understand instructions from the approaching pilot on VHF, which will include the course and speed he or she wishes you to follow – hearing the radio will be impossible once the helicopter is overhead.

- **Boat position** Align the boat head-to-wind (or nearly so), where possible, with all sails lowered, and ensure all crew wear lifejackets.

- **Winchman** If a winchman is lowered from a helicopter, follow his or her instructions exactly.

Glossary

A, B, C

aft Towards, at, or near the stern.

ahead In a forward direction.

anchor A heavy device attached to a boat by a rope (anchor warp) or chain cable and lowered overboard to secure a boat to the bottom.

anchorage An area with good holding ground where it is sheltered and safe to drop anchor.

anemometer An instrument that measures wind speed.

anticyclone Area of relatively heavy, sinking air that results in high pressure.

antifouling paint Special paint applied to the hull to prevent underwater fouling from weed and barnacles.

apparent wind The combination of true wind (that which we feel when stationary) plus the wind produced by motion.

astern (1) Backwards. (2) Outside and behind the stern of the boat.

backing the jib To sheet the jib to windward.

backstay Wire leading from the masthead to the stern.

balanced helm When a boat has a balanced helm, if you let go of the tiller, it will continue on a straight course. See *weather helm* and *lee helm*.

barometer Instrument used to register atmospheric pressure.

batten A light wooden, fibreglass, or plastic strip that slots into a pocket sewn into the aft edge (leech) of a sail.

beam reach Sailing with the wind blowing directly over the side of the boat.

bearing The direction of an object from your boat, or between two objects, measured in degrees relative to north. See *heading*.

bearing away Turning the boat away from the wind; opposite of luffing (or luffing up).

beating To sail to windward close-hauled, and zigzagging to reach an objective to windward.

Beaufort Scale A descriptive scale used for measuring wind strengths.

berth (1) A place to park alongside a quay or pontoon, or in a marina. (2) A bed in the cabin.

bight (1) Bend in the shore making cove, bay, or inlet. (2) Bend in a rope.

bilge (1) The rounded parts of the hull where the sides curve inwards to form the bottom. (2) The area where water collects inside the boat.

binnacle A pedestal in which a compass is fitted and on which the wheel is usually mounted.

boathook Pole with hook used to pick up mooring buoy or ring when mooring or berthing.

boom A horizontal spar or pole, used to extend the foot of a sail and to help control the sail's angle in relation to the wind.

boom vang (or kicking strap) A tackle or strut that prevents the boom from rising under wind pressure in the mainsail.

bow The forward end of a boat; opposite of stern.

bower anchor The main anchor on a boat.

bowline (pronounced "bow-lynn") A knot used to make a loop in the end of a rope or to tie to a ring or post.

bowsprit A spar projecting from the bow of some boats, allowing sails to be secured further forwards.

breast rope A mooring rope running at right angles to the boat, from bow or stern, sometimes used in addition to the four main warps to hold the boat alongside.

broach When a boat accidentally turns broadside to the waves.

broad reach Sailing with the wind coming over the port or starboard quarter of the boat.

buoy A floating marker used for navigation.

buoyage A system of navigation marks used to identify hazards and safe channels.

burgee A small triangular flag flown from the top of a mast, serving to indicate apparent wind.

cabin The living quarters below deck.

capsize When a boat tips over to 90° or 180°.

cardinal marks Forms of buoyage, used to indicate large or individual hazards in the water.

chart A nautical map.

chart datum The level from which soundings (depths) and drying heights are measured.

cleat A wooden or metal fitting that is used to secure ropes.

clew The lower aft corner of a fore-and-aft sail.

clew outhaul The rope or wire that adjusts the position of the clew and the tension in the foot of the mainsail.

close-hauled Sailing as close to the wind as possible, with the sails pulled in tight.

close reach The point of sailing between close-hauled and a beam reach.

clove hitch A knot used for short-term mooring to a ring or post, or for hitching fenders to a rail.

coachroof The raised cabin roof in the middle of the boat.

cockpit The working area, usually towards the stern of a boat, from which the boat is steered.

companionway A ladder or steps leading down from the cockpit to the cabin.

compass north The direction in which a compass points. If there is no local magnetic interference (see *deviation*), it will point to magnetic north.

control line A rope or line that adjusts a sail or part of the rig – such as the cunningham.

convection currents Air currents formed due to the land heating up and cooling down.

course made good The course achieved after allowing for leeway and tidal set and drift.

course steered The course actually steered by the helmsman and read off from the compass.

crew Either everyone on board, or everyone except the helmsman.

cringle A metal or plastic eye sewn into a sail.

crossing turn The term used when one part of a rope crosses another.

cruising chute See *gennaker*.

cunningham A control line for adjusting tension in the luff of a mainsail or jib.

D, E, F

danbuoy A floating marker pole with flag that is attached to a lifebuoy to improve visibility.

depression An area of low pressure.

depth sounder A device to measure distance from the seabed to the instrument's transducer.

deviation The difference between magnetic and compass north as a result of the effect of local magnetic fields on the boat's compass. Deviation varies with the boat's course, and is measured in degrees, east or west of magnetic north.

dinghy A small boat usually designed to be used by one or two people.

dip-pole gybe Method of gybing a spinnaker on larger cruisers and cruiser-racers.

direction Measured clockwise as an angle relative to north. See *heading* and *bearing*.

dismasting When the mast breaks. See *jury rig*.

displacement The weight of the water displaced by a floating hull.

downhaul A rope for hauling down sails or for controlling a spar such as the spinnaker pole; opposite of uphaul.

downwind (or offwind) All courses that are further away from the wind than a beam reach are known as downwind, or offwind, courses; opposite of upwind.

DR Dead reckoning position. It is plotted on a chart by drawing the course steered from the last known position and measuring off the distance sailed according to the log. See also *EP*.

drift The strength of a tidal stream; the distance the stream will move a floating object in an hour.

drogue An object towed, usually over the stern of a boat as a way of reducing its speed in heavy weather.

ebb tide When the tide is going out, between high and low water; opposite of flood tide.

eddies Circular current, the area of reversed current that forms behind a rock or headland in a current or tidal stream.

EP Estimated position. A DR (dead reckoning) position plus tidal set and drift. EPs are plotted at regular intervals on a chart and compared with a fix to identify any errors in plotting.

EPIRB (emergency position indicating radio beacon) Transmits distress signals to satellites that are part of the GMDSS.

fairlead A bolt, ring, or loop that guides a rope.

fathom An old unit of length for measuring water depth. One fathom is 6ft (1.8m).

fender A protector hung over the side between the boat and a pontoon or another vessel.

fiddles The raised lips on worktops in the cabin.

figure-of-eight A stopper knot, used to prevent a rope end running out through a block or fairlead.

fin keel A single, central, fixed, ballasted keel.

flogging When a sail flaps noisily it is said to be flogging.

flood tide The tide that is coming in; opposite of ebb tide.

fluke The barb or hook of an anchor.

foot The bottom edge of a sail.

fore At, near, or towards the bow.

foredeck The part of the deck nearest the bow.

forestay A wire that leads from the mast to the bow fitting. A headsail may be attached to it.

G, H, I

galley A boat's kitchen.

gennaker A sail that is a cross between a genoa and a spinnaker. Sometimes called a cruising chute.

genoa A large headsail that overlaps the mast and usually sweeps the deck with its foot. See *jib*.

gimbals Fittings that allow an object (such as a galley stove) to swing so as to remain upright when the boat heels.

GMDSS (Global Maritime Distress and Safety System) A set of standards to which modern radio sets, satellite communication systems, and EPIRBs conform.

goosewinging Sailing directly downwind (running) with the mainsail set on one side and the headsail set on the other.

GPS A global positioning system receiver that uses information from a network of satellites to determine and display a boat's position accurately.

GRIB Gridded binary data files; small files of weather information easily transmitted over the Internet.

ground track The course followed, relative to the seabed. See *water track*.

GRP Glass-reinforced plastic (fibreglass), from which many boat hulls are made.

guardrails Another term used for lifelines. See *lifelines* (1).

gunwale (pronounced "gunnel") The top edge of the side of the hull.

guy A rope that controls the spinnaker on the windward side. It runs through the end of the spinnaker pole.

gybing Turning the stern of the boat through the wind. See *tacking*.

halyard A rope or wire that is used to hoist a sail, flag, or other signal.

hank A metal or plastic hook that is used to secure a sail to a stay.

hatch A cover over an opening on deck.

head The top corner of a triangular sail, or the top edge of a four-sided sail.

heading The direction in which you are steering the boat measured by a compass. See *bearing*.

heads Sea toilet or the compartment that contains the toilet and washing facilities.

headsail A sail set on the forestay; a jib.

head-to-wind The point at which the boat is heading straight into the wind with the sails luffing.

heaving-to Bringing a boat to a halt, usually by sheeting the headsail to windward. After the event, a boat is described as "hove-to".

heel (1) When a boat tilts over to one side, it heels. (2) The heel of the mast is its bottom end.

helmsman The person who steers the boat.

hoist To raise a sail or flag.

horn cleat A metal, wooden, or plastic cleat with two horns around which the rope is wrapped to create sufficient friction to hold the rope fast.

hull The main body of a boat.

IALA International Association of Lighthouse Authorities, which organizes buoyage.

in-irons Stuck head-to-wind with sails flapping and no steerage.

inversion (1) Weather – when warm air lays on top of cold air. (2) Boat – capsizing so mast points vertically down.

ISAF International Sailing Federation – the international governing body of sailing.

isobars Lines on weather maps that connect points of equal pressure.

J, K, L

jackstays Lengths of webbing or wire that run the length of both sidedecks, to which the crew attach their tethers when working on deck.

jib A triangular headsail (a sail set in front of the forward mast).

jib sheets Ropes used to trim (or "sheet") the jib.

jury rig A makeshift rig that you construct to get you to safety following a dismasting.

katabatic winds Sinking currents of cold air that run down the slopes of mountains.

kedge anchor A lighter anchor than the main (or bower) anchor.

keel The lowest part of a sailing boat, used to resist sideways drift (leeway).

kicking strap See *boom vang*.

knot The unit of speed at sea, defined as one nautical mile per hour.

latitude The angular distance north or south of the equator. The lines of latitude are the grid lines on a map or chart running east to west, and parallel to the equator. See *longitude*.

lazy guy A leeward guy left slack (not in use) when using a spinnaker.

lazyjacks Restraining lines rigged from the mast to the boom to retain the mainsail when it is lowered and stowed on the boom.

leeboards (lee-cloths) Wooden boards (or canvas cloths) fitted along the inboard edge of a sea berth, to prevent the occupant from being thrown out of the berth in rough conditions.

leech The aft edge of a sail.

lee helm If a boat turns to leeward when you let go of the tiller or wheel, it has lee helm. See *weather helm* and *balanced helm*.

lee shore A shore onto which the wind is blowing; opposite of weather shore.

leeward Away from the wind; opposite of windward.

lifelines (1) Safety rails or wires fitted around the deck edge, supported by stanchions. (2) Another term for *tether*.

longitude The angular distance west or east of the Greenwich meridian. The lines of longitude are the grid lines on a map or chart running north to south. See *latitude*.

luff (1) The forward edge of a triangular sail. (2) A sail luffs, or is luffing, when its luff shakes due to the sail not being pulled in sufficiently. (3) To turn towards the wind.

luffing (1) When a boat is turned towards the wind (also known as luffing up). (2) When the luff of a sail shakes or flaps.

lying a-hull Drifting with all sail stowed.

M, N, O

magnetic north The direction to which a magnetic compass points. Magnetic north differs from true north and moves over time.

magnetic variation The angular difference between magnetic north and true north, which alters year by year as the magnetic poles move.

mainsail (pronounced mains'l) The principal fore-and-aft sail.

mainsheet The rope attached to the boom and used to trim (or adjust) the mainsail.

marlinspike A pointed tool used to loosen knots and assist in splicing rope.

mast A vertical pole to which sails are attached.

MAYDAY This is an internationally recognized radio distress signal for use when you are in grave or imminent danger. It takes priority over any other kind of message. See *PAN PAN*.

mean direction The term used to describe the average wind direction.

meridian A line of longitude that runs from north to south poles.

mooring A permanent arrangement of anchors and cables, to which a boat can be secured.

multihull A boat with more than one hull. A catamaran or a trimaran.

nautical mile The unit of distance at sea, defined as one minute (1') of latitude. It is standardized to 1,852m (6,076ft).

navigation lights Lights shown by a boat that indicate relative course, position, and status such as sailing, fishing, or towing.

neap tides Tides with the smallest range between high and low water; opposite of spring tides.

no-sail zone Since boats cannot sail directly into the wind, there is a no-sail zone on either side of the direction of true wind. The closest that most boats can achieve is an angle of 45° on either side.

occluded When a cold front overtakes a warm front, the front becomes occluded.

offshore wind A wind that blows off the land.

offwind See *downwind*.

onshore wind A wind blowing onto the land.

outboard engine An engine mounted externally on a boat.

outhaul A rope, such as the mainsail clew outhaul, which adjusts the tension in the foot.

overfalls Rough water caused by the tide pouring over a rough or precipitous seabed.

P, Q, R

painter A mooring rope attached to the bow of a small boat.

PAN PAN This is an internationally recognized distress signal that takes priority over all except a MAYDAY message.

passage A journey between two ports.

pile moorings Wooden or metal stakes (piles) driven into the sea bed, to which mooring warps are tied.

pilotage Navigation by eye, compass, and chart, when in sight of land.

pinching Sailing too close to the wind inside the no-sail zone.

plotter A device for plotting a course on a paper chart.

point of sailing The direction in which a boat is being sailed, described in relation to its angle to the wind.

pontoon A floating platform to which boats can be moored.

port The left-hand side of a boat, when looking forwards.

port tack A boat is on port tack when the wind is blowing over the port side and the boom is out to starboard. See *starboard tack*.

prop walk The effect of a turning propeller, which pushes the stern of the boat sideways in the same direction in which the propeller rotates.

pulpit An elevated and rigid metal rail around the bow of a boat.

pushpit An elevated and rigid metal rail around the stern of a boat.

reaching Sailing with the wind roughly at right angles to the fore and aft line of the boat. See *beam reach* and *broad reach*.

reef To reduce sail area when the wind becomes too strong to sail comfortably under full sail.

reef knot A knot that is used for tying the ends of rope of equal diameter, as when putting in a reef.

reef points Lines sewn to the sail to tie up the loose fold in a reefed sail.

rigging The system of wires and ropes used to keep the mast in place and work the sails.

roller furling This is a mechanical system to roll up a headsail or mainsail.

roller reefing This is a mechanical system to reef a headsail or mainsail.

round turn A complete turn of a rope or line around an object.

rowlocks (pronounced "rollocks") U-shaped fittings that support the oars and act as a pivot when rowing.

rudder A movable underwater blade that is used to steer the boat, controlled by a tiller or wheel.

run/running Sailing directly downwind (that is, with the wind right behind you, or nearly so) on either a port or starboard tack.

S, T, U

safe track The course you follow through constricted water.

seacock A valve that can be shut to close a through-hull fitting.

seizing Binding two lines together, or a rope to a spar, or a loop in a rope.

sheet Rope attached to the clew of a sail, or to a boom, used to trim (adjust) the sail.

sheet bend A knot used to join two ropes.

shrouds The wire ropes on either side of the mast that support it sideways.

side deck The deck at the side of a boat.

skeg A projecting part of the hull that supports the rudder.

slip line A doubled line with both ends made fast on the boat so that it can be released and pulled from on board.

slot The gap between the luff of the mainsail and the leech of the headsail.

spinnaker A large, light, downwind sail set from a spinnaker pole.

spinnaker pole A pole used to extend the spinnaker tack away from the boat.

splicing Joining two lines, or creating a loop in one, by interweaving the strands of rope.

spreaders Small poles extending outwards from one or more places on the mast. Shrouds run through the outer ends.

springs Mooring warps to help prevent the boat from moving ahead or astern when moored.

spring tides Tides that have the largest range between high and low tides. See also *neap tides*.

stanchion An upright post used to support the guardrails.

standing part The part of a rope that is not being used to tie a knot.

starboard The right-hand side of a boat, when looking forwards.

starboard tack The course of a boat when the wind is blowing over a boat's starboard side and the boom is out to port. See *port tack*.

steerage way Having enough speed through the water so that the rudder can be used to steer.

stern The rear or after part of a vessel; opposite of bow.

storm jib A small, strong headsail used in very strong winds.

tack (1) The forward lower corner of a fore-and-aft sail. (2) Under sail, a boat is either on starboard tack or port tack. See *tacking*.

tacking Turning the bow of the boat through the wind. See *gybing*.

tackle An arrangement of a line led through two or more blocks to move objects or handle heavy loads.

tender A small boat used to ferry people and provisions to and from a larger boat.

tether The line or strap of a safety harness that is attached to a jackstay, rail, or other strong point on deck.

tidal atlas Small charts showing tidal stream directions and rate of flow.

tidal drift The strength of a tidal stream.

tidal range The difference between a tide's high and low water levels.

tidal set The strength or speed of a tidal stream.

tidal stream A flow of water caused by the rise and fall of the tide.

tide The regular rise and fall of the sea's surface.

tide tables A record of the times and heights of high and low water for every day of the year.

tiller A rod by which the rudder is controlled, for steering.

topping lift A rope running from the masthead to the boom end used to support the boom when the mainsail is not hoisted.

transit Two prominent marks that can be aligned to determine that a boat lies on a certain line.

traveller A slide that travels along a track, used for altering sheet angles.

trim To let out or pull in a sheet to adjust a sail.

true north The direction of the True North Pole. See also *magnetic north* and *compass north*.

true wind The speed and direction of the wind you feel when stationary. See also *apparent wind*.

trysail A small, strong replacement for a cruiser's mainsail that is used in severe weather.

uphaul A rope for adjusting the height of the spinnaker pole; opposite of downhaul.

upwind All courses that are closer to the wind (heading more directly into it) than a beam reach are called upwind courses; opposite of offwind or downwind.

V–Z

vector A line drawn to indicate both the direction and magnitude of a force, such as a tidal stream.

VHF (very high frequency) A common radio system used on boats.

wake Waves generated astern by a moving vessel.

warp Any rope used to secure or move a boat.

watch (1) A division of crew into shifts. (2) The time each watch has duty.

water track The course to steer through the water to achieve a ground track after allowing for the effects of any tidal stream.

waypoints Important points along your route that are often programmed into GPS or chartplotter systems.

weather helm If the boat, under sail, turns to windward when you let go of the tiller, it has weather helm. See *lee helm* and *balanced helm*.

weather shore When the wind blows off the land, the shore is called a weather shore; opposite of lee shore. See also *offshore wind*.

whipping To bind the ends of a rope with thin cord (whipping twine) to prevent it unravelling.

winch A device to provide mechanical advantage for pulling in sheets and halyards.

windage The drag caused by the parts of the boat exposed to the wind.

windlass A mechanical device used to pull in a cable or chain, such as an anchor rode.

windward Towards the wind; opposite of leeward.

working end The part of a rope used for tying a knot.

Index

S

Acknowledgments

Dorling Kindersley would like to thank:
Editorial assistance: Sreshtha Bhattacharya
Design assistance: Chhaya Sajwan, Shanker Prasad, Devan Das, Dhirendra Singh
Picture researcher: Aditya Katyal

Author's acknowlegments: The author would like to thank Sam Fuller for her assistance in the preparation of this book.

PICTURE CREDITS

The publisher would like to thank the following for their kind permission to reproduce their photographs:

(Key: a-above; b-below/bottom; c-centre; f-far; l-left; r-right; t-top)

11 PPL: Gary John Norman (br). 12 Patrick Eden: (cl). Musto: (cr). 14 Orca Bay: (cl). Musto: (cr). 17 McMurdo : (cr). 20 Musto: (bl). 22 Steve Sleight: (cr). 23 Blue Water Supplies: (bl). Secumar: (tl, cla). 24 Steve Sleight: (tl, c). 25 McMurdo : (clb). 26 Kos Picture Source: David Williams (bl). 27 Sunsail/Pat Collinge/ Richard Neil/Jonathan Smith. 35 Jeremy Evans: (b). 36 Jeremy Evans: (cl, bl). 84 Jim Baerselman: (bl). 85 J/Boats UK: (tl). Rick Tomlinson: (bl). 122-123 Getty Images: Lotte Grønkjær. 125 Jeremy Evans: (bl, c). 127 Steve Sleight: (tl, tr). 132 Steve Sleight: (b). 135 Cathy Meeus: (bl). Jeremy Evans: (tl, cl). 143 Jeremy Evans: (b). 144 Patrick Eden: (bl). 145 Janneau: (tl, cl, bl). 148 Janneau: (bl). 149 ITT Industries/Rules/Jabsco: (cl, bl). 150 Mastervolt: (cl). 151 Alubat & Northsea Maritime: (tl). 153 Mastervolt: (bl). 154-155 Getty Images: Thierry Dosogne. 156 Sunsail/Pat Collinge/ Richard Neil/Jonathan Smith: (c). 159 Garmin Ltd.: (c). 162 Patrick Eden: (cl, c). 163 Corbis: Skyscan (bl). 168 Imray-Iolaire: (cl). 169 Jeremy Evans: (cl). 170 The United Kingdom Hydrographic Office and The Hydrographic Office of France: (bl). 171 The United Kingdom Hydrographic Office and The Hydrographic Office of France: (tl, tc, tr, clb, cb, crb). 173 Jeremy Evans: (tl, bl). 174 Garmin Ltd.: (br). Plastimo/ Navimo UK Ltd: (clb). 175 Garmin Ltd.: (tl, cl, bl). 176 Garmin Ltd.: (tr). NASA Marine: (bl). Raymarine: (cr, clb). 177 Garmin Ltd.: (t). Maxsea: (bl). 185 Raymarine: (tl). 190 Corbis: Onne van der Wal (c). Dehler Yachts: (br). 191 Steve Sleight: (bl). 192 Corbis: (cl). Steve Sleight: (bl). 195 Getty Images: Abner Kingman (t). UK Sailmakers: (b). 197 Corbis: Karlheinz Oster (bl). 198-199 Getty Images: Elyse Butler. 201 US National Weather Service: (c). 202 NASA Marine: (tl, cl, bl). 203 Courtesy of Fugawi: (t). Mannix: (br). Petticrow: (bl). 205 NERC Satellite Receiving Station, University of Dundee: (t). 207 FLPA: Steve McCutcheon (crb); R Thompson (clb). 210 FLPA: (bl); Larry West (cl). 211 FLPA: Chris Demetriou (bl); Maurice Nimmo (cl); Steve McCutcheon (t). GeoScience Features Picture Library: (clb). 213 Getty Images: David C Tomlinson (b). 215 Alamy Images: Patrick Eden (t). 216-217 Getty Images: DAJ. 220 Steve Sleight: (bl). 224 Sara Coombes: (cla). 225 Steve Sleight: (bl). 228 Jeremy Evans: (cl). 229 Jeremy Evans: (cl). 230 Steve Sleight: (cl, clb, bl). 231 Patrick Eden: (tl, tr, bl, br). 262-263 Alamy Images: Mike Robinson. 279 Corbis: Sygma / Pascal Le Segretain (b). 280 PPL: Barry Pickthall (c). 281 Alamy Images: Images & Stories (t). 282 Getty Images: Stringer (c). 286 McMurdo : (tl, tc, tr, bl, bc, br). 287 Alamy Images: Chris Cooper-Smith (t). Secumar: (cl). 289 Getty Images: AFP / Stringer (bl). 290 Alamy Images: ARGO Images / Keith Pritchard (c). 291 Alamy Images: Bluegreen Pictures / Gary John Norman (b). Corbis: ZUMA Press / Charlie Neuman (tl).

Jacket images: Front: Alamy Images: Ivan Synieokov crb; Beken Of Cowes Ltd: clb; Back: Patrick Eden: cla; Spine: Beken Of Cowes Ltd.